50

to improving your
academic writing
STEPS

Study Book

Chris Sowton

Garnet
EDUCATION

For Fitzy, who was there at the beginning, and for Olivia and Amy, who were there at the end.

Acknowledgement
Text on page 19 reprinted from Keck, C. (2006). The use of paraphrase in summary writing: A comparison of L1 and L2 writers. *Journal of Second Language Writing*. 15, 4: 261–278. Copyright 2006, with permission from Elsevier.

Published by
Garnet Publishing Ltd
8 Southern Court
South Street
Reading RG1 4QS, UK
www.garneteducation.com

Copyright © Chris Sowton 2012
Reprinted 2014

The right of Chris Sowton to be identified as the author of this work has been asserted in accordance with the Copyright, Designs and Patents Act 1988.

ISBN: 978-1-85964-655-7

British Library Cataloguing-in-Publication Data
A catalogue record for this book is available from the British Library.

Production
Project manager: Sarah MacBurnie
Project consultant: Rod Webb
Editorial: Fiona Dempsey, Sam Lacey, Rachel Lovering, Peter Finn
Design and layout: Sarah Church, Mike Hinks, Bob House

Printed and bound
in Lebanon by International Press: interpress@int-press.com

Contents

Unit F. Developing your writing style

Unit G. Using functional language in your writing

Unit H. Enriching your vocabulary

Unit I. Improving your grammar

Unit J. Finalizing your writing

Introduction

Purpose of this book

50 steps to improving your academic writing is primarily intended for students who are new to or inexperienced in academic writing. It has been designed with one specific aim in mind: to provide the user with the skills and knowledge to write an essay in the context of university systems.

Principally, the book is a self-study book which students can use themselves in order to develop their skills. However, it may also be used in the classroom by teachers of English for Academic Purposes as part of a wider course.

Structure of the book

50 steps has ten units of five steps each. Each unit is based on a different aspect of academic writing. Details of these units, alongside a general overview of the topics which they cover, are presented below.

- **Unit A. Understanding academic convention**
  Providing an overview of the key characteristics of academic writing.

- **Unit B. Researching your essay**
  Analyzing the best strategies for gathering and recording background information.

- **Unit C. Preparing to write**
  Focusing on what you need to do before you embark on your essay.

- **Unit D. Organizing your text**
  Looking at the key principles of text and essay organization in academic English.

- **Unit E. Making your writing more 'academic'**
  Highlighting key aspects of good academic style.

- **Unit F. Developing your writing style**
  Helping you make your writing sound more professional and appropriate.

- **Unit G. Using functional language in your writing**
  Presenting useful examples of language for specific functional purposes.

- **Unit H. Enriching your vocabulary**
  Extending your understanding of key academic vocabulary.

- **Unit I. Improving your grammar**
  Focusing on areas of grammar common in academic writing.

- **Unit J. Finalizing your writing**
  Making your essay as good as it can possibly be.

Structure of each step

Each of the 50 steps has the same six parts, which are as follows:

- **A. Reflection**: Evaluation of your existing understanding of the topic through targeted questions.

- **B. Contextualization**: Demonstration of the importance and relevance of the topic through presentation of the learning point in context.

- **C. Analysis**: Explanation of the topic, delivered by answering the specific questions posed in part B.
- **D. Activation**: Application of what you have learnt through a range of test activities.
- **E. Personalization**: Provision of practical strategies which can be used to apply what you have learnt to your own academic writing.
- **F. Extension**: Indication of other steps in the book which may provide additional support. This also refers to the resource materials to be found at the back of the book.

The answer key to the questions posed in part D, Activation, can be found on pages 207–224. In addition, on pages 225–236 you will find a glossary, which will help explain key words and terms useful for academic writing. The resource materials on pages 237–272 include photocopiable documents, a range of additional information, extension activities and useful hyperlinks.

How to use this book

Each of the steps should take you approximately one hour to complete. Evidently, exactly how long you spend will depend on the precise details of the step and your existing level of knowledge.

The structure of the book means that you can decide how best to use it. If you are already aware of your areas of weakness in academic writing, and feel you only need support in certain key areas, then you should focus on those particular steps. If, however, you feel you need more support, it will be more beneficial to follow through the book from beginning to end.

However you use this book, it is important that you try to apply what you learn as much as you possibly can. Academic writing is *not* something which you can learn and then ignore. In order to improve your writing, you must constantly try to apply the knowledge and skills you gain.

How is writing different from speaking?

> 'If we spoke as we write, we should find no one to listen.
> If we wrote as we speak, we should find no one to read.'
>
> T. S. Eliot

A Reflection

How is language used differently in speaking and writing?

- *Write 'S' for words to use in spoken and 'W' for those to use in written English.*

  um *S*   then ___   I mean ___   consequently ___   er ___   L8R ___

B Contextualization

What are the key differences between speaking and writing?

- *By analyzing the 'spoken' text and the 'written' text below, both of which focus on the same subject matter, complete the column on the right.*

Spoken text: Speaking is *[pause]* er something we learn without really thinking about it *[volume drops]* usually from our mums and dads, but writing is something we really have to think about. It is *[pause]* um an expar-expertise not everybody has. *[intonation rises]* Understand? Let me put it another way. Loads of people still can't write *[points finger]*. Now.

Written text: Speaking is a skill which we develop subconsciously (usually from our parents). Writing, however, has to be consciously developed. It is an expertise which, surprisingly, many people still do not possess. This is true even in the 21st century!

Question	Speaking	Writing
How is the skill acquired?	Natural, unconscious process, usually from parents.	*Conscious, time-intensive process, mainly at school.*
How is the language joined together?	Simple LINKING DEVICES (e.g., *and/but*).	
How formal is the grammar?	Flexible.	
How can extra meaning be communicated?	E.g., BODY LANGUAGE, including HAND MOVEMENTS.	
How is emphasis created?	Changes in volume/tone.	
Is variety possible?	Different accents acceptable.	
How do you interact with the audience?	Audience is often known; can clarify meaning instantly.	
Can you change what you said?	No – you cannot delete speech.	

UNIT A Understanding academic convention

Step 1

c Analysis

What are the different uses of language in speaking and writing?

In terms of language, speaking and writing differ in two main ways: the **method of delivery** and **level of formality**.

Method of delivery

Speech is immediate and usually unplanned. As such, we need to gain time for thinking and we use fillers such as *um*, *er* and *I mean*. Writing can be edited and rewritten many times. Therefore, it has no need for such words.

Level of formality

Three historic languages have, in particular, given academic English the vocabulary which it has today: ANGLO-SAXON, FRENCH and LATIN. Words from the first are everyday words that are more likely to be found in speech (e.g., *then*). However, words from French and especially Latin are often a feature of writing (e.g., *consequently*).

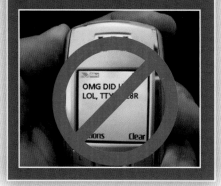

Note: Text English

Text English – the abbreviated type of language which is often found in text messages and e-mails (and on Facebook and Twitter) – is unacceptable in academic writing. Although it is technically 'writing', many of its features are closer to speaking.

What are the major differences between speaking and writing?

How is the skill acquired?

As children, we acquire spoken language naturally, when we are exposed to the language of those around us, such as our parents. Writing, however, is a much more difficult skill to learn. The process is more complicated and takes a long time. This is why writing is often considered more important and prestigious. When learning writing in a second language, the process is even more difficult – so do not worry about your problems with English!

How is the language joined together?

Spoken language tends to use simpler forms of linking words (e.g., *and*, *but*), whereas written language typically uses more complex forms (e.g., *however*, *therefore*).

  ▣ Speaking: But writing is something ...
  ▣ Writing: Writing, however, has ...

How formal is the grammar?

Grammar has more flexibility in speech than in writing. In the majority of writing, you are expected to use full sentences which are 'grammatically correct' (i.e., every sentence must have a subject and a verb). In speech, this is not always necessary.

  ▣ Speaking: Now.
  ▣ Writing: This is true even in the 21st century!

How can extra meaning be communicated?

There are many ways to communicate your meaning in speech without using language (e.g., BODY LANGUAGE). Obviously, in writing, these techniques are not available. This means that your writing has to be as specific and clear as possible. In the example below, the writer has to use particular words (*surprisingly*) and punctuation (an exclamation mark – *!*) to do the same job as pointing a finger for emphasis.

- Speaking: Loads of people still can't write [*points finger*].
- Writing: It is an expertise which, surprisingly, many people still do not possess. This is true even in the 21st century!

How can specific emphasis be created?

In speech, there are a range of effects by which we can indicate EMPHASIS. These include:

- **Volume** (e.g., soft/loud)
- **PITCH/TONE** (e.g., rising/falling)
- **TEMPO** (e.g., slowly/quickly)

Speech	Writing
Voice gets louder	!
Tone rises	?
Pitch/voice drops	( ) or …
Shorter pause	,
Longer pause	. or ;

In writing, we have to use punctuation to perform the same role. A brief comparison of the two media is presented in the table. The example below is from the text.

- Speaking: … [*volume drops*] usually from our mums and dads …
- Writing: (usually from our parents).

Is variety possible?

Spoken language varies greatly from region to region. Indeed, two speakers of the same language may find it very difficult to understand each other. To take the example of the word *about*: its written form does not change, but it can be said in different ways. For example, someone from London would typically pronounce the word as /əˈbaʊt/ (to rhyme with 'shout'); a Glaswegian might pronounce it /əˈbuːt/ (to rhyme with 'flute'). Writing, on the other hand, is more standardized. Different types of English (e.g., AMERICAN ENGLISH and BRITISH ENGLISH) only have very small differences in spelling.

How do you interact with the audience?

When speaking, we almost always know who we are speaking to. In writing, however, our words might be read by anyone. Our audience, therefore, has to be considered more carefully beforehand, and VAGUENESS and AMBIGUITY must be avoided. In addition, when writing you only have one opportunity to make yourself understood, whereas in speaking you can explain yourself as many times as necessary. Here, the speaker is able to rephrase what they have just said, so that the other person can understand.

- Speaking: [*intonation rises*] Understand? Let me put it another way.

Can you change what you said?

Once something has been said, it has been said. It cannot be 'deleted' (though of course it can be clarified). In writing, texts can be edited and redrafted as often as necessary. In this example, the speaker tries twice to pronounce this difficult word correctly. When writing, however, he or she can look the word up in a dictionary, or use spellcheck, to get it right first time.

- Speaking: It is … an expar- expertise …

D Activation

The sentences below are all examples of spoken English. Rewrite them to make them more typical of written English.

1. 'Speaking and writing are really really different skills … um … there are three ways this is true – how they're learnt, what they contain, and how they're done.'

_____

_____

2. 'It's clear, isn't it, that yer grammar has gotta be better in writing.'

_____

_____

3. 'The main differences in speaking and writing [*intonation rises*]? Difficult question.'

_____

_____

4. 'Things don't really change in writing, wherever you are, but in speaking they can change loads.'

_____

_____

E Personalization

 In your mother tongue, discuss an academic subject with a friend.

- Record this conversation.
- Following this, write a short summary (c. 100 words) on the same topic.
- Compare the recording and the written summary, and identify the differences between the two.

Review some of your previous writing. Does it sound more like speech? Can you identify any words which should not be there? In particular, you may want to check for:

- the influence of TEXT ENGLISH
- sentences which are not grammatically correct
- repetition of the same language
- informal linking words

F Extension

Step 21 focuses on strategies for increasing the FORMALITY of your language – a crucial difference between speaking and writing.

Step 43 analyzes punctuation – a skill specifically required for writing as opposed to speaking.

Unit J (Steps 46–50) looks in detail at the issue of PROOFREADING, and how you can ensure your final written text avoids some of the problems listed above.

How is academic writing different from other forms of writing?

'Talent alone cannot make a writer.'

Ralph Waldo Emerson

A Reflection

What are the key characteristics of academic writing?

- *Select the appropriate term – more or less – in the middle box.*

Generally speaking, academic writing	is more / less objective	than other forms of writing.
	uses more / less referencing	
	is more / less complex	
	has a more / less formal structure	

B Contextualization

Compare and contrast the following pieces of writing.

- *On the left is an e-mail written by a student. On the right is an essay extract about the same topic.*

E-mail (standard writing)

Essay (academic writing)

What is academic English?

Dear Professor Plum,

Please find below my answers to your questions.

I believe academic English and general English are different for the main reason that they have very different goals. Lectures and seminars need a different approach to general spoken English. And, of course, academic essay writing is not the same as standard writing.

I think there are 4 main areas where I can see big differences between standard writing and academic writing. They are:
- You should not be subjective.
- You should be more complex.
- You should have more structure.
- You should use academic style and systems.

Best wishes,
Sophia

Characteristics of academic English

'Academic English' is differentiated from 'general English' in its focus on 'those communication skills in English which are required for study purposes in formal education systems' (Jordan, 1997: 1). Within these systems, there are three main areas of focus: the lecture, the seminar and the essay, each of which has a specific set of sub-skills which are required for successful performance. It is essays where the most significant distinction between academic English and general English is made. Generally speaking, there are four main areas where differences between standard writing and academic writing can be seen: the inherent objectivity of academic writing, its complexity, its formality of structure and its adoption of academic style.

UNIT A Understanding academic convention

Step
2

c Analysis

What are the key characteristics of academic writing?

It is almost impossible to define good academic writing *exactly*. However, it is certainly possible to identify some key characteristics. The ones listed on the right are four of the most important features.

> Academic writing ...
> - is more objective
> - is more complex
> - has a more formal structure
> - uses more referencing

Academic writing is more objective

Phrases such as *I think*, *I believe* and *In my opinion* should not be used in academic writing. Academics are not looking for what you think or believe – they want to see what you can show, demonstrate and prove through evidence.

Three specific strategies for achieving OBJECTIVITY (illustrated in more detail in Steps 21–23) are outlined below:

- ■ Standard writing: *I think there are 4 main areas where I can see big differences between standard writing and academic writing.*
- ■ Academic writing: Generally speaking[1], there are[2] four main areas where differences between standard writing and academic writing can be seen[3] …

Strategy 1: HEDGING LANGUAGE (*generally speaking*) increases the 'distance' between the writer and the text, thereby creating more objectivity.

Strategy 2: Empty introductory phrases (*there are*) provide a platform for objective statements.

Strategy 3: The PASSIVE VOICE (*can be seen*) removes the need for a subject in the sentence. This can be particularly useful to avoid using *I*.

Academic writing is more complex

As a general principle, academic writing is more complex than other forms of writing. This is because academic writing often discusses difficult, challenging ideas which can only be expressed with particular grammar and language. Areas where this complexity may be seen include:

Formality of language

Academic language is more formal than the vocabulary used in other writing.

- ■ Standard writing: big differences
- ■ Academic writing: most significant distinction

> **Note**
> Do not mistake 'complex' and 'complicated'. Academic writing should *not* be complicated. It should be relatively easy to follow, written in a clear, direct style. Therefore, you should *not*:
> - use long, difficult words which you do not understand.
> - use difficult grammatical structures that you are not confident with.
> - make strong statements about issues which you are unable to justify.

Grammatical structures

There are particular grammatical forms which appear more frequently in academic writing than other writing. For example: the **PASSIVE VOICE**, **NOUN PHRASES** and, as below, **RELATIVE CLAUSES**.

- Academic writing: A specific set of sub-skills which are required for successful performance.

Density of language

In the passage on page 11, the average number of letters per word of the e-mail is 4.8, whereas it is 5.4 for the sample of academic writing. This 'density' can be achieved through a greater use of **CONTENT WORDS** (such as verbs and nouns) rather than **STRUCTURE WORDS** (such as prepositions and conjunctions). In the example below, the adjective form found in general writing is substituted with a verb form in academic writing.

- Standard writing: Academic English and general English are different …
- Academic writing: 'Academic English' is differentiated from 'general English' …

Academic writing has a more formal structure

All writing has some kind of structure. The structure of academic writing is more formal than other types of writing. The following characteristics may be observed:

- The text as a whole has a specific, formalized structure – the **INTRODUCTION**, **MAIN BODY** and **CONCLUSION**.
- The text must have **COHESION** and **COHERENCE** – it must link together clearly so that it is possible to follow the writer's argument.
- Paragraphs should be roughly the same length throughout, so there is a good overall balance.
- Paragraphs often follow a similar structure – topic sentence, outline of argument, supporting evidence, short conclusion and transition to the next paragraph (see Step 18 for more detail).

Academic writing uses more referencing

Building on the ideas of other people is one of the central features of academic writing. In order to show where these ideas come from (and to avoid **PLAGIARISM**), a reference system is used (note: the reference system used throughout this book is the Harvard referencing style).

- Standard writing: I believe academic English and general English are different for the main reason that they have very different goals.
- Academic writing: 'Academic English' is differentiated from 'general English' in its focus on 'those communication skills in English which are required for study purposes in formal education systems' (Jordan, 1997: 1).

D Activation

Look at the following pairs of sentences. In each case, decide which is more typical of academic English, and explain why.

1a. I think that the first-person pronoun is not commonly used in academic English.

1b. The first-person pronoun is not commonly used in academic English.

Reason: _____

2a. There are a lot of scholars who argue that structure is important in academic writing.

2b. Scholars such as Shih (1986) and Canagarajah (2002) argue that structure is important in academic writing.

Reason: _____

3a. 'Hedging language' is never found in standard written English.

3b. 'Hedging language' is more likely to be used in academic English than standard written English.

Reason: _____

4a. Academic English has a higher lexical density and grammatical complexity than standard English.

4b. Standard English uses simpler grammar and fewer long words than academic English.

Reason: _____

E Personalization

■ **Look at an essay you have written in your mother tongue.**
- Compare this to a piece of your non-academic writing (e.g., e-mail, letter, report). What differences do you notice?
- Are these differences the same as or different from the ones in English?

■ **Look at an essay you have written in English.**
- Are there any aspects of it which are not 'academic'? How could you improve any of the 'non-academic' elements?

■ **Read an article/book extract in your subject area.**
- Identify examples of characteristics of academic writing (the passive voice, formality, hedging language, etc.).

F Extension

■ Steps 4 and 5 look at how you can use other people's ideas in your writing and **reference** appropriately.

■ Step 18 explains the characteristics of a **good paragraph** – a key component of good academic structure – while Steps 19 and 20 examine the introduction and conclusion.

■ Unit E (Steps 21–25) focuses specifically on strategies to make your writing more academic, particularly on: making your essays more **formal**, increasing the **objectivity** of your writing, using **hedging language** and structures and making your writing more **complex**.

What is plagiarism?

'Fine words! I wonder where you stole them?'

Jonathan Swift

Reflection

Are there differences between how plagiarism is seen in your country and the UK?

- *Tick if the statement reflects normal practice, put a cross if not, and a question mark if you are unsure. How can you explain any differences?*

Statement	Normal practice in my country	Normal practice in the UK
I can use other people's original ideas without reference.		
I need to reference ideas which are commonly known or accepted.		
I can use/adapt the research of my friends.		
I can copy and paste information from the Internet into my essay without saying where it is from.		
I can submit the same piece of work twice, e.g., on a different course/module.		
I can pay someone to check through/proofread my essay to make minor improvements.		

B Contextualization

Which aspects of the original sources are plagiarized in the student's first draft?

Original sources

1. 'Students were less certain about the concept of using someone else's ideas (Qu.1b), with 40% of students not acknowledging that this was plagiarism' (Dawson and Overfield, 2006).

2. 'A similar point could be made about Chinese academic norms, which are the result in part of a long tradition of reproducing Confucian teachings in civil service exams. The philosopher's words were known by and belonged to everyone' (Sowden, 2005: 227).

3. 'We need to strike a balance between being sensitive to students' feelings, understanding potential cultural differences, and being clear and helpful in the messages we give through our feedback' (Hyland, 2000: 381).

First draft of student writing

40% of students think that using someone else's ideas without reference is acceptable.

Often, it is East Asian students who find this a particular problem, because in the Confucian system knowledge is seen as something which is shared by society (Sowden, 2005).

It may also be a challenge for teachers when giving feedback, as they are often unaware of how to strike a balance between being sensitive to students' feelings, understanding potential cultural differences, and being clear and helpful in the messages they give.

c Analysis

If you come from a country whose university system is similar to the UK's, there may be many similarities in your answers on page 15. However, many countries have very different views about knowledge. These differences may be in areas such as:

- what the purpose of university education is
- where 'knowledge' comes from
- how 'experts' should be treated

These differences have a direct impact on the issue of plagiarism, and for many students this can be very confusing. It is important to emphasize that this does not mean one university system is better than another, simply that they are different. Since you are being assessed in an English-medium institution, you will need to understand and follow the procedures and practices of that institution.

'I can use other people's original ideas without reference.'

This is not *normal practice in the UK.*

Using other people's ideas without reference and pretending that they are your own is known as *plagiarism*. Plagiarism refers not only to text, but also to other people's words, data, diagrams, photographs, etc. Plagiarism is taken extremely seriously by the academic community. Punishment can range from a deduction of marks for your essay through to expulsion from the university. Nowadays, many universities use highly sophisticated computer programmes to detect cheating (such as Turnitin – www.submit.ac.uk), so if you do plagiarize, it is likely you will be caught.

> **Note**
> 'Plagiarism is a form of cheating and a serious academic offence ... A substantiated charge of plagiarism will result in a penalty being ordered ranging from a mark of zero for the assessed work to expulsion from the College.'
> **Extract from the plagiarism statement of King's College London**

Of course, you are expected to use other people's ideas in your writing. Quoting, paraphrasing and summarizing are the best ways that you can do this and avoid plagiarism. These skills are discussed in detail in Step 4 and Step 5.

'I need to reference ideas which are commonly known or accepted.'

This is not *normal practice in the UK.*

Information which is 'commonly known', as opposed to somebody's 'exclusive discovery', does not need to be referenced. Sometimes, however, it may be difficult to know which category information is in. Knowledge which is generally considered to be 'common' includes that which is well known in either your field of study or in the wider world (for example, it can easily be found in a general work of reference such as a dictionary or encyclopaedia). As a general rule, if you are in doubt, it is better to be cautious and provide a reference.

'I can use/adapt the research of my friends.'

This is not *normal practice in the UK.*

There are some types of collaboration which, as a student, you are allowed to do, such as group project work. Such work is performed together and credit is received equally. You may not use or borrow someone else's ideas without their knowledge, or even if that person gives you permission.

'I can copy and paste information from the Internet into my essay, without saying where it is from.'

This is not *normal practice in the UK.*

A distinction has to be made between 'searching' and '*re*searching'. At a British university, you are not assessed on your ability to find information, but rather on your ability to understand and process it. Be careful when downloading information from the Internet that you would like to paraphrase or quote in your essay. Mixing up your own words and original material is dangerous. This kind of ACCIDENTAL PLAGIARISM is treated just as seriously as deliberate plagiarism.

'I can submit the same piece of work twice e.g., on a different course/module.'

This is not *normal practice in the UK.*

This kind of plagiarism, often referred to as **self-plagiarism**, is also unacceptable. Every piece of work which you present for assessment should be unique.

'I can pay someone to check through/proofread my essay to make minor improvements.'

This is normal practice in the UK.

The key word here is *minor*. Normally you may use proofreaders to improve the grammar or language in your essay. However, as soon as the proofreader makes significant or fundamental changes to your essay – for example expressing his or her own point of view in 'your' essay – then plagiarism has occurred.

Essay-writing services: a warning

Using an essay-writing service – a phenomenon which has become increasingly popular in the last few years – is completely unacceptable. Since the overwhelming majority of essays which you can buy are already known to electronic software, you will be caught anyway, and the process will also have cost you a considerable amount of money.

Plagiarism in context

First draft of student writing	Problem
40% of students think that using someone else's ideas without reference is acceptable.	This data comes from an original piece of research, and therefore the source needs to be provided, i.e., '(Dawson and Overfield, 2006)'.
Often, it is East Asian students who find this a particular problem, because in the Confucian system knowledge is seen as something which is shared by society (Sowden, 2005).	This is, arguably, common knowledge. The basic principles of Confucianism are well known in academic circles (and can easily be found in a general reference book). Therefore, the source does not need to be acknowledged.
It may also be a challenge for teachers when giving feedback, as they are often unaware of how to strike a balance between being sensitive to students' feelings, understanding potential cultural differences, and being clear and helpful in the messages they give.	This is someone's original idea, and therefore needs to be referenced, i.e., '(Hyland, 2000: 381)'. The student has copied and pasted the author's words and provided no reference. This is clearly plagiarism.

D Activation

Look at the following sentences and underline the correct statement.

1. Plagiarism **is/is not** considered to be a serious offence by universities.
2. If found guilty of plagiarism, you **can/cannot** be expelled from the university.
3. I **am/am not** allowed to copy and paste material directly from electronic sources into my essay.
4. I **am/am not** allowed to discuss my essay with a friend.
5. Universities **do/do not** have a range of electronic software to detect plagiarism.
6. I **have to/do not have to** reference every single fact in my essay.
7. If I pay someone to proofread my essay, he or she **can/cannot** change the content and ideas as well.
8. I **can/cannot** resubmit a piece of my work for assessment.
9. I **should/should not** use other people's ideas in my essays.

E Personalization

▣ **Make a list of the differences which exist between the UK and your home country in terms of plagiarism. Knowledge of these specific differences will help you to avoid plagiarism.**

▣ **Go to the website of the university you are attending (or hope to attend) and read its plagiarism declaration form.**

▣ **Read through your last essay. Are there any parts in the essay where you feel:**
   - you have used somebody else's ideas without proper acknowledgement?
   - you have copied and pasted information directly from the Internet?

   If so, what strategies could you use to solve these problems?

F Extension

▣ Step 4 and Step 5 focus on QUOTING, PARAPHRASING, SUMMARIZING and REFERENCING, which represent the main ways of avoiding plagiarism. In addition, Step 31 analyzes **reporting verbs**, which can be a useful tool for explaining what other people have said.

▣ Step 8 develops your **critical thinking skills**, so that you can manipulate, adapt and utilize your source material.

▣ Step 10 provides tips on **note-taking**. Good note-taking skills are one of the best ways to avoid accidental plagiarism.

▣ Step 14 extends your knowledge on **brainstorming** and **outlining**. These skills can help with your time management; poor time management is a major factor which results in students plagiarising.

▣ Appendix 4, Step 3 provides hyperlinks to the plagiarism statement from King's College London and to a plagiarism detection system website.

How can I use other people's ideas in my writing?

'If I have seen a little further, it is by standing on the shoulders of giants.'

Sir Isaac Newton

A Reflection

Thinking about your current practice, which of the following statements are true for you?

Statement	True	False
'I find it difficult to include a range of sources in my work.'		
'I do not understand the difference between quoting, paraphrasing and summarizing.'		
'I often use long quotations (more than 25 words).'		

B Contextualization

How does the passage on the right use other people's ideas?

- *Consider the improvements in comparison with the passage on the left. What strategies were used?*

Passage using only the student's ideas

> The term paraphrasing is generally not understood very well. It is normally understood as meaning a mixture of quotations, summary and paraphrase. Many people think that paraphrasing, summarizing and quotation are skills that students can use when using original material in their writing. The large amount of information which is available both on the Internet and in books, and which university students can access, shows the importance of paraphrasing – in particular, how paraphrasing can be used to avoid plagiarism.

Passage incorporating other people's ideas

> Typically, paraphrasing is discussed as part of a 'triadic model' of 'paraphrase, summary, and quotation' (Barks and Watts, 2001: 252). For example, Campbell (1990) and Johns and Mayes (1990) suggest that paraphrasing is one of a number of strategies (including summary and quotation) that students can use when integrating source texts into their writing ... The ubiquitous online and paper writing resources available to university students also emphasize the importance of paraphrase, specifically as a strategy for avoiding plagiarism (Yamada, 2003).
>
> **Keck, C. (2006). The use of paraphrase in summary writing: A comparison of L1 and L2 writers. *Journal of Second Language Writing*. 15, 4: 261–278.**

c | Analysis

> **What are some of the basic skills when quoting, paraphrasing and summarizing?**

Understand why a range of sources is important

This is a common problem for many students, whether native or non-native speakers of English. Since non-native speakers will often take a long time to read and understand source materials, it is common to find only two or three sources used in an essay. However, your teachers may expect you to use 8–10 sources, or possibly more.

> **Two important points:**
> - You do not need to read all of your reading list.
> - You do not need to understand everything in every source.

When using sources, you need to achieve a balance between breadth and depth. If you are inexperienced in reading, this can be very challenging. To do this, you need to adopt a range of strategies, including the ability to reflect upon and criticize writing (see **Step 8**) and to carry out targeted, critical reading, whereby you focus only on the information you need (see **Step 9**).

Ensure that you understand the difference between the three skills

Note: the specific referencing conventions for quotations, paraphrases and summaries are discussed in **Step 5**.

- **Direct quotation** is when you use exactly the same words as somebody else:
  Typically, paraphrasing is discussed as part of a 'triadic model' of 'paraphrase, summary, and quotation' (Barks and Watts, 2001: 252).

- **Paraphrasing** is when you rewrite text from another piece of writing, using your own words:
  The ubiquitous online and paper writing resources available to university students also emphasize the importance of paraphrase, specifically as a strategy for avoiding plagiarism (Keck, 2006).
  The original text (Yamada, 2003: 249) was as follows: 'The information in these sites is usually electronic versions of writing manuals or handouts distributed by these colleges.'

- **Summarizing** is when you condense whole paragraphs, pages, articles or even books down to a single sentence:
  Campbell (1990) and Johns and Mayes (1990) suggest that paraphrasing is one of a number of strategies (including summary and quotation) that students can use when integrating source texts into their writing.

Be careful about the length of quotations which you use

Often, students use long quotations because it is an easy way to increase their word count. Wherever possible, this should be avoided. Long quotations give the impression that the student cannot think critically and is unable to separate what is useful from what is not. Many quotations will be fewer than ten words. As a general rule, you should justify any quotation which is longer than 15 words. Ask yourself:

- Do I *really* need all the words?
- What is *essential* in this quotation?
- Might *paraphrasing* or *summarizing* be a better option?

How can these skills improve your writing?

Quoting, paraphrasing and summarizing can be beneficial to your writing in three main ways: they add **clarity**, **authority** and **support**.

■ **Clarity**: Experts in the field may often be able to say things in a more specific, precise way than you.

■ **Authority**: As the quotation by Sir Isaac Newton at the beginning of this step suggests, a good essay will build on the work of experts in the field. Also, you need to demonstrate that you have a good overall understanding of the topic, and that you are considering the issues from all angles.

■ **Support**: A good balance of theory and evidence is required in academic writing. Published works can add relevant support to your own thoughts and reflections about a particular subject.

What different strategies are there for paraphrasing?

There are two key strategies for successful paraphrasing: changing the words and changing the grammar. In both cases, the *idea* should remain the same, but the specific *detail* should be different. Often both strategies will be used together, i.e., a good paraphrase will often involve changes to both the words and the grammar.

Strategy 1: Changing the words

Replacing words from the original text with SYNONYMS is the simplest and most common way to paraphrase. However, note that synonyms do not mean *exactly the same* as each other. They only have a *similar* meaning. You must be careful not to misrepresent somebody's opinion by poor use of synonyms.

In the example from page 20, the following changes were made:

Where can I find synonyms?
- Microsoft Word thesaurus (shift F7)
- A synonyms dictionary
- A range of websites, e.g.:
  www.thesaurus.com
  www.wordsmyth.net

Yamada (2003)	Keck (2006)
electronic	online
writing manuals or handouts	paper writing resources
distributed by these colleges	available to university students

Strategy 2: Changing the grammar

Altering the grammar in the original text can be done in two main ways: changing the VOICE (either active into passive, or vice versa) and changing the WORD CLASS. In both cases, the emphasis of the original may change slightly. For example, an alternative way of paraphrasing Yamada (2003) would be as follows:

■ **Original:** The information in these sites is usually electronic versions of writing manuals …

■ **Paraphrase:** The usual site information is electronically produced writing manuals (Yamada, 2003).

D Activation

Paraphrase the following sentences, each of which is taken from Keck (2006).

1. 'Such investigations are likely to play a crucial role in our larger efforts to help university students become confident and successful academic writers.'

   _____

   _____

2. 'The study aimed to establish a reliable, replicable method.'

   _____

   _____

3. 'Many believe that the teaching of paraphrasing can help students to move beyond copying as a textual borrowing strategy.'

   _____

   _____

4. 'Judgments of paraphrase acceptability depend upon a number of factors, including, but not limited to, the length of the borrowed phrase, word frequency, and the grammatical structure of the paraphrase.'

   _____

   _____

 **E Personalization**

■ **Consider your most recent piece of academic writing and the ways in which you used other people's ideas.**

■ **Look at your references:**
   • How many sources did you use? Was this sufficient?
   • Do your sources reflect a variety of opinions on the subject?

■ **Look at the direct quotations:**
   • What percentage of the essay did they take up?
   • Were there any which were longer than 15 words? If so, can you justify them?

■ **Look at the paraphrasing:**
   • Were they genuine paraphrases, or did you just copy and paste?

F Extension

■ Step 5 provides guidance on how to **reference** properly.

■ Step 8 helps you develop your **critical thinking skills**, to decide what part of other people's writing you should use in your own writing.

■ Step 31 provides guidance on ways in which you can **report** what other people have written about a particular subject.

■ Appendix 3, Step 4 lists an analysis of the different word classes of common academic words and the passive forms of English tenses. This information may be useful when paraphrasing.

How can I reference properly?

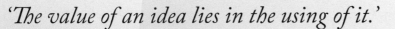

'The value of an idea lies in the using of it.'

Thomas Edison

A Reflection

Match the following words/phrases with the appropriate definition.

Paraphrase	The exact words of another author which you use in your essay.
In-text citation	Additional information found at the bottom of a page (end of the essay).
Bibliography	Detailed description of all the sources/influences for your essay.
References	A rewrite of an original piece of writing, in your own words.
Direct quotation	A list of the sources which you quote in your essay.
Footnotes (endnotes)	A reference in the text of your essay to the source you have paraphrased or quoted from.

B Contextualization

What are the main referencing conventions for the 'Author–Date' (or Harvard) system?

- *Using the information below as a guide, complete the table which follows.*
- *Is this the system you have used/will use? If not, what are the main differences?*

In-text citation	References
Chernin (1988) argues that the origins of the Harvard system are largely unknown.	Chernin, E. (1988). The 'Harvard system': A mystery dispelled. *British Medical Journal*. 297: 1062–1063.
Most researchers 'want us to know more than just facts' (Turabian et al., 2007: 6).	Turabian, K., Booth, W., Colomb, G. and Williams, J. (2007). *A Manual for Writers of Term Papers, Theses, and Dissertations*. 7th ed. Chicago: University of Chicago Press.
Anglia Ruskin University uses Harvard as their default referencing system (Anglia Ruskin University, 2010).	Anglia Ruskin University (2010). *Referencing*. http://libweb.anglia.ac.uk/referencing/referencing/harvard.htm. Retrieved 05/04/10.

IN-TEXT CITATION	
Paraphrase/summary	
	(Author Surname(s)/Author Surname et al., year: page)
REFERENCES	
Book	
	Author Surname, Initial. (year). Article title. *Journal Title*. Volume, part: pages.
Website	

C Analysis

What key terminology is used in referencing?

Paraphrase: a rewrite of an original piece of writing, in your own words.

In-text citation: a reference in the actual text of your essay to the particular source that you have paraphrased or quoted from.

References: a list of the sources which you quote in your essay.

Bibliography: detailed description of all the sources/influences for your essay.

Direct quotation: the exact words of another author, which you use in your essay.

Footnotes (endnotes): additional information found at the bottom of a page (end of the essay).

> **Note**
> Two useful Latin phrases for in-text citations:
> * et al. 'and others'
>   When there are more than three authors, use the first and replace the others with 'et al.'.
> * ibid. 'in the same place'
>   When a reference comes from the same place as the one immediately before it, 'ibid.' can be used in its place.

What are the main principles of referencing?

Throughout the world, there are many hundreds of different referencing systems in use. For example, in the Humanities and Social Sciences, the 'Author–Date' (or Harvard) system is that most frequently used. It is important that you check in your handbook or with your department as to what referencing system your institution uses.

Nowadays, referencing is not quite as difficult as it used to be. Many British universities provide students with a range of software which makes the process much easier. You should check with your university library staff/computer service to see what is available. The three common programs in general use at British universities are:

* Refworks (www.refworks.com)
* Endnote (www.endnote.com)
* Reference Manager (www.refman.com)

If you do not have access to any of these sites, there are several more which may provide similar services, such as CiteULike (www.citeulike.org). You may need to pay to use these programs properly. The programs offer you the chance to download the citations you would like to use, or to input the information manually, using the referencing system your institution uses.

> **A note on brackets and editions**
> * Notice the different use of brackets in the example on page 23 – Chernin (1988) vs (Turabian et al., 2007: 6). When an author's name appears in the normal flow of the text, the brackets only go around the year (with or without page number); when the paraphrase or quotation appears at the end of a sentence, brackets go around the name as well.
> * If one or more updated versions (editions) of a book were printed after the original version, it helps to state in your reference which edition you are referring to – for example, Turabian et al. (2007) is in its seventh edition (see part B).

What is the Harvard referencing system?

In-text citation

Paraphrase: Author Surname(s) (year)
Chernin (1988) argues that the origins of the Harvard system are largely unknown.

Direct quotation: (Author Surname[s],/Author Surname et al., year: page)
Most researchers 'want us to know more than just facts' (Turabian et al., 2007: 6).

References

Book (multiple authors): Author Surnames, Author Initials. (year). *Title of Book*. Edition. City of Publication: Publisher.
Turabian, K., Booth, W., Colomb, G. and Williams, J. (2007). *A Manual for Writers of Term Papers, Theses, and Dissertations*. 7th ed. Chicago: University of Chicago Press.

Journal: Author Surname(s), Initial(s). (year). Title of article. *Title of Journal*. Volume, part: pages.
Chernin, E. (1988). The 'Harvard system': A mystery dispelled. *British Medical Journal*, 297, 6655: 1062–1063.

Website: Organization (year). *Title of Website*. URL. Date retrieved.
Anglia Ruskin University (2010). *Referencing*.
http://libweb.anglia.ac.uk/referencing/referencing.htm. Retrieved 05/04/10.

What other referencing systems are there?

As noted above, there is no universal system for referencing. As a student, there are three golden rules to follow:

- **Follow the guidelines of your department:** look in your handbook, talk to your teachers or the administrative staff and find out which is used.
- **Be consistent**: do not mix and match the systems that you use. This is something which can irritate university teachers.
- **Ensure that your in-text citations match your references**: anything that you quote in the text must also appear in your references.

This is a list of other commonly used referencing systems and their key features. For each, URLs for websites where further information can be obtained are included.

Modern Languages Association www.mla.org. The MLA system is widely used in North America, particularly in the humanities.

Modern Humanities Research Association www.mhra.org.uk. The MHRA system is widely used in the United Kingdom, particularly in the arts and humanities.

Chicago www.chicagomanualofstyle.org. This footnote-based system is often used in historical journals and the social sciences.

American Psychological Association www.apastyle.org. APA is similar to Harvard as it also uses author–date order, and is used predominantly in the social sciences.

Vancouver www.nlm.nih.gov/citingmedicine. Also known as the 'Author–Number' system, it is commonly used in the physical sciences (particularly medicine).

Oscola www.law.ox.ac.uk/publications/oscola.php. A system specifically used in law.

D Activation

Look at the following essay extract and the accompanying references.
Identify the six mistakes.

According to (Gibaldi and the Modern Language Association of America 2003), good referencing is important because it enables you to become part of the academic community. This view is supported by Tara (2010), who argues that the success or failure of a PhD can rest on good references. Oshima and Hogue (1991), meanwhile, emphasize the importance of referencing in avoiding plagiarism when stating 'if you neglect to mention whose ideas you are using, you are guilty of … plagiarism.'

References

Brabazon, T. (2010). How not to write a PhD thesis. *Times Higher Education Supplement*, 28 January.
www.timeshighereducation.co.uk/story.asp?sectioncode=26&storycode=410208.

Gibaldi, Joseph, and Modern Language Association of America. *MLA Handbook for Writers of Research Papers*. 6th ed. New York: Modern Language Association of America, 2003.

E Personalization

- **Check your department's handbook to see which system is used.**
  - Learn about this system. A simple Internet search will identify the information you need. Look at books and articles which use this system to see how it works in context.

- **Check whether your university uses any electronic referencing systems. This can save you time. If not, there is a range of both free and paid-for software which you may consider obtaining.**

- **Examine your recent writing and assess the quality of your referencing. Ask yourself the following questions:**
  - Did I use more than one system?
  - Did all my in-text citations appear in my references?

F Extension

- Step 3 and Step 4 outline the reasons for using **source material** in your writing which you will need to reference.

- Unit J describes strategies for **proofreading**. It is important to check your use of references, as this is often an area where unnecessary mistakes are made.

- Appendix 4, Step 5 lists hyperlinks for all the websites on pages 24–25, along with others which provide detailed information about referencing systems.

How do I choose my source material?

> *'The way to do research is to attack the facts.'*
>
> Celia Green

A Reflection

What are the advantages and disadvantages of using the following sources to research your essays?

- your reading list
- Wikipedia®
- Google Scholar
- academic journals
- academic books
- general books on the subject
- online podcasts/lectures

B Contextualization

Imagine that you have been asked to answer this essay question: 'What are the characteristics of good academic writing?' Details of one of your sources are below.

- *Consider the following four questions about this source.*

  1. Is it relevant?
  2. Is it authoritative?
  3. Is it recent?
  4. Is it reliable?

Title	EAP: Issues and directions
Authors	Ken Hyland, Liz Hamp-Lyons
Publication	*Journal of English for Academic Purposes*, 1, 1: 1–12
Keywords	English (second language); English for academic purposes; scholarly journals; second language instruction; second language learning

Extract from abstract

The field of English for Academic Purposes has developed rapidly in the past 25 years to become a major force in English language teaching and research. Drawing its strength from broad theoretical foundations and a commitment to research-based language education, EAP has begun to reveal some of the constraints of social contexts on language use and to develop ways for learners to gain control over these.

Contents

1. EAP, ESP and *JEAP*
2. What is EAP?
3. The growth of English for Academic Purposes
4. Users of 'academic' English
5. 'Academic literacy'
6. Disciplinary variation or similarity
7. The concept of 'community'
8. New genres and new technologies
9. Accommodation or critique
10. Conclusions

Sample

First sentence: 'The growth of English as the leading language for the dissemination of academic knowledge has transformed the educational experiences of countless students, who must now gain fluency in the conventions of English language academic discourses to understand their disciplines and to successfully navigate their learning.'

Random sentence from middle: 'However, the full implications of this communications revolution are not yet apparent or completely understood, and we still have a long way to go before we can be sure we are using its potential most effectively in our teaching.'

C Analysis

Strengths and drawbacks of certain source materials

Your reading list
- ✓ The people who will be marking your essay – experts in their field – have recommended this list. You should trust their opinion.
- ✗ The list may be extremely long and unrealistic and may reflect your lecturer's bias/interest.

Wikipedia® (en.Wikipedia.org)
- ✓ Can be a good starting point for research, especially if you know little about the subject.
- ✗ It is not considered an appropriate academic source as it may be subjective and biased.

Google Scholar (scholar.google.co.uk)
- ✓ Identifies purely academic sources (e.g., books, abstracts, articles, theses), providing an indication of how popular/respected they are among the academic community.
- ✗ You may have to pay to read some of the material which it identifies.

Academic journals
- ✓ Easy to search, should be available through your university and up-to-date.
- ✗ Can be difficult/technical/focused on very specific issues.

Academic books
- ✓ Tend to be authoritative and well-respected.
- ✗ Texts can be long and difficult to understand.

General books on the subject
- ✓ May offer a useful introduction to the subject (if they are written in a non-academic style).
- ✗ May not be considered appropriate academic sources and may trivialize certain issues.

Online podcasts/lectures
- ✓ A good resource if your listening skills are better than your reading skills.
- ✗ Can be time-consuming – difficult to get a quick overview (unlike a reading text).

How can I choose my source material?

Besides asking the four questions noted on page 27, talk to people on your course or who took the course last year. They may be able to provide useful recommendations.

Question 1: Is it relevant?
You will have a lot of reading. As a non-native speaker, this may take a long time. You will probably not have time to read everything you want to – so be selective. Everything you read should be directly related to your essay title.

Strategy 1: Read the ABSTRACT

This gives an overview of the book/paper, probably including the research topic; the specific study area; methodology; key findings. A brief analysis will indicate how appropriate the source is.

☑ 'The field of English for Academic Purposes' – relevant to the essay question.

☑ 'Broad theoretical foundations' – implies it will be wide-ranging and quite general.

☑ 'To develop ways for learners to gain' – suggests it might be student-focused.

Strategy 2: Read the TABLE OF CONTENTS/INDEX/KEYWORDS

A table of contents gives an overview of the book's chapters; the index indicates specific ideas. Both can be used to focus research on the sections of most value to you.

☑ '4. Users of "academic" English' and '5. "Academic literacy"' – these sections indicate that they might be particularly useful in answering your essay question.

☒ '1. EAP, ESP and *JEAP*' and '6. Disciplinary variation or similarity' – these sections use abbreviations/technical language, indicating that the intended audience may be experts.

Strategy 3: Read an extract

Are you the intended audience of the book? Is the level too easy or too difficult? If you cannot understand much from the extract, the book will be of little use to you.

❓ By looking at a sample of the writing, you must make this judgement yourself.

Question 2: Is it authoritative?

There is no point in using the ideas of people who are not respected in your academic field.

Strategy 4: Identify the publishers

If the book/article has been published by a well-respected publisher (e.g., a good UNIVERSITY PRESS, a major publishing company), you can assume the publication has a certain quality. These publishers are unlikely to publish material they think is factually inaccurate or extremely biased. If, however, it is by a VANITY publisher, its 'authority' may be less.

❓ *Journal of English for Academic Purposes* – a respected journal in its field; experts in the field have judged this article to be of the necessary quality. However, the journal is aimed at professionals, so the level may be inappropriate for a student.

Question 3: Is it recent?

Scholarship moves forward quickly. In some subjects (e.g., robotics), even five years is a long time. You must judge whether the information is still relevant to your topic.

Strategy 5: Look at the date the book was published

❓ '2002'. Although in ten years the core principles of academic writing will probably not have changed much, some of the content about 'new technologies' may not be relevant. You may want to compare this source with more recent sources as well.

Question 4: Is it reliable?

Since people can publish material more easily than ever before (mainly via the Internet), reliability is an increasingly important issue. **Step 7** and **Step 8** focus on these issues.

D Activation

Which types of sources would be most useful if …

1. … you have no idea about a particular subject?

_____

2. … you want specific academic information about a topic?

_____

3. … you have a good understanding of the topic and want to deepen your understanding?

_____

4. … you are tired of/bored with reading and want a change?

_____

 ## E Personalization

 ### What is your current practice?

- Make a list of the sources which you used for a recent essay.
- Ask yourself the four questions given in part B.
- Make yourself a table (see below – this can be photocopied from Appendix 1, Step 6, Document 1) and fill it in accordingly with a tick, a cross or a question mark.

Source	Relevant?	Authoritative?	Recent?	Reliable?	Comments	Read?
Name of source	✓ ? X	✓ ? X	✓ ? X	✓ ? X	Any relevant comments which might help you decide whether to read the source later.	✓ ? X

- The information in the right-hand column will help you prioritize which sources you are going to use first.

F Extension

- Step 7 examines the advantages and disadvantages of using the **Internet** for research.
- Step 8 enhances your **critical thinking skills**, enabling you to make better judgements about your sources.
- Step 13 develops your ability to understand **essay titles** and therefore how to be more selective in your reading.
- Step 49 looks in more detail at **abstracts**, which can be useful in deciding whether or not to read a source.
- Appendix 4, Step 5 provides hyperlinks for websites which may help you research your essay.
- Appendix 1, Step 6, Document 1 provides the table from part E above in photocopiable form, to help you evaluate your potential source material.

How should I use the Internet for research?

'*Getting information off the Internet is like taking a drink from a fire hydrant.*'

Mitch Kapor

A Reflection

Consider the following statements about researching essays on the Internet, as opposed to using printed sources. Do you agree or disagree with them?

1. It is easier to find the information I want.   Agree / Disagree
2. It is more difficult to judge whether the information is academic or not.   Agree / Disagree
3. The sources are more likely to be subjective.   Agree / Disagree
4. I am more likely to commit plagiarism accidentally.   Agree / Disagree
5. The information is more relevant.   Agree / Disagree

B Contextualization

Look at the following websites and decide which would be useful for researching your essays. Add in your comments and assess their suitability (✓, ? or ✗).

URL	Description	Comments	Suitability
journals.cambridge.org	An online journal database.	*Wide range, relevant topics, academic focus*	✓
www.guardian.co.uk	Centre-left 'quality' newspaper.		
www.richarddawkins.net	Personal website of the well-known academic Richard Dawkins.		
metalib.kcl.ac.uk	Internal website of the library service of King's College London.		
answers.yahoo.com	Online forum for people to ask questions about any subject.		
www.archiveshub.ac.uk	A collection of archives held in UK universities and colleges.		
en.Wikipedia.org	Encyclopaedia to which the public can contribute.		
www.sciencedirect.com	An online science database.		
www.jstor.com	Wide-ranging online journal database.		
www.dailymail.co.uk	Right-wing, mid-range newspaper.		

Analysis

What are the advantages and disadvantages of using the Internet for research?

It is easier to find the information I want.

In theory, the ability to search electronically for information allows you to target the information you want. Rather than time-intensive investigations of printed material, you can type a few terms into a search engine and, seconds later, be presented with lots of information. However, while some of this information will be useful, much of it will be useless. As the quotation at the beginning of this step suggests, searching the Internet for information can be a very long and difficult process. When used wisely (e.g., using the hyperlinked references at the end of a journal), the Internet can be an extremely valuable and powerful tool, but be careful.

Keywords and journals

Keywords are particularly useful for searching journals. They help you narrow down your focus of research and identify other articles which may be of relevance and interest. For example, searching for the general term 'academic writing' on a journal site can lead to more specific terms, such as: 'English for Academic Purposes'; 'second language writing development'; 'second language writing'; 'disciplinary writing and instruction'; and 'cross-cultural rhetoric'.

It is more difficult to judge whether the information is academic or not.

Getting an academic paper or book published can be a long and exhausting process. It has to be drafted and redrafted many times, often following the advice of other specialists in the field. Publishers also take a financial risk when printing books, so are unlikely to invest in anything of poor quality. Articles in good journals are always PEER-REVIEWED. In short, therefore, if something is *printed* or appears in a journal (print or electronic), there is a better chance of it being a good *quality* piece of writing (even if you disagree with its ideas).

A quick checklist for websites

Domain: what is the Internet suffix? Is it an educational site (e.g., .ac.uk or .edu)? Is it from an organization (.org) or a governmental body (.gov)? Or is it from a company (.co.uk or .com)?
Appearance: Does it look academic (font, layout, colours etc.)? Does it look professional?
Style: Is the language academic? Does it contain references to academic articles? Does it sound knowledgeable about the subject?

On the Internet, however, anyone who has a basic understanding of HTML can set up an Internet site in a few minutes and publish whatever they like. There is no checking, no evaluation and no financial investment. While you can easily find out more information about the writer of a book or article, many Internet sites are anonymous. As a general rule, information on the Internet is more likely to be biased, subjective and unreliable (see below), which means that it is inappropriate for use in an academic essay.

One solution is that rather than using a general search engine (such as Google, Yahoo or Bing), you should use Google Scholar (see Step 6). This will guarantee that you only search academic sources.

The sources are more likely to be subjective.

Setting up a website is relatively easy and cheap, so online material will often be written by groups with a particular opinion on the subject you are researching. Such groups may present a one-sided argument which is selective in its evidence. Sometimes the stance is clearly suggested by the name of the website – www.createdemocracy.com would seem to be clearly pro-democracy. Other sites, however, have more ambiguous addresses. You could not know that www.migrationwatch.co.uk is anti-immigration from the address alone.

I am more likely to commit plagiarism accidentally.

This is certainly a danger. If you are in a hurry to finish an essay, the temptation to 'copy and paste' sections from an online article can be difficult to resist. However, as discussed in Step 3, you are almost certain to be caught if you do this. Alternatively, you might copy and paste parts of an article into your notes/essay with the intention of paraphrasing/summarizing it later – only to be unable to identify which parts are yours and which are from the original. This kind of ACCIDENTAL PLAGIARISM is dealt with in exactly the same way as intentional plagiarism. Ignorance is no defence.

The information is more relevant.

In the modern age, people are writing about events as they happen, through newspaper websites and blogs. In the academic community, however, there is a general feeling that it is necessary for some time to pass in order to judge events properly. While the quotation from Zhou Enlai may be extreme, it contains an element of truth.

> *It is too early to judge.*
> Zhou Enlai (in 1960), when asked his opinion about the 1789 French Revolution.

Another reason people feel that Internet information is more relevant is that, through sites with online forums and groups, you can post a specific question and, if you are lucky, get a specific answer back very quickly. Sometimes these answers may be useful, interesting and of good quality, but very often they will not be. You have to ask yourself who is replying to your question, what qualifies them to give an opinion, and where they got their information from (it could be plagiarized). Even though the information may provide you with a 'quick fix', it may not be what you are really looking for.

What types of website can be used in academic writing?

☑ **Journal websites:** The overwhelming majority of good-quality journals can now be found online at websites such as www.jstor.com or www.sciencedirect.com. On these sites it is possible to read and download thousands of articles, books and book reviews.

☑ **Academic databases:** Sites such as www.archiveshub.ac.uk contain many useful academic resources. Often these are subscription-based, but it is likely you can access them through your university.

☑ **University intranets:** Your own university's website (often accessed via the library pages) can often direct you towards a number of extremely useful websites (e.g., metalib.kcl.ac.uk), including academic databases and journals.

Remember the ABC of using the Internet for research:
Assess: is the information on the site relevant and reliable?
Bookmark: if you are going to use the website, make sure you can (a) access it quickly and (b) have a record of where you got the information from.
Choose: do not just copy and paste information because it is easy – decide which of the source material you have is genuinely useful.

? **Newspapers and magazines:** These sources of information may be non-academic, and are more likely to be subjective. For example, a 'quality' newspaper, www.guardian.co.uk, has centre-left political views; www.dailymail.co.uk, on the other hand, is right-wing and less formal.

? **Blogs:** Some specialists are very active blog users (e.g., www.richarddawkins.net), but often the information found on blogs will be poorly researched and highly subjective.

✗ **Wikipedia® and online forums:** While sites such as en.Wikipedia.org or answers.yahoo.com may be useful starting points for your research (if you have little or no understanding of the topic), you should only use them as a platform to go on to more appropriate sites.

Step 7

D Activation

Assess the usefulness of the following websites for academic research, based on the results of web searches given.

1. **EBSCOhost – world's foremost premium research database service**
EBSCOhost (ebscohost.com) serves thousands of libraries and other institutions with premium content in every subject area.

2. **32504 university essays & university coursework documents …**
Academic DB is the UK's largest university essay and coursework database.

3. **Economist.com**
Authoritative weekly newspaper focusing on international politics and business news and opinion.

4. **BBC – Homepage**
Breaking news, sport, TV, radio and a whole lot more. The BBC informs, educates and entertains – wherever you are, whatever your age.

5. **Answers.com: Wiki Q&A combined with free online dictionary …**
Wiki Q&A combined with free online dictionary, thesaurus and encyclopaedias.

E Personalization

Examine the Internet source material which you used in recent essays (you may find this information in the browsing history of your Internet browser).

- According to the criteria listed above, do you think these sources were suitable for academic writing?

If you are a regular user of Wikipedia®:

- Look at some of the references used and go back to the original source.

Identify which online academic resources you have access to through your institution.

- What general academic resources are there? Explore these resources so you know exactly what is available.

F Extension

Steps 3, 4 and 5 looked at the issues of **plagiarism** and **referencing**. When taking any kind of notes, but especially notes from electronic sources, it is important that you understand these topics. If you are still unclear, revisit these steps.

Step 8 helps sharpen your **critical evaluation skills**, which are essential when using web-based information.

Step 10 explains how you can **take notes** more effectively, which is important when using any kind of resource material.

Step 13 looks at how you can fully understand your **title**. Because of the huge amount of information on the Internet, it is important that you focus on information which is directly relevant.

Appendix 2, Step 7, Activity 1 is a short additional test of your knowledge on how to use the Internet appropriately for researching essays.
Appendix 4, Step 7 lists the hyperlinks you considered in part B. Check their suitability for your research purposes.

What critical thinking skills do I need to develop?

> '*There is nothing either good or bad, but thinking makes it so.*'
>
> **William Shakespeare** (*Hamlet* Act 2, Scene 2)

A Reflection

Which of these three definitions of 'critical thinking' do you think is correct?

- Critical thinking means reading what experts have said and presenting a general summary of their ideas.
- Critical thinking means saying that everything you read is wrong.
- Critical thinking means not being afraid to challenge what experts have said, and using this as a way of shaping your own view about a topic.

B Contextualization

Look at the two pieces of writing below. The first is purely descriptive (i.e., it only summarizes what other people have said, offering no authorial opinion), whereas the second is more analytical.

- *Why is the second text a more appropriate piece of academic writing?*

Descriptive writing

Fisher and Scriven describe critical thinking as 'a skilled, active interpretation and evaluation of observations, communications, information, and argumentation' (1997: 20). Russell states that 'the intelligent are full of doubt' (1998: 28). Facione et al. (2000: 101) argue that without scrutiny, the following type of texts would be common: 'intellectually *dishonest* (e.g., in the use of data), *intolerant* (e.g., of opposing ideas), *inattentive* (e.g., to implications of proposals), *haphazard* (e.g., procedurally), *mistrustful of reason* (e.g., hostile toward sound scientific inquiry), *indifferent* (e.g., toward new findings), and *simplistic* (e.g., naively dualistic).' Orwell has the following attributed to him: 'During times of universal deceit, telling the truth becomes a revolutionary act.'

Analytical writing

Critical thinking is a notoriously difficult term to define, although Fisher and Scriven's classification of it as 'a skilled, active interpretation and evaluation of observations, communications, information, and argumentation' (1997: 20) captures many of its essential details. Echoing Russell's truism that 'the intelligent are full of doubt' (1998: 28), Facione et al. (2000: 101) argue that without this doubt, academic study would allow biased, prejudiced and illogical texts to not be scrutinized properly. Although the saying attributed to Orwell that 'during times of universal deceit, telling the truth becomes a revolutionary act' may be a little too political for the academic context, the idea is still a strong one.

References

Facione, P., Facione, N. and Giancarlo, C. (2000). The disposition toward critical thinking: Character, measurement, and relationship to critical thinking. *Informal Logic, 20,* 1: 61–84.

Fisher, A. and Scriven, M. (1997). *Critical Thinking: Its Definition and Assessment*. Norwich: Centre for Research in Critical Thinking.

Russell, B. (1998). *Mortals and Others: Bertrand Russell's American Essays 1931–1935*. London: Routledge.

UNIT B Researching your essay

c Analysis

Why is critical thinking important?

Critical thinking is a term which you will frequently read and hear during your time at university. Feedback for student essays often says that they 'lack critical thinking'. However, little guidance may be given as to what this means, or how you can improve. Although it is difficult to give an *exact* definition of the term, it is possible to identify some key characteristics. Three important ideas – identified here as the '3 Cs' – are as follows:

The word *critical*
Although the word *critical* has a purely negative connotation in day-to-day English, in academic language it means 'evaluative' or 'analytical'.

Challenge: Do not be afraid of questioning what 'experts' and scholars have written about a particular topic. They are not always right.

Consider: Reflect on what you have read, and identify what your POSITION is. As the second text in part B shows, good academic writing is analytical rather than just descriptive (i.e., it says *why* and *how*, not just *what*, *when* and *where*).

Combine: Having read a range of sources, you need to synthesize your ideas. Good academic writing analyzes the issues from all angles and is based on a wide range of evidence and sources.

Critical thinking is much more important in the British university system than in many other countries (see Step 3). In some cultures, it is not considered good practice to challenge the views of authorities and well-respected writers. In the UK, however, a culture of SCEPTICISM exists: you are encouraged to test and challenge ideas. Of course, any criticisms you make must be supported by evidence: you cannot disagree with something without saying *why*. As such, many students find critical thinking difficult, and find it strange when their essays (which would have received good marks in their home academic system) score poorly. When looking at texts critically, there are several important questions which you can ask, including:

* Are there NECESSARY AND SUFFICIENT CONDITIONS for the claims which are being made (i.e., based on the evidence which exists, are the conclusions reasonable)?

* Does the text show BIAS? For example, does the author have particular beliefs which may unfairly influence his or her writing? Or, if the research has been funded by a particular organization, might this influence the results?

* Is the text censored? Has the government, or another agency, hidden any of the information?

This is not to say that you should avoid any material which may be affected in these ways, but you should be careful about how you use it. Sources which might be considered 'propaganda' are, academically speaking, much weaker.

Three golden rules for successful critical thinking

Be rational: if you are not prepared to change your view about a subject, you should not be studying at university. You should be prepared to follow your reason, wherever it takes you.
Be open-minded: one of the great opportunities of studying at university in a foreign country is to broaden your perspective. As Socrates himself said, 'I am a citizen not of Athens, but of the world' – follow the logic to get to the truth.
Be radical: do not be afraid to adopt controversial positions if you believe them to be right. Just because a view is unpopular, or is different to what the majority think, does not make it wrong. What makes it wrong is if it lacks evidence. After all, the ideas of Darwin and Einstein were once ridiculed.

Developing your critical thinking skills

The following technique, known as the Socratic method (named after Socrates, the Greek philosopher who developed it), is an effective way of testing the truth of statements. This system is based on the idea of SCEPTICISM, and proceeds as follows:

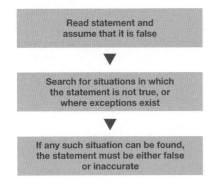

E.g., 'All foreign students have poor critical thinking skills.'

There are many thousands of overseas students at British universities who, every year, graduate with excellent degrees. If they all had poor critical thinking skills, this could not happen.

Thus, the statement is false and could be challenged in an essay: 'Sowton's assertion lacks evidence'; 'Sowton's claim is false.'

Additionally, your reaction can be modified in two ways:

- **Expanding your objection**: you might criticize the evidence or methodology which the author used – or you might present COUNTER-EVIDENCE which strengthens your opposition. For example:
  - Sowton's study not only focused on a small sample but also used ambiguous questions.
  - The data gathered do not support Sowton's conclusion.
  - The high number of foreign students at UK universities demonstrates the weakness of Sowton's argument.
- **Offering a concession**: you might try to explain the reason why the writer came to a wrong decision. For example:
  - Although many students come from countries where critical thinking is not valued as highly as in the UK, Sowton's conclusions are still too extreme.

Using critical thinking in your own proofreading

Critical thinking can also play an important role in checking your own writing. For example, the sentence above can be improved by repeatedly using the Socratic method, until a suitable sentence is produced.

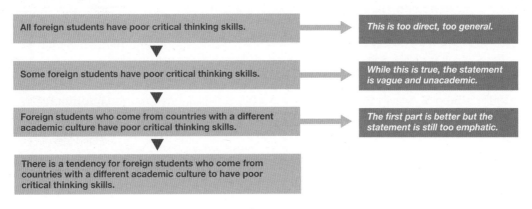

Step
8

D Activation

Read the following passage and highlight any assertion which you feel can be challenged using the strategies listed overleaf. In each case, explain *why*.

> Students from countries which can broadly be said to have a 'Confucian system' (particularly China, Japan and South Korea) have difficulty with critical thinking because of the academic cultures found in these countries. I have taught many people from this part of the world, and they always seem to have difficulties. Clearly, therefore, your mother tongue is also an important factor. In my opinion, French and German speakers also have significant problems in this respect. Recent research (e.g., Smith, 2001; Barton 2004) indicates that it is not only overseas students who have problems with critical thinking, but British students as well. This research is supported by **www.criticalthinkingcourses.com**.

E Personalization

▢ **Examine a recent essay you have written and:**
- highlight any unsupported arguments, or arguments which have weak supporting evidence
- challenge these arguments (following the Socratic method outlined overleaf)
- rewrite them accordingly

▢ **Consider whether you yourself:**
- have any particular bias (e.g., political, national, cultural) which may influence either your reading or writing

▢ **If you decide you have, consider how you can reduce this bias, or at least minimize it.**

F Extension

▢ Steps 6 and 7 analyzed the best way to **choose your source material**, both print and online, a process which is greatly aided by good critical thinking skills.

▢ Step 9 focuses on the development of **reading skills** – including critical reading – an idea closely related to this step.

▢ Step 23 looks at **hedging language**, which is useful when you need to modify your statements.

▢ Step 25 concentrates on the ways in which you can develop your **arguments** clearly, a process which requires good critical thinking skills.

▢ Unit J focuses on **proofreading**, where critical thinking skills are imperative.

▢ Appendix 2, Step 8, Activity 2 provides a list of controversial, unsupported **quotations** by so-called 'experts' – your job is to challenge them using your critical thinking skills.

How can I read more efficiently?

> *'Reading is thinking with someone else's head instead of one's own.'*
>
> **Arthur Schopenhauer**

A Reflection

Look at the following statements about reading and tick the ones which apply to you. In each case, consider *why*.

- ☐ I often have to read a passage two or three times to understand it.
- ☐ I always read in **CHRONOLOGICAL ORDER**.
- ☐ I read every single word in the text.
- ☐ I spend lots of time looking up new words.

B Contextualization

Look at the text in the box below:

1. **Read the title** and predict the text's focus.
2. **Write down 2–3 bullet points** in the box on the right about what you want to learn from this text.
3. **What is the focus going to be?** Read the topic sentence (the first sentence of the paragraph).
4. **Read the full text** in no more than three minutes, but:
   - *do not read every single word*: divide the text into phrases
   - *do not use a dictionary*: guess at the meaning of unfamiliar words
   - *focus particularly on* **SIGNPOSTING LANGUAGE**: this may help your understanding

What specific strategies can improve reading skills?

In trying to develop reading skills, there are four key areas which students should try to improve: understanding, flexibility, speed and comprehension. Greater understanding comes through more active involvement in the text. Rather than just hoping that understanding will develop passively, it is imperative to examine the text analytically – whether autobiography, academic essay or newspaper article. Increased flexibility comes from not slavishly following the linear order of the text, but by adapting your reading strategies accordingly (e.g., reading the conclusion first). Turning to the issue of speed, focusing on the content-carrying words of the language, and reading in clusters of words (i.e., two-, three- and four-word phrases) can be beneficial. Finally, greater comprehension can be realized by focusing more on your prediction skills and your general understanding of the English language, and less time on your electronic dictionary. In brief, while reading may appear to be an insurmountable problem, by adopting a few key strategies, significant improvements can be made.

Analysis

Academic reading: an overview

There are two main reasons we read: for pleasure and for information. Hopefully, your academic reading is both pleasurable and informative, although it is more likely to be the latter! Academic reading differs from other types of reading in that the texts tend to be longer and more challenging. This means that you have to be an ACTIVE READER to understand the texts in as much detail as possible.

For many students, reading is the strongest of the four skills. However, many still face significant challenges when starting at British universities. Reading lists can be very long, and the texts may be far more difficult than anything you have seen before. Even confident readers may need to make several important modifications to their reading skills.

Developing your reading skills

Achieving greater understanding: I often have to read a passage two or three times to understand it.

As a student, you do not have time to reread long texts. It is normal to reread certain difficult sentences or paragraphs, but if you need to read whole texts again and again in order to understand them, the problem is more serious. In your reading, you need to achieve a balance between breadth (i.e., to gain a good overall understanding of the subject) and depth (i.e., a reasonable level of detail). Becoming an ACTIVE READER is the best way to achieve a greater understanding of the text. There are two main strategies for doing this:

Strategy 1: Predict content. Use the TITLE, SUB-HEADINGS, ABSTRACT and KEYWORDS to predict what you think will be included in the text. This will 'warm-up' your brain, and you may find that you already have some knowledge of the topic.
Title: What specific strategies can improve reading skills?
You may be able to predict what might follow using your knowledge of reading skills in your mother tongue and your previous experience of learning English.

Strategy 2: Ensure you know why you are reading the text. It is important that you know *why* you are reading a text. Ask yourself what you want to learn from it. You tend to get more out of a text if you are actively searching for answers as you read it. For this particular text, you might ask:
- What general skills can I develop and use in my reading?
- What are the major problems non-native speakers face in reading academic texts?

Achieving greater flexibility: I always read in chronological order.

Academic reading is not like reading a novel: you can read the information in the order which works best for you. You should think of it like making orange juice: you want to squeeze out all the useful information you can (the juice) and then throw the rest away.

Strategy 3: Read the 'high-value' parts of a text first. For example, the topic sentence (the first sentence of a paragraph, which outlines its theme), the introduction and the conclusion. SKIM-READING is a skill which can be usefully employed here.
In trying to develop reading skills, there are four key areas which students should try to improve: understanding, flexibility, speed and comprehension.
This sentence provides a clear overview of the theme of the paragraph – and makes it clear that there are four particular issues which will be discussed.

Achieving greater speed: I read every single word in the text.

Reading every word in a text is simply not an option. Not only does it take too long, it actually makes comprehension more difficult. It is important to see how the text works as a whole, rather than as a series of individual words. Two useful strategies for increasing your speed are as follows:

Strategy 4: Read in PHRASES. It is usually possible to break English texts up into phrases of two, three or four words. Looking at the first three sentences, it is clear that these phrases will often be adjectival phrases and NOUN PHRASES (four key areas, greater understanding) and VERB PHRASES (to develop, will develop passively).

Strategy 5: Focus on CONTENT WORDS (e.g., nouns and verbs) rather than STRUCTURE WORDS (e.g., prepositions and conjunctions). As such, by focusing on them, you are more likely to gain a general understanding of the information which really matters. The following example is taken from the penultimate sentence of the text. It is much easier to understand the main idea of the text which contains only the content words.

Structure words only	Content words only
Finally, _____ can be _____ by _____ more on your _____ and your general _____ of the _____	_____, greater comprehension _____ realized _____ focusing _____ prediction skills _____ understanding _____ English language, ...

Achieving greater comprehension: I spend lots of time looking up new words.

An understanding of how words work, and how they relate to each other, can help in your comprehension of the text – in particular, how the text develops and how the sentences are organized.

Strategy 6: Guess the meaning of words. Constantly looking up words is very time-consuming, and just because you have an electronic dictionary, it does not mean you have to use it. There are many clues within the text which you can use to guess at the meaning of unfamiliar words. Most of the time, an approximate meaning of the word is enough – you do not need to know the *exact* meaning.

- **Contextualization:** guess the meaning of the word from the context. Put in a likely synonym and see whether it makes sense.
  ... reading in *clusters* of words (i.e., two-, three- and four-word phrases) can be beneficial ...
  Imagine *clusters* was not there; what would you put in its place? Perhaps *groups*. This meaning is confirmed by the definition which follows (i.e., two-, three- and four-word phrases).

- **Prefixes and suffixes:** the beginning and ending of the word may contain parts which tell you something about it.
  Autobiography: written by a person about their own life (*auto* = 'self', *bio* = 'living', *graphy* = 'writing').

- **Word family:** although you may not be able to recognize the word, you may recognize words which have the same ROOT, helping you to guess its meaning.
  Analytically: this word may be unfamiliar, but *analysis* is relatively common. From this (and out of knowledge that ~ly is a common suffix for adverbs), it is possible to understand that *analytically* means 'looking at something closely and in detail'.

Strategy 7: Look for cohesion. Good writers use a range of language in the text to tell the reader where it is going. This SIGNPOSTING LANGUAGE can be an extremely useful 'map'.
Turning to the issue of speed: indicates that the author is moving on to a different subject.
In brief: indicates that a summary will follow.

D Activation

Read the following sentence from part B and complete tasks 1–4.

> '[Increased flexibility] comes from not slavishly following the linear order of the text, but by <u>adapting</u> your reading strategies accordingly (e.g., reading the conclusion first).'

1. Using square brackets, divide the sentence into meaningful phrases (e.g., increased flexibility).
2. Underline the CONTENT WORDS in the text (e.g., adapting).
3. Without using a dictionary, guess the meaning of the following words:
    *   Slavishly
    *   Linear
    *   Accordingly
4. Is there anything in the passage which can help with cohesion (e.g., but, indicating contradictory information)?

E Personalization

*   **Analyze the source material which you used for recent essays and ask yourself:**
    *   how long did it take to read?
    *   were there any texts which I found particularly difficult? If so, could I have read any of them more effectively?
*   **Practise the strategies identified in part D with a short text.**
*   **Identify your reading speed.** There are many websites where you can get this information – e.g., www.readingsoft.com. Knowledge of this can help you plan better and be more realistic about how much background reading you can do.
*   **For your next piece of reading, set yourself a time limit and stick to it. The time limit should be challenging but reasonable.**

F Extension

*   Step 12 looks at **time management**, crucial because reading takes up such a high percentage of your time as a student.
*   Step 18 focuses on **topic sentences**, which can be an extremely useful tool in reading more quickly.
*   Steps 19 (**introductions**), 20 (**conclusions**) and 49 (**abstracts**) all focus on high-content, fact-focused parts of the essay.
*   Steps 29 (**cohesion**) and 30 (**linking devices**) provide extra explanations on SIGNPOSTING LANGUAGE.
*   Appendix 1, Step 9, Document 2 is a photocopiable document based on part B, which you can use before reading a text.
*   Appendix 3, Step 9 lists high-frequency **prefixes** and **suffixes** in academic English; Appendix 4, Step 9 provides a link to a reading evaluation website.

How can I take notes effectively?

*'I don't like the sound of all those lists he's making –
it's like taking too many notes at school; you feel
you've achieved something when you haven't.'*

Dodie Smith

A Reflection

Which of the following are true for you? Consider where these problems may originate.

1. I am dissatisfied with the way in which I currently take notes. Agree / Disagree
2. I find it difficult to distinguish what is and isn't important. Agree / Disagree
3. I can take notes well in my own language, but not in English. Agree / Disagree
4. When I look at my notes afterwards, they make no sense. Agree / Disagree

B Contextualization

Below are some well-taken notes from a lecture. Analyze them, then complete the table.

Topic[1]	The importance of note-taking at university	Lecturer[2]	Miss Inga Structure
Relevance[3] 1,500-word essay (due next week) is on 'good academic skills'		Date[4]	25 June 2011

Summary[5]	Main notes
Definition of note-taking	+[6] NT[7] is: – brief[8] – clear[8] Ss take 2[6] long to wrt[7] notes [6] O[6] time left to write essays: 'drowned in data'[9]
Why is NT important?	2 v. imp[7] reasons for NT: Edu: 2 dvp yr ideas[8] Prac: 2 use 4 essays & exams[8]

Note	Aspect	How can this feature improve the quality of your notes?
1	Topic	For organizing your notes properly and remembering the main focus.
2	Lecturer	
3	Relevance	
4	Date	
5	Summary	
6	Symbols	
7	Abbreviations	
8	Bullets/lists	
9	Quotation	

c Analysis

What common problems are associated with note-taking?

I am dissatisfied with the way in which I currently take notes.

Note-taking can be an extremely frustrating activity. However, since you will spend a significant percentage of your academic life taking notes, it is a skill which you have to develop. As with all skills, it will not improve by itself; it is something which you have to work hard at. While this step provides guidance on strategies you can use, it is important that you develop a system which works well for you. To do this, you will need to reflect on how you learn most successfully, as this will differ from person to person.

There are three main problem areas for overseas students regarding taking notes: **content**, **language** and **usage**.

Content: I find it difficult to distinguish what is and isn't important.

First of all, let us consider what the word *notes* actually means. *The Oxford English Dictionary* defines the word as a 'brief record of facts, impressions or topics'. The word 'brief' is particularly important. Problems often stem from students writing too much. In reading, this is a problem because your notes may often be as long as the text itself. In listening, if you write too much, you may always feel that you are 'behind' the lecturer, i.e., writing down the lecturer's last point when he or she has already started a new one.

When deciding whether you should note something or not, ask yourself the following questions: is it *relevant* or is it *valuable*? You need to prioritize information which is *directly* applicable to your subject area. You should also note down information which you consider to be particularly interesting or authoritative – for example, a phrase or a sentence which perfectly summarizes an idea. In short, do not be afraid to do less.

Language: I can take notes well in my own language, but not in English.

Wherever possible, it is better to take notes in English. This will:

* enable you to practise the target language, English.
* ensure there are no 'mistranslations'.
* be more time-efficient, since you will be writing the essay in English.

However, in situations where you are finding the process difficult, and you feel that using your mother tongue would be helpful, it is better to use it. Remember, the primary purpose of note-taking is to remember information, not to practise language.

Usage: When I look at my notes afterwards, they make no sense.

There is nothing more upsetting than spending a long time taking notes, and then being unable to understand them when you look at them again. It makes you feel that the whole activity is pointless, and that you have wasted your time. There may be several causes of this problem:

* you cannot read your own handwriting.
* you cannot understand your own SHORTHAND.
* you cannot understand the logical development of ideas.

The suggestions which follow may help minimize such problems.

What is good note-taking practice?

As noted, note-taking is a very 'personal' concept. The model suggested here may not be applicable to everyone, but the good features of these notes should be considered. A transcript of the lecture from which the notes were taken appears below.

Transcript of lecture extract

The question which must first be addressed is: what do we actually mean by note-taking? It is a term which is frequently used but commonly misunderstood. In my opinion, there are two critical factors for good note-taking. Notes should be brief and they should be clear. One of the main problems faced by students is that they spend far too much time writing their notes, meaning that they have very little – if any – time left to actually write their essay. They are drowned in data. Moving on to the actual importance of notes, I would say that there are two major benefits. Firstly, the educational: taking notes can help stimulate your thoughts and develop your ideas. And, secondly, notes have a practical use: you need to be able to recall key information to incorporate into your essays and to prepare for your exams.

Topic

The importance of note-taking at university.

Lecturer

You need to know the name of the lecturer if you want to paraphrase or quote ideas from the lecture in your own essay.

Relevance

Thinking about *why* you are listening to this lecture, or reading this particular article, is extremely important. This will help you decide what kind of knowledge you hope to gain and what notes you need to take. It will make your listening more proactive.

Date

Needed so you can clearly organize your notes – especially if lectures are in a sequence.

Summary

When you read through your notes later, a summary on the left-hand side to remind yourself of key points can be useful. Try writing this summary as questions so your notes effectively become a series of questions and answers, useful for information recall.

Symbols

Symbols are a quick, easy, dynamic way to write down information. In the example notes, + means 'good', – denotes 'leads to/causes', and 0 represents 'nothing, no'. There are a number of symbols in common usage, but you may also wish to use your own personalized system. You might consider using *textspeak* (the language used in writing text messages) – e.g., *2 use 4 essays* (= to use for essays). **However, only use textspeak in your notes.**

Abbreviations

Various abbreviations are commonly used in academic writing, such as 'e.g.', 'etc.', 'i.e.', and 're:'. Writing other shortened forms (e.g., 'wrt' and 'NT') can save time. Be sure you can remember what the full word is. Normally this will be obvious from the context – e.g., 'wrt' clearly means 'write' and 'NT' means 'note-taking'.

Bullet points/lists

It tends to be much easier to remember information when it is presented in list form. It can help you categorize and organize information.

Quotation

If you hear (or read) a short phrase or extract which is extremely powerful and summarizes an idea very clearly, you may want to write it down word for word.

D Activation

Read the following text and make notes on it. A sample set of notes is provided in the answers section on page 212. A blank note-taking form, which you should use, can be photocopied from Appendix 1, Step 10, Document 3. Do not take longer than ten minutes to do this.

As they listen, students are expected to take notes, which will allow them to retrieve information later. Lecturers may try to help this process by indicating the overall structure and purpose of the lecture in visuals and handouts. They may vary their intonation to indicate the end of one section and the start of a new one. They may use textual signalling language: macro-markers, which state how the sections of the lecture fit together or link to other parts of a course, and micro-markers such as *but, well, now, so.* As well as signalling relations in meaning, these are also used to indicate where the lecturer moves to a new idea. However, students with a low proficiency level for listening may be unable to recognize the function of intonation, or distinguish signalling language from content language. They may find it difficult to listen, read and take notes at the same time. They may fail to recognize that they should supplement information contained in visuals and handouts with interpretive and evaluative comments made by the lecturer.

Extract from Alexander, O., Argent, S. & Spencer, J. (2008). *EAP Essentials.* **Reading: Garnet Education: 220.**

E Application

▣ **Look at the notes from the last lecture/piece of reading you did.**
- Do you understand them? If not, why not? Consider what improvements could be made.
- Do the same for notes you wrote six months ago. Do you understand them?

▣ **Having used the sample notes from this chapter ...**
- what did you like about them? How will you change your note-taking habits?
- what did you not like about them? What will you not change?

▣ **Compare your notes with those of a friend or colleague who went to the same lecture, or who read the same text.**
- Can you learn anything from her or his note-taking system?

▣ **Take some time after the lecture to edit your notes – an extra few minutes can have long-term benefits. Do not just put them in a file, never to be seen again.**

F Extension

▣ Step 12 looks at **time management** – an important crossover as note-taking consumes so much of your time as a student.

▣ Step 13 develops your ability to understand the **titles** of your assignments – knowledge of which will enable you to take more relevant notes.

▣ Step 31 analyzes the language which can be used to **report** what others have said.

▣ Appendix 1, Step 10, Document 3 is a photocopiable blank template form for note-taking, as outlined in part B.

▣ Appendix 3, Step 10 suggests more symbols and abbreviations which you might consider using when taking notes.

How does my mother tongue affect my writing?

'You live a new life for every new language you speak.'

Czech proverb

A Reflection

What problems might your mother tongue cause when you try to write in English?

- *Select the appropriate term for each sentence.*

    1. Sentences in my mother tongue are generally shorter than / the same length as / longer than in English.
    2. The grammar is similar to / different from that of English.
    3. The vocabulary comes from a source similar to / different from English.
    4. The word order is the same as / different from that of English.
    5. In my mother tongue, the way a word is said is the same as / different from the way it is written.

B Contextualization

Look at these sentences. In each, there is a mistake caused by MOTHER-TONGUE INFLUENCE.

- *Identify each mistake and decide which of these mistakes you are likely to make.*

    1. Many students have the idea that sentences in English should be extremely long, but that is not always true, and many sentences written by non-native speakers seem to go on for a very long time, but that can make it very difficult to follow exactly what is going on.

       Overly long sentence, with too many clauses – should be divided up into two sentences.

    2. The articles are particular problem for many students because an articles do not always exist in your the mother tongue.

    3. In many Romance languages (e.g., Spanish and Italian), it is meritorious to use Latin-based words as the norm.

    4. The use of collocations is well related to a language's culture.

    5. Spelling kan be hard becos inglish wurds are often ritten diffrently to how they sownd.

    6. I learn the past simple already in high school.

    7. Word order be can seen as a problem big for many students.

c Analysis

What problems can be caused by mother-tongue influence?

Some of the mistakes you make in English may be caused by the influence of your mother tongue. Additional problems which may be caused include:

- ■ **AVOIDANCE**, where you deliberately do not use particular grammar/language because you are worried you will use it incorrectly.

- ■ **FOSSILIZATION**, where you have been making mistakes for such a long time that they now seem natural to you, and you cannot identify the mistake.

To counteract these problems, you need to understand the characteristics of your own language and to analyze both its similarities to and differences from English. However, it is also important to emphasize that the influence of your mother tongue is only one of many factors which impacts on your learning of English. The purpose of this step is to raise awareness of some of the other major factors, focusing on three areas where mother-tongue influence can often be seen: **grammar**, **language** and **style**.

> **Positive transfer**
> Although the focus of this step is on some of the problems caused by **MOTHER-TONGUE INFLUENCE** (resulting in **NEGATIVE TRANSFER**), it is important to note that **POSITIVE TRANSFER** also exists – i.e., that it may be easier for you to learn certain aspects of English because of similarities to the grammar or language of your mother tongue.

What grammatical differences may be seen?

No two grammar systems are exactly alike. Since the grammar of your mother tongue has such a big influence on the way you speak, it can be difficult to forget about it when using English. This is particularly evident in students' use of **verbs** and **ARTICLES**, and **WORD ORDER** choices.

Verbs

I learn the past simple already in high school. The way in which different languages express time varies considerably. English may use one tense, whereas another language may use a completely different tense (see Step 41).

Articles

The articles are particular problem for many students because an articles do not always exist in your the mother tongue. Many languages have no article system (see Step 44) but use other methods to express 'definiteness'. As articles are so common in English they may be involved in the mistakes you see most frequently.

Word order

Word order be can seen as a problem big for many students. English, like around 75% of the world's languages, has a basic Subject–Verb–Object order. However, many languages, including Japanese, Korean and Turkish, are Subject–Object–Verb. In other languages (such as Russian), word order is less important because they use **INFLECTION** to show 'who is doing what to whom'. **MOTHER-TONGUE INFLUENCE** means students sometimes write English sentences following the word order of their mother tongue, as in the example above. Such students may also use 'postpositions' rather than **PREPOSITIONS** (e.g., *I am going school to* instead of *I am going to school*) or to place **AUXILIARY VERBS** after **MAIN VERBS** (e.g., *I going am* instead of *I am going*).

What language differences may be seen?

Vocabulary

In many Romance languages (e.g., Spanish and Italian), it is meritorious to use Latin-based words as the norm. English has borrowed many words from Romance languages, especially French. Speakers of Romance languages such as Spanish or Italian may want to use the English word that is related to a word in their own language – but the Romance-derived word may be considered overly formal in English. The example here – 'meritorious' – sounds too formal, even in academic writing ('better' or 'good practice' would be more suitable).

Spelling

Spelling kan be hard becos inglish wurds are often ritten diffrently to how they sownd. In English, the sound and the spelling do not always match. This contrasts with many other languages, which are 'written exactly as they sound'. This causes serious problems with regard to knowing how to spell certain words. It is, therefore, important to check a good dictionary and/or to make use of computer spellcheckers.

> **'Ghoti'**
> This is how you can spell *fish*, according to George Bernard Shaw – using the *gh* from *enough*, the *o* from *women* and the *ti* from *motion*.

Collocations

The use of collocations is well related to a language's culture. All languages use particular COLLOCATIONS (words which frequently appear together with other words). Using collocations can be difficult, as they are hard to predict. In this example, the phrase *well related* would not be used; the normal collocation is *strongly related*. This is one reason why it is important to try to think in English, rather than translate directly from your mother tongue.

What stylistic differences may be seen?

As previous steps have outlined, English academic writing has a particular style, which may be different to the academic writing style in your country.

Sentence length

Many students have the idea that sentences in English should be extremely long, but that is not always true, and many sentences written by non-native speakers seem to go on for a very long time, but that can make it very difficult to follow exactly what is going on. In many cultures, long sentences are seen as evidence of good academic writing. British academic style, however, tends to prefer a simpler, more direct style in which long sentences are avoided. One particular problem which some students have, as in this example, is the overuse of *and* and *but*.

Idea development

There are some who believe that different cultures have different ideas about the way in which a piece of writing should develop. It is important to consider the way in which ideas are presented in your mother tongue, and compare that with English (see Step 17).

Concept of knowledge

As outlined in Step 3, some cultures tend to view 'knowledge' in different ways from others.

D ## Actlvation

Look through the following passage and identify the mistakes which have been made.

> In addition to an influence of your mother tongue, one populer theory about second language acquisition is the 'natural order hypothesis'. This theory states that when learning any language (whether your first or second language) there is a order specific in which grammar is learnt. It is argued that there is a high relationship between ~*ing*, plural ~*s* and the verb *to be*. A vivid understanding of this grammar comes before, for example, irregular past forms. This theory has been developed initially by Stephen Krashen.

Problem area	Example from the text	Problem area	Example from the text
Verbs		Vocabulary	
Articles		Spelling	
Word order		Collocations	

E Personalization

 Analyze your own language according to the criteria listed below.

Area	Academic English	My language	Pos/Neg transfer
Verbs	12 x forms (3 x tenses, 4 x aspects); active/passive voice		
Articles	Frequently used, definite and indefinite		
Word order	Subject–Verb–Object the norm		
Choice of vocabulary	Words from different sources, especially native Anglo-Saxon; French; Latin		
Spelling	Spelling and sound do not necessarily match		
Sentence length	Shorter, more concise sentences generally preferred		

For any cases of negative transfer which you have identified, try to find some examples in a recent piece of your writing and identify how you can solve the problem.

F Extension

- Step 3 looks at **plagiarism**, a subject which highlights some of the problems which come from differences in academic cultures.
- Step 38 looks specifically at **collocations**, which are typically highly language-specific.
- Unit I helps you with aspects of grammar, which students often find difficult.
- Appendix 1, Step 11, Document 4 is a photocopiable table for analyzing mother-tongue influence.
- Unit J focuses predominantly on **proofreading**. Good knowledge of this skill can help edit out some of those mistakes which are caused by mother-tongue influence.

How can I manage my time effectively?

'All work and no play makes Jack a dull boy.'

English proverb

A Reflection

Consider the following statements and state whether you agree/disagree with them.

1. I never have enough time to do everything I want.   Agree / Disagree
2. I have trouble meeting my deadlines.   Agree / Disagree
3. I spend all my time reading and never have time to write my essays.   Agree / Disagree

B Contextualization

The following table contains extracts from the diary of Ming, a first-year undergraduate student. In the table which follows, assess her time-management skills.

Monday	**Thursday**
Check e-mail (1430–1500)	Brainstorm/plan essay in café (1500–1600)
Background reading for essay (1500–1800)	Write essay (1600–2200)
Filing (2000–2130)	Proofread essay (2330–0200)
Tuesday	**Friday**
Talk to Ayumi about her essay (1100–1130)	Review notes (1100–1200)
Instant Messenger (1130–1200)	Plan week ahead [Outlook] and alter as necessary (1200–1230)
Background reading for essay (1200–1800)	Lunch (1230–1300)
Meet friends (1900–2130)	Read (1300–1415)
Wednesday	**Saturday**
Background reading for essay (0800–1200)	Day off. No work.
Lecture 2 (1300–1500)	

Good time management	Poor time management
Saturday has been taken as a day off – it is important to rest.	

Analysis

Time-management overview

The issue of time management is a critical one to be a successful student. The most important aspect of time management is planning. This section will identify reasons why planning is important and introduce strategies for time management which you can experiment with.

I never have enough time to do everything I want.

Causes:	Explanations/impacts:	Solutions:
You are trying to achieve too much	It is understandable that you want to do as well as possible, but you have to be realistic in your goals. In addition to the 'knowledge' challenge, you have the 'language' challenge.	You must prioritize your workload – focus on the tasks which are (i) most important and (ii) have the closest deadline. Sometimes you must make difficult decisions about how much time you can spend on a particular task.
You are not working efficiently	It is difficult to 'juggle' lots of different tasks, especially if you have not had experience of this before. When you have a lot to do, it can be difficult to know where to start. Sometimes it can feel as if you are not achieving anything.	You need to develop **INFORMATION-MANAGEMENT SYSTEMS** which can support what you do. Initially, it may take time to get familiar with these systems, but over time they will save you time (see below and **Appendix 4, Step 12** for more details).

I have trouble meeting my deadlines.

Causes:	Explanations/impacts:	Solutions:
You are looking at things on a short-term basis	If you only plan your workload over the short term, you will forget your deadlines – the danger is that you will only remember them when it is too late.	You need to plan for the medium and long term as well – plan not only for the day, but for the week, month and course as a whole.

I spend all my time reading and never have time to write my essays.

Causes:	Explanations/Impacts:	Solutions:
You feel that you do not know enough about the subject	It may be that you lack confidence in your own knowledge, and you do not feel you know enough to start writing. But there has to be a point where you stop reading and start writing, otherwise you will not produce anything. Do not be afraid to stop reading.	You need to be more selective and focused in your reading (see Steps 6 and 9). In addition, you should decide how much time you can spend reading for an essay and follow this plan – 40% of the time available should be for reading, 60% for writing.

Top ten tips for managing your time

Tick the tips which relate to you. Examples from part B are used.

1. Be honest about what you do.

Background reading for essay (Mon 1500–1800; Tue 1200–1800; Wed 0800–1200) 'Spending time in the library' does not always equate to 'reading for your essay'. Progress should be measured by outcomes rather than activities. I need to do this. ☐

2. Work when you know you are most effective.

Filing (Mon 2000–2130) Most people find that working on complex, difficult tasks (e.g., reading a difficult text) is better earlier in the day. Time-intensive but relatively simple tasks (e.g., filing) may be better when your brain is more tired. I need to do this. ☐

3. Work where you know you are most effective.

Brainstorm/plan essay in café (Thu 1500–1600) Some work best in their room, some in cafés. For some people, this may depend on the type of work involved. I need to do this. ☐

4. Change the task when you start to feel bored.

Range of activities (Fri 1100–1415) When a task starts to make you feel tired, do something different. For example, writing an essay when you have no motivation will result in bad writing and you will just have to rewrite it. I need to do this. ☐

5. Be prepared to be flexible.

Plan week ahead [Outlook] and alter as necessary (Fri 1200–1230) You do not have to follow your schedule if it is not working. It is only a guide. I need to do this. ☐

6. Manage your time day by day and also by task.

Brainstorm/plan/write/proofread (Thu all day) TASK MANAGEMENT is important: plan out an individual task, developing a series of mini-deadlines. I need to do this. ☐

7. Involve your friends and colleagues.

Talk to Ayumi about her essay (Tue 1100–1130) It can be useful to involve others. Creating artificial deadlines (e.g., showing a draft to a friend) can help you focus on important tasks. I need to do this. ☐

8. Do not be distracted.

Check e-mail (Mon 1430–1500); Instant Messenger (Tue 1130–1200) When you are working, work; when you are relaxing, relax. I need to do this. ☐

9. Use electronic calendars.

Plan week ahead [Outlook] and alter as necessary (Fri 1200–1230) Many people find electronic calendars a useful tool for managing schedules. I need to do this. ☐

10. Take time off.

Day off. No work. (Sat all day) It is important to take time off. The brain needs to be refreshed. Being a good student is about quality, not quantity. I need to do this. ☐

D Activation

Answer the following questions to test your understanding of this step.

- *Try to answer the questions without referring to part C.*

1. Why is it important to plan in the medium and long term as well as the short term?

   If you only plan in the short term, you may well forget your deadlines.

2. What two criteria should you use to judge your priorities?

3. Why might it be inefficient to work on the same task for a long period of time?

4. Why is it important to get a balance between working and relaxing?

5. Why should you measure your progress by *outcomes* rather than *activities*?

6. How can you involve friends/colleagues in managing your time?

7. What does 'task management' mean?

8. Why are electronic calendars useful?

E Personalization

- Ensure that you have checked through the top ten tips outlined in part C and ticked the ones that apply to you.
- Think back over today, or the last week, and write down what you did and when you did it. It is important to know your current practice before you can consider how to change.
- Get to know yourself better. Complete the following sentences.
  - The time(s) when I work best is/are: _____
  - The place(s) where I work best is/are: _____
- Limit your social use of the Internet and your mobile phone to specific periods of the day. This may help you divide your work/personal time.

F Extension

- Step 6 presents techniques for you to be more focused in **choosing your source material**.
- Step 9 provides suggestions on how to **read more effectively**, which will enable better time management.
- Appendix 4, Step 12 details time-management hyperlinks.

How can I understand my title?

'The longer the title, the less important the job.'

George McGovern

A Reflection

Look at the following titles (1–4 below) taken from pieces of academic writing.

- *Identify the general purpose of a title.*
- *Decide which of these titles work best.*

1. Evaluate the impact of different mother tongues on the acquisition of English as a second language at British universities in the early 21st century, paying particular attention to students from the Far East.
2. The coursebook: future continuous or past?
3. Skills all round.
4. Why are essay titles important?

B Contextualization

Read the following essay titles.

- *In each case, decide what the question is specifically asking you to do. In what ways would your approach be similar or different?*

Title	What is it asking you to do?
1. Why are essay titles important?	
2. Assess the extent to which a good title can contribute to successful academic writing, focusing particularly on the humanities.	
3. Outline the different types of essay title which exist.	
4. 'Essay titles have hidden depths' (Andrew Northedge). Discuss.	
5. Academic essay titles: critically important or significantly overrated?	
6. Summarize the key aspects of a good essay title.	
7. Discuss the advantages and disadvantages of setting your own essay title.	
8. Justify the importance of essay titles.	

UNIT C Preparing to write

c Analysis

What is the purpose of an essay title?

The purpose of a title in a piece of academic writing is threefold:

- to indicate the general direction of your essay
- to focus attention on a specific topic
- to get the reader interested in your essay

It is likely that most of the time (especially at the beginning of your course), you will be answering questions which have been set by your teachers. Therefore, you will need to understand *exactly* what they are asking you to do. Later in your course (especially if you have to write a dissertation), you will write your own title. At that time, it is important that you follow the same principles outlined below.

Titles should be written in a concise style, using powerful, meaningful words. They should contain enough information so that the reader can predict what the essay is going to focus on (unlike Title 3 in part A), but not so much that they are confused before they start (e.g., Title 1). Titles 2 and 4 are both written in appropriate language, though clearly for very different audiences – the former for a general audience, the latter for an expert audience.

> ### A note on subheadings
> A subheading is a kind of 'mini-title' which you may find in the main body of a piece of academic writing. Opinion is divided as to whether you should use subheadings or not. They can be useful to inform the reader what the focus of a particular section may be. However, others would argue that this is what a topic sentence should do. Some subjects – particularly the sciences – use subheadings more frequently than others.

Whatever the title you are given, the most important thing an essay can do is answer the question. No matter how good your answer, if the information is not relevant you will not score highly. Therefore, a detailed understanding of the title is crucial.

What different models of essay titles are there?

Very few essay titles are completely straightforward. Generally, they contain two or more components, each of which is critical. These components can be categorized as follows:

Topic – what is the question about?

Focus – what is the specific aspect you are examining?

Instruction – how should you look at the question?

Limitations – are there any restrictions to your investigations?

For example, in the context of some of the essay titles found in part B:

No.	Topic	Focus	Instruction	Limitation
2	A good title	How do they contribute to successful academic writing?	Assess	the humanities
3	Different types of essay title	N/A	Outline	N/A
5	Academic essay titles	Are they important or not important?	Discuss (by implication)	N/A

Titles in descriptive essays

Summarize the key aspects of a good essay title.

Certain courses may favour this kind of question, which asks you to demonstrate that you have understood a particular issue. There is an assumption that the information contained in the question is true. You are not expected to challenge this, but show what you know about the topic. This type of question may also be found in examinations, where you are being tested on your knowledge of the subject matter rather than on your ability to research it and develop an argument. Common instruction verbs of this type are found in the box below.

account for　define　describe　explain　outline　summarize　assess

Alternative descriptive type: *wh~*questions

Why are essay titles important?

Questions using the standard question words are common in day-to-day and academic English. 'What', 'how' and 'why' are common; 'Where' and 'when' are less common.

Titles in evaluative essays

Discuss the advantages and disadvantages of setting your own essay title.

Evaluative essays look at two sides of a particular issue. As an author you must decide what your view is – do you agree with one side or the other, or do you have a balanced view? As well as the verbs in the box below, other phrases you might find in evaluative essays include: 'pros and cons' and 'strengths and weaknesses'.

compare and contrast　evaluate　discuss

Titles and formatting

Capitalization: often just the first word of the title, but some capitalize all the important words (i.e., the content words).

Formatting: you can embolden, italicize and underline the title if you wish, but do only one of these.

Full stops: titles should not have a full stop but should have a question mark (if appropriate).

Justification: should be centred.

Quotation marks: for quoted material only.

Alternative evaluative type: statement and colon

Academic essay titles: critically important or significantly overrated?

The information to the left of the colon indicates the topic, while the information to the right asks a specific question. This type of question is often the basis for presentations/lectures as well.

Titles in argumentative essays

Justify the importance of essay titles.

In an argumentative essay, you are generally expected to take a position, then defend this position. The verbs used are important for identifying exactly what you are being asked to do.

justify　argue　assess　state

Alternative argumentative type: quotation and discuss

'Essay titles have hidden depths' (Andrew Northedge). Discuss.

A well-chosen quotation, often from a well-known scholar in your field, is presented. You are then asked to consider what this quotation means and whether you agree or disagree with it. The instruction word 'discuss' is commonly used. Note: you may need to reflect on the impact and meaning beyond the quotation – not just the literal words which are there.

D Activation

You have been asked to write an essay on 'The dominance of the English language in the 21st century'. Write a title according to each of the templates on page 57.

Template	Example
1. Descriptive (verb)	Account for the dominance of the English language in the 21st century.
2. Descriptive (wh~question)	
3. Evaluative (verb)	
4. Evaluative (statement and colon)	
5. Argumentative (verb)	
6. Argumentative (quotation and discuss)	

E Personalization

 Read through previous essays which you have written and ask yourself:

- did I answer the question in the most appropriate way?
- what should I have included/not included in my response?
- was the focus of my essay correct?

If you are creating your own essay title:

- write out a number of examples and choose the one you prefer. It may take several drafts to get it exactly right.
- check with a friend that the title is clear and makes sense.

F Extension

- Step 6 – a good understanding of a book or article's title can help you in **selecting your source material**.
- UNIT J – **proofreading**. One of the key criteria (many would argue *the* most important) for a good academic essay is that you answer the question. Strategies for checking whether you have done this are presented in this section.
- Appendix 3, Step 13 lists several genuine academic titles within four different academic fields.

How can I brainstorm ideas and develop an outline?

'The outline is 95 per cent of the book. Then I sit down and write, and that's the easy part.'

Jeffery Deaver

A Reflection

The following are statements frequently made by students about planning.

• *Which do you agree with?*

1. There is no point in planning an essay.   Agree / Disagree
2. Planning takes too much time.   Agree / Disagree
3. I do not know how to plan.   Agree / Disagree

B Contextualization

Read these two paragraphs from the essay 'Academic essay titles: critically important or significantly overrated?'

• *Which paragraph was planned and which was unplanned?*

Paragraph 1

Answering the question is the most important thing an essay can do. One particularly common problem which students face is that they answer the question they *wanted* to get, rather than the one they actually got. This is a serious error. The result of this is irrelevant detail and unfocused argument. It is commonly known that essays which do not directly address the question posed receive poor marks.

Paragraph 2

You have to answer the question when you write an essay. If you do not, then lots of the essay will not be relevant and the argument will be unfocused. Students often try to answer the question which they wanted to have rather than the question which they actually have in front of them. This is a really big mistake and you're almost certain to get lower marks.

• *How did you make your decision? Explain, focusing on specific aspects of the text.*

_____

_____

_____

_____

_____

UNIT C Preparing to write

Step
14

59

C Analysis

Why should I plan my essays?

There is no point in planning an essay.

This statement is simply wrong. As can be clearly seen from the texts in part B, Paragraph 1 (which has been planned) is far better than Paragraph 2 (which has not). Just by looking at Paragraph 2 you can see that it is:

1. Disorganized

If you do not, then lots of the essay will not be relevant and the argument will be unfocused. The arguments appear in a STREAM OF CONSCIOUSNESS, rather than carefully developed.

2. Poorly written

This is a really big mistake and you're almost certain to get lower marks.
The style is extremely informal. The text sounds more like a conversation than a piece of academic writing.

In short, writing an essay without having an outline is like going somewhere new without a map.

Planning takes too much time.

There are two reasons why this statement is untrue. The first is that when you develop good planning techniques, the planning process is actually relatively quick. It does *not* take hours and hours to plan your essay; the majority of essays can be planned in less than an hour. Secondly, whatever time you spend on planning is time well spent. The quality of your first draft will be far better, meaning that the editing and proofreading stages will be much easier. Planning is important in all academic writing situations – even exams. In exams, five minutes spent planning an essay is definitely better than five extra minutes of writing.

How can I plan my essays?

I do not know how to plan.

If you feel you have no idea how to begin the planning process, do not worry: you are not alone. There are few things more terrifying than a blank piece of paper staring at you. However, by following the three-stage process outlined here, planning can become a simple and effective process.

Stage 1: Brainstorming

Brainstorming is a process where you simply write down all the information you know about a particular topic. Brainstorming can help you identify what you know (and, importantly, do *not* know) about a subject. There are three key principles to brainstorming:

- **Quantity**: specific detail and accuracy are not important at the brainstorming stage. You are simply trying to empty your head of everything you know on the subject.
- **Variation**: a range of different ideas is to be encouraged – quotations, data, arguments, ideas, background information. They all help to shape and develop your argument.
- **Combination**: once you have listed all your ideas, it becomes much easier to see the main themes, and therefore to build your argument.

Some people prefer to brainstorm on a computer, some by hand. You should do whatever you feel most comfortable with. The most popular method of brainstorming is the MIND MAP (or CLUSTER DIAGRAM), like the example below. Using Post-it® notes and putting them on a wall (where you can rearrange and order them) is also useful.

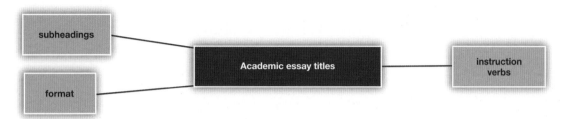

Stage 2: Creating an outline

Once you have brainstormed your ideas, you may come to one of two conclusions: either you are ready to develop your outline and start writing your essay, or you do not know enough about the subject. If it is the latter, then you need to read more to develop your knowledge. There is no point trying to start writing an essay if the content is not going to be good enough.

When you look at your brainstormed ideas, do not be afraid to delete many of them. Try to find links between topics (and combine ideas). An outline should contain brief information about what the focus of each of the sections is going to be. For shorter pieces of writing (e.g., less than 15 paragraphs), this may be on a paragraph-by-paragraph basis. To decide how many paragraphs an essay should have, use the following equation: *80% of essay length/150*. The first figure relates to the essay length minus 10% for the introduction and 10% for the conclusion; the second figure relates to the average length of each paragraph. So, in a 1,500-word essay, this would mean around eight body paragraphs.

> ### Two top tips for writing outlines
> The outline should be written in simple language – bullet points can be particularly useful. Do not just keep your essay outline on your computer: print it out and put it on your wall.

Stage 3: Expanding your outline

A third stage, which develops the outline further, is to either (a) write brief notes about what will be included or (b) write the accompanying topic sentence for each paragraph. For example:

Basic outline	Expanded outline
Introduction	*Topic sentence:* This essay will argue that understanding the title of your essay is absolutely critical to producing a good piece of writing.
Answering the question	*Topic sentence:* Answering the question is the most important thing an essay can do.
What different titles mean	*Notes:* Ref. to diff. types of essay – language analysis (esp. verbs) – examples from various subjects.
Consideration of counter-arguments	*Topic sentence:* However, there are others who argue that the title is simply a guide, and that your style of writing is more important.
Conclusion	*Notes:* Summary of key points – how can this knowledge be applied?

Many people omit this stage, but it can be useful. It can be particularly helpful if you are having problems in areas such as coherence, logical development or structure.

Activation

Create an expanded outline for an essay from the brainstormed notes here. The outline should be five paragraphs long (introduction – three body paragraphs – conclusion).

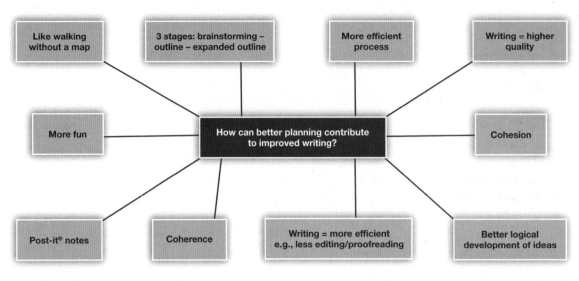

Basic outline	Expanded outline
1.	
2.	
3.	
4.	
5.	

Personalization

- If you do not plan your essays at the moment, consider the reasons for this. Think of possible solutions, based on the information in this step, and try to implement them.
- Practise this three-stage process (brainstorming – outline – expanded outline) on a topic you know extremely well. This will help you focus on developing the relevant skills.
- Compare an essay which you wrote, and you planned well for, with a piece of writing that you did not plan. Identify the differences in quality between the two.

Extension

- Step 10 focuses on **note-taking**, a skill which is closely related to brainstorming and outlining.
- Step 12 develops your **time-management skills** – an important skill as many students feel they do not have enough time to brainstorm and outline their essays.
- Step 16 looks at **different types of academic essays**. It is important that your outline has a structure appropriate for the kind of essay you are writing.
- Appendix 3, Step 14 provides other ideas and activities for brainstorming and outlining.
- Appendix 4, Step 14 gives a useful online resource which can help in this area.

What is a thesis statement and how do I write one?

'Statements are sentences, but not all sentences are statements.'

Willard Quine

A Reflection

Look at the following definition and introduction to an essay entitled: 'Is a thesis statement important in an essay?'

• *According to the definition, can you identify the 'thesis statement'?*

Thesis statement: A sentence in an academic essay which presents the central argument of the essay in concise language.

According to Reid (2000: 77), the thesis statement is the 'strongest, clearest statement in the essay', a view shared by the Online Writing Lab (2010) who, in addition, make a distinction between thesis statements used in analytical, expository and argumentative pieces of writing. While there are a number of important aspects in an essay, such as structure, cohesion and the logical development of ideas, the thesis statement is related to all of these features. For, without a thesis statement, an essay has no controlling idea or central focus, making the development of ideas an extremely challenging proposition. Divided into three parts, this essay looks first at the structure of a thesis statement. Subsequently, section two examines the language which should be employed, and section three common problems related to the writing of thesis statements.

References:

Online Writing Lab (2010). *The Purdue Online Writing Lab*. http://owl.english.purdue.edu. Retrieved 08/04/10.

Reid, J. (2000). *The Process of Composition*. New York: Addison Wesley Longman.

• *Having identified the thesis statement, can you identify its key characteristics?*

B Contextualization

These thesis statements were rejected. Match the draft with the teacher's comments which identify the problem.

1. The centrality of the thesis statement in the essay is an incontrovertible truth, for without it the epistemological evolution of the argument is an impossibility.

   The thesis statement should not be a question.

2. In this essay, I will look at the importance of thesis statements.

   Too simple. This is a very vague generalization.

3. Thesis statements which use informal, vague language lead to the breakdown of the entire academic structure.

   Too long and complex. You need to simplify the language.

4. Without the thesis statement, the entire purpose of the essay is completely and utterly lost; the result of this is chaos – the essay is just an anarchic collection of words.

   Too specific. The scope of a thesis statement should be wider.

5. What, then, is the reason why thesis statements are so important?

   Too emotive. You should not use such passionate language.

c Analysis

What is a thesis statement and why is it important?

As the example below from part A suggests, the thesis statement is the most important sentence in your essay.

☑ For, without a thesis statement, an essay has no controlling idea or central focus, making the development of ideas an extremely challenging proposition.

Two main functions of the thesis statement are to:

*   state your position with regard to the essay title
*   provide an overview of the essay and the direction in which it is going

Some other key characteristics of a thesis statement are listed below.

*   It is always found in the introduction, generally towards the end.
*   It should not just be a fact, but rather an idea which can be developed and built upon.
*   It should be referred to again in the conclusion.
*   Some thesis statements use *I*, but note that in many subject areas (or for many teachers), it may not be preferred (see Step 22).

What are some common problems associated with thesis statements?

Thesis statements are known for being difficult to get right, so do not worry if you find writing them challenging. The important thing is to learn from your mistakes and to understand the feedback you are given. The example rejected thesis statements from part B represent the most common student problems in relation to this topic.

Thesis statements should not be too long and complex.

✗ The centrality of the thesis statement in the essay is an incontrovertible truth, for without it the epistemological evolution of the argument is an impossibility.

Like all academic writing, a good thesis statement should be relatively easy to understand. Since it is such an important part of the essay, its meaning has to be transparent and clearly written. You should be careful with the grammar and language which you use in your thesis statement, and be sure that you do not make any basic errors. Generally speaking, thesis statements should not contain information such as data, quotations or references.

Thesis statements should not be too general.

✗ In this essay, I will look at the importance of thesis statements.

This version of the thesis statement does not really say anything. It neither states the writer's position, nor provides an overview of the direction in which the essay is going. Bad thesis statements, such as this, often just paraphrase the essay title. This is *not* the purpose of a thesis statement.

Thesis statements should not be too specific.

X Thesis statements which use informal, vague language lead to the breakdown of the entire academic structure.

The thesis statement is not the place to provide specific details about your viewpoint. This thesis statement, for example, focuses in too much detail on one very specific aspect of the essay. This sentence is perfectly well written, but it sounds more like a TOPIC SENTENCE than a thesis statement. Getting the balance between generality and specificity is difficult, and you may need to redraft your thesis statement several times to get this right (see below).

Thesis statements should not be too emotive.

X Without the thesis statement, the entire purpose of the essay is completely and utterly lost; the result of this is chaos – the essay is just an anarchic collection of words.

Your academic writing in general should not be too emotive; this is especially true for your thesis statement. Evaluative language – words which strongly express your opinion but in a more academic way – can be extremely useful in thesis statements.

Thesis statements should not be written as a question.

X What, then, is the underlying reason why thesis statements are so important?

As its name suggests, the thesis statement should be a *statement*. Your title will generally be written in a question format – the thesis statement is the place where you present your reaction to the title.

How can I edit my thesis statement?

Do not be surprised if you edit your thesis statement several times as you write your essay. Your ideas will develop and change as the essay progresses. Since your thesis statement is directly linked to the main thrust of your essay, it will have to change as well. An example is presented below for several drafts of a thesis statement for the essay title: 'Global warming: myth or reality?'

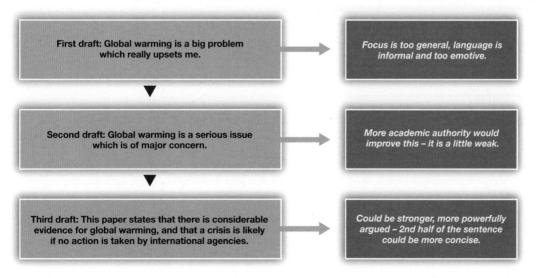

First draft: Global warming is a big problem which really upsets me.

Focus is too general, language is informal and too emotive.

Second draft: Global warming is a serious issue which is of major concern.

More academic authority would improve this – it is a little weak.

Third draft: This paper states that there is considerable evidence for global warming, and that a crisis is likely if no action is taken by international agencies.

Could be stronger, more powerfully argued – 2nd half of the sentence could be more concise.

The final draft of the thesis statement – written in powerful language which clearly shows the attitude of the writer and the importance of the topic – appears on the following page.

D Activation

Write an appropriate thesis statement for the following essay titles. An example is done for you.

Essay title	Thesis statement
1. Global warming: myth or reality?	This essay will strongly argue that the scientific evidence for global warming is overwhelming, and that if multilateral action is not taken, a crisis will occur.
2. 'All higher education should be completely free' (Angela Fitzpatrick). Discuss.	
3. Assess the impact of overseas students on British universities.	
4. Is democracy the best political system?	

E Personalization

Look back at essays you have written recently and ask yourself:

- did you include a thesis statement? Is it obvious?
- if you did include one, is the language appropriate, according to the criteria outlined above?

Note: If the language is not appropriate, try editing it so that it says exactly what you want it to say.

Write a thesis statement for your next essay. Give it, and the essay title, to a friend and ask him or her to:

- suggest what they think the main focus of the essay is.
- predict what they think your opinion on the topic is.

If there is any difference between what your friend understands and what you really think, your thesis statement may not be clear enough.

F Extension

- Step 13 analyzes **essay titles**, which should be directly related to your thesis statement.
- Step 19 looks at the **introduction** to an essay, where the thesis statement is presented, and Step 20 at the **conclusion**, where it is answered.
- Step 21 focuses on the issue of **formality**, a particularly important aspect of a thesis statement.
- Appendix 3, Step 15 presents four sample thesis statements, taken from a range of different essays.

What different types of academic writing are there?

> 'An essay in its highest form is now expected to be reflective, elegant and philosophical.'
>
> The Oxford Companion to the English Language

A Reflection

Look at the titles 1–5 below.

- *In what ways do you think the approach and contents of each essay would differ?*
1. Outline the main types of academic writing in common use in British universities.
2. Assess the essay-based system of assessment which is common in most British universities.
3. Justify the importance of the essay as a means of assessment.
4. A critique of *50 steps to improving your academic writing* by Chris Sowton.
5. What are the most common types of writing in my subject area?

B Contextualization

Match the type of writing (on the left) to its description (on the right).

- *Then look again at the titles in part A and decide which title relates to each type of writing.*

An argumentative essay …	… is a piece of writing, often used in the sciences, which tests your knowledge about a particular concept.
A critique …	… is writing which you do yourself (not for assessment) to remember information and develop your own learning skills.
A descriptive essay …	… is a much longer piece of writing (usually >8,000 words) which tends to be used at Master's level.
A dissertation …	… both summarizes and offers critical analysis of an academic article or book.
An exam essay …	… tends to be relatively short and very focused, testing your ability to recall key information.
An evaluative essay …	… is often set by teachers to test your understanding of a particular topic – e.g., a process, idea or theory.
Reflective writing …	… tries to persuade the reader that a particular point of view (i.e., your opinion) is correct.
A short-answer question …	… compares and contrasts the different sides of a topic. It may support one side or another, or else take a balanced overview.

UNIT D Organizing your text

Step
16

67

Analysis

What are some of the common types of academic writing?

Although it is impossible to generalize for all subjects and for all universities, it is generally agreed that the essay is the most common means of assessment in the British academic system. Note that the language used to describe the types of essay below may not be the same as you have read elsewhere; there is no generally agreed definition.

An argumentative essay …

… tries to persuade the reader that a particular point of view (i.e., your opinion) is correct.

Sometimes known as 'expository' or 'persuasive' essays, argumentative essays are the most common type of essay which you will encounter at university. A good argumentative essay will demonstrate:

- understanding and consideration of a wide range of sources (see Steps 3–7).
- critical analysis of and reflection on the source material (see Steps 8–9).
- a clear argument (see Steps 14, 15 and 25).

- This demonstrates that …
- The evidence for this is …
- Clearly, the data indicate …
- This can be proved by …
- It is impossible to escape the conclusion that …

A critique …

… both summarizes and offers critical analysis of an academic article or book.

A critique is a task which may be set by your teacher in order both to test your ability to understand an important text, and to reflect critically on this text. A good critique will highlight the main points of a text (identifying the author's key findings) and will also clearly state your own position regarding this text – whether you agree or disagree with it. Poor critiques tend to have no critical analysis and are just summaries of the text.

A descriptive essay …

… is often set by teachers to test your understanding of a particular topic – e.g., a process, idea or theory.

Descriptive essays may be common at the beginning of your course, where the teacher wants to check that you have understood a particular topic. They expect less critical analysis than evaluative or argumentative essays. Often they may be used to provide a definition of a key process (e.g., reforming the education system), idea (e.g., civil law) or theory (e.g., Einstein's general theory of relativity).

- There are X main types of …
- X can be defined as …
- Firstly … secondly … thirdly …
- This process/idea/theory has X steps/stages/parts.

A dissertation …

… is a much longer piece of writing (usually >8,000 words) which tends to be used at Master's level.

Dissertations can be divided into two main types: empirical and library-based. Empirical dissertations conduct original research, whereas library-based dissertations use material which has already been published. Students decide their own topic (and therefore title), usually in discussion with their personal tutor. An even longer piece of writing, used at the doctorate level, is known as a thesis.

An exam essay …

… tends to be relatively short and very focused, testing your ability to recall key information. Exam essays will generally fall into one of the three essay categories above (argumentative, descriptive and evaluative) and they will share the same principles. However, there are three major differences:

- **Fact-based, not argument-based**: generally speaking, exam essays focus more on your ability to recall information rather than to make a powerful argument.
- **Simple referencing**: you are not expected to reference in the same way – e.g., direct quotations and paraphrases. Clearly, if you can remember such information, and it is relevant, you should include it. Normally, knowing the person's name is enough (e.g., Smith's theory of X …).
- **Shorter introductions and conclusions**: whereas in a 'normal' essay they will each be c. 5–10% of the essay length, in exams they will be much shorter (perhaps just two sentences). Indeed, in some essays an introduction may not be necessary at all.

An evaluative essay …

… compares and contrasts the different sides of a topic. It may support one side or another, or else take a balanced overview. Sometimes known as a 'compare-and-contrast' or 'discursive' essay, this type of essay evaluates a question. You, as a writer, must consider all aspects of the question, and decide which side (if any) you agree with. Note that it is possible to take a more balanced view in this kind of essay (e.g., you may agree 70% with one side and 30% with another). Evaluative essays can take two main forms:

- Whereas X is …Y is …
- X is different from Y in that …
- X and Y share a number of similarities …
- On balance, it can be argued that …

- **Type 1:** Introduction – arguments for X – arguments against X – conclusion.
- **Type 2:** Introduction – topic 1 arguments for and against (repeat for topics 2, 3, 4, etc.) – conclusion.

Reflective writing …

… is writing which you do yourself (not for assessment) to remember information and develop your own learning skills. REFLECTIVE WRITING is a type of writing which you do only for yourself. As the name suggests, reflective writing may help you to reflect on (i.e., *think about*) an academic topic without having to use academic language. Reflective writing can be described as an informal academic diary.

- I thought that …
- It seemed to me …
- From this I understood …
- This reminded me of …
- This idea was first discussed in …

A short-answer question …

… is a piece of writing, often used in the sciences, which tests your knowledge about a particular concept.
Short-answer questions are used by teachers to check your understanding of what has recently been learnt. Often your answers will comprise just a single paragraph. Therefore, writing in a concise, focused way is very important.

Step
16

Activation

Read the following thesis statements and decide which type of writing they would be most appropriate for.

- Then refer to part A and decide which title would be most appropriate.

Thesis statement	Type of essay
There are generally considered to be three main types of essays (as well as other writing forms) used in British universities; I will investigate each of these in turn.	
This essay analyzes the advantages and disadvantages of the essay, arguing that although it is not a perfect means of assessment, it is the best system which exists.	
The essay is a short, dynamic and powerful piece of writing which has been important for hundreds of years in the British academic system.	
Having summarized the main points of this article, I will challenge its main findings, which are based on poor data, unreliable sources and bad arguments.	

 Personalization

- 🔲 **What essays are most common in your subject area?**
  - Check with your teachers/other students/the departmental handbook.
- 🔲 **Are you following the rules for each type of writing?**
  - Show your recent essays to a friend or colleague. Without telling them, ask them to guess what type of writing it was. If they cannot do this, it may be that your focus is not right.

Extension

- 🔲 Step 10 examines **note-taking** – the type of essay which you write will determine what information you note.
- 🔲 Step 13 looks at **titles**, which will be directly related to the type of writing you are expected to produce.
- 🔲 Step 14 focuses on the skills of **brainstorming** and **outlining**. The outline you eventually produce will be directly related to the particular type of writing.
- 🔲 Step 22 looks at **reflective writing** in more detail.

How is text organized in academic writing?

'Order is never observed; it is disorder that attracts attention.'

Eliphas Levi

A Reflection

What are the functions of the parts of speech in English?

- *Based on your analysis of the passage below, complete the table with the appropriate information.*

> The organization of text in academic writing can initially appear a mystery. However, careful study soon reveals that the basic principles are relatively simple. Therefore, it is important to focus your attention on developing your understanding of this knowledge.

Part of speech	Example(s) from passages	Further information
Noun		
	appear; reveals; is;	
		Describes (modifies) the noun/pronoun.
	initially; soon	
		Can replace a noun.
Conjunction		
Preposition		

B Contextualization

Read these two passages. Decide which sounds more 'natural' and typical of academic English.

Passage A

Important in the development of discourse analysis is the work of text grammarians. Such grammarians view texts as elements strung together in definable relationships ... closely related to such work is that of J. Firbas and F. Danes in the Prague School in the 1970s ... There has also been research on anaphora, topic progression, and ... grammatical choices at clause level (such as tense, voice, aspects and modality).

Passage B

Text grammarians have played an important part in the development of discourse analysis. Elements strung together as definable relationships are the way in which grammarians view texts ... In the 1970s in ... the Prague School were J. Firbas and F. Danes, whose work is closely related to this... Tense, voice, aspects and modality (grammatical choices), as well as anaphora and topic progression, have been some of the major research areas.

Texts from, and adapted from McArthur, T. (ed.) (1992). *The Oxford Companion to the English Language.* Oxford: Oxford University Press.

Analysis

What is the function of each main word class in English?

A good understanding of the different types of words (parts of speech) is integral to understanding the key principles of organization in English.

Part of speech	Example(s) from passage	Further information
Noun	organization; text; mystery; study	Refers to a person, place or object which forms the subject or object of the sentence. Generally appears with an ARTICLE or DETERMINER.
Verb	appear; reveals; is; developing	Describes what the subject does – relating to events, actions, states of being.
Adjective	basic; simple	Describes (modifies) the noun.
Adverb	initially; soon	Describes (modifies) adverbs and adjectives.
Pronoun	it	Can replace a noun.
Conjunction	however; therefore	Links sentences together.
Preposition	of; in	Precedes nouns and pronouns, indicating a range of different relationships including space, time, cause, agent, possession.

Key organizational principles:
- the basic word order of English is SUBJECT–VERB–OBJECT
- adjectives come before nouns
- the position of adverbs is flexible – if in doubt, place them in MID-POSITION
- prepositions come before nouns

What are the key principles of organization in English?

Having looked at word order, we now turn to how content is organized in English. Two main principles govern this: old information comes before new information; and topic (general information) comes before comment (specific information); see below. Examples of good practice come from passage A, the original piece of writing on page 71.

Principle 1: old information precedes new information

'Old' information here means information the reader is already familiar with. This information may already have been discussed in a previous paragraph, or may be 'common knowledge' and need no introduction. New information – the information which we are waiting for – comes at the end of the sentence. This principle is known as END-WEIGHTING.

Old information	New information
Such grammarians	view texts as elements strung together in definable relationships
Closely related to such work	is that of J. Firbas and F. Danes

Here, 'new information' quickly becomes 'old information' as the text progresses. This adds to the cohesion of a text by creating a chain between ideas.

Principle 2: topic precedes comment

We need to understand what the topic is before we move on to making a comment about it. Compare this to looking at a painting in an art gallery: most people would look at the whole painting first – to get an idea of what it is about – before looking at the interesting details.

Topic	Comment
Important in the development of discourse analysis	is the work of text grammarians
Grammatical choices at clause level	(such as tense, voice, aspect and modality)

In academic writing, this will often express itself as theory–example. This principle is particularly important in relation to increasing the cohesion of your written text (see Step 29).

Useful phrases which can introduce a topic:
- considering …
- regarding …
- talking of …
- speaking of …
- with regard to …
- as for …

What flexibility is there in the order that text is organized?

As noted above, academic writing in English follows two main principles in terms of its organization. However, depending on the particular emphasis you may want to put on a sentence, there is some flexibility. For example, some sentences may be FRONT-WEIGHTED rather than END-WEIGHTED (i.e., the new information precedes the old information) and in others the comment may come before the topic. The reasons for doing this are:

- **Surprise**: doing the unexpected is a good way of generating interest
- **Explanation**: justifying a situation before it happens, so the reader is prepared
- **Persuasion**: putting your key information first may help to convince your reader
- **Clarity**: changing the structure of the sentence may aid understanding

Front-weighting can be done in various ways, as shown below. These strategies are developed in more detail elsewhere – predominantly Unit E (see Steps 21–25).

Strategy 1: Changing the order of CLAUSES will change the emphasis of the sentence.
End-weighted (EW): I am not clear about how text is organized because of my difficulties in English.
Front-weighted (FW): As a result of my difficulties in English, I am not clear how the text is organized.

Strategy 2: Clefting (using cleft sentences) places a particular clause at the beginning of the sentence, giving it prominence.
EW: The emphasis of the sentence is changed by clefting.
FW: What clefting does is to change the emphasis of the sentence.

Strategy 3: Using the passive places the object at the beginning of the sentence, changing the emphasis.
EW: The Online Writing Lab at Purdue University has created many academic writing resources.
FW: Many academic writing resources have been created by the Online Writing Lab at Purdue University.

D Actlvatlon

Write a paragraph describing your area of study, paying close attention to the two principles outlined on pages 72–73.

 # E Personalization

Consider whether your writing follows the two key principles of organization in English.

- Go through and mark it appropriately to check – 'O' for old information, 'N' for new, 'T' for topic and 'C' for comment.
- Wherever you do not follow these principles, try to present the information in a more orthodox way.

In your writing, consider whether there are any points where you use front-weighting strategies.

- If not, practise them. Look through your previous writing and identify sentences which may benefit from this.

F Extension

- Steps 28 and 29 look at COHERENCE and COHESION, both of which are fundamental to good text organization.
- Step 30 focuses on LINKING DEVICES – useful pieces of language which clearly show relationships within the text.
- Step 43 discusses **punctuation**, an important aspect of text organization.
- Unit J examines **proofreading strategies**, which may assist you in checking that your writing has suitable organization and that WORD CLASSES are used appropriately.

What are the characteristics of a good paragraph?

'A sentence should contain no unnecessary words, a paragraph no unnecessary sentences.'

William Strunk

A Reflection

Select the statement in each case which is most typical of your current practice.

1. How do you currently make decisions about when you use paragraphs?
   a) After I have written 10–12 lines of text and it looks a bit long.
   b) Through a process of logical, ordered reason.
   c) Complete guesswork.
2. How many ideas do you include in each paragraph?
   a) One.
   b) More than one.
   c) Not sure.

B Contextualization

Put the sentences in order to form a coherent paragraph.

- In summary, the paragraph has to be planned carefully so that all these aspects are covered fully.
- Logical development is closely related to the idea of coherence, but places a greater emphasis on content rather than language and grammar.
- If this idea is too specific or too general, then your paragraphs may be too long, short or ambiguous.
- Paragraph unity can be achieved through the quality of your controlling idea (as expressed by your topic sentence).
- It is commonly argued that a good paragraph has three specific aspects: unity, coherence and logical development.
- This essay now turns to the specific unit of the paragraph.
- Moreover, the use of linking words (e.g., *therefore*, *however* and *in conclusion*) is considered one of the best ways to ensure that this happens.
- Coherence may, in particular, be developed by appropriate use of referents, such as pronouns, determiners and restatements.

 **Analysis**

What is a good paragraph?

This essay now turns to the specific unit of the paragraph. It is commonly argued that a good paragraph has three specific aspects: unity, coherence and logical development. Paragraph unity can be achieved through the quality of your controlling idea (as expressed by your topic sentence). If this idea is too specific or too general, then your paragraphs may be too long, short or ambiguous. Coherence may, in particular, be developed by appropriate use of referents, such as pronouns, determiners and restatements. Logical development is closely related to the idea of coherence, but places a greater emphasis on content rather than language and grammar. In summary, the paragraph has to be planned carefully so that all these aspects are covered fully. Moreover, the use of linking devices (e.g., *therefore*, *however* and *in conclusion*) is considered one of the best ways to ensure these three characteristics.

Paragraphs are the building blocks of writing, giving shape and meaning. Without them, it would be extremely difficult to follow the argument. They are particularly important in academic writing, where the ideas are complex. As in the example above, three key aspects of good paragraphs, like that above, are:

Unity

Unity, coherence and logical development

One paragraph = one idea. This will give each paragraph a clear unity throughout. Importantly, a paragraph is not defined by its length. A paragraph should be as long as it needs to be, but in academic writing, many paragraphs will be around 100–150 words long.

Coherence

Now turns to … closely related to … greater emphasis … rather than … in summary … moreover …
Each paragraph should develop your overall argument, helping to answer your question in some way. A good paragraph is composed of several sentences which link together well. Similarly, a piece of writing is composed of several paragraphs which connect clearly to each other.
A transition phrase at the start of the paragraph (e.g., *this said*, *having looked at*) and/or a transition sentence at the end can help integrate the overall text.

Logical development

If this idea is …
A good paragraph will develop an idea logically, which in academic English generally means theory first, followed by examples, or a general idea, followed by a more specific analysis.
In Step 17 you looked at these principles in more detail.

What problems are common in paragraphs?

It is too long: It may be that your paragraph contains more than one idea. If so, dividing the paragraph in two may be the appropriate solution.

It is too short: Do you explore the idea in enough detail? Is the central idea enough for one paragraph or do you need to combine it with another idea?

It is not clear how the ideas link together: You may need to plan the paragraph in more detail (see part E). It may also help to use more linking devices (see Step 30).

The main theme is not clear: Have you written a clear topic sentence? Alternatively, you may have more than one controlling idea and need to revise your focus.

What kind of sentences might you find in a paragraph?

Like an essay, a paragraph needs planning before you begin to write it. Although there is no fixed order in which sentences in a paragraph should come, some principles are outlined below. The diagram indicates the order in which these sentences tend to appear.

Transition sentence from previous paragraph 1

This essay now turns to the specific unit of the paragraph.
Links between paragraphs are very important. A short sentence (or a few words, combined with your topic sentence) at the start of the paragraph can often make this transition clear.

Topic sentence 2

It is commonly argued that a good paragraph has three specific aspects …
The topic sentence is the most important sentence in the paragraph. It almost always appears as either the first or second sentence of the paragraph. Its function is to:

- illustrate the central theme of the paragraph
- act as a platform for the rest of the paragraph
- get the reader interested and give an idea of the direction in which the paragraph is going

Topic sentences tend to be relatively short, concisely written and full of CONTENT WORDS.

Supporting sentences 3

Paragraph unity can be achieved through the quality of your controlling idea …
Your supporting sentences follow your topic sentence, and develop the main ideas outlined. Supporting sentences can have several different functions (e.g., *defining*, *showing cause and effect*, *comparing and contrasting*), many of which are covered in Unit G. These sentences may use a range of devices – argument, counter-argument, quotations, examples and evidence – to develop the central theme. There is no limit to how many supporting sentences you can include, but be careful not to go into too much detail in one paragraph.

Summary sentence 4

… the paragraph has to be planned carefully so that all these aspects are covered fully.

The penultimate or last sentence of a paragraph will often give a short summary of the main point of the paragraph. It may well act as a 'bridge', referring to the topic sentence.

Transition sentence to next paragraph 5

… the use of linking devices (e.g., *therefore*, *however* and *in conclusion*) is considered one of the best ways to ensure these three characteristics.

To improve the cohesion of your writing, you may wish to include a transition sentence to the next paragraph. This may be in the form of an 'open statement', later developed in more detail.

Step
18

D Activation

Which of the following is the best topic sentence? What is the problem with the other two?

1. When writing topic sentences, there are two very important aspects to consider, namely, content (which provides a summary for the rest of the paragraph) and language (which has to be clear and focused in order to express your point properly).

2. When creating topic sentences, there are two particularly important aspects to consider: content and language.

3. The topic sentence is an interesting part of the paragraph.

Having checked your answer, write a paragraph based on this topic sentence.

E Personalization

Look at a paragraph of an essay you have recently written and evaluate it according to the table below.

Factor	Guideline target	Self-feedback
Length	c. 100–150 words	
Unity	One central idea	
Transition	Is it linked to the previous/ next paragraph?	
Topic sentence	Is it clear and well-written?	
Supporting sentences	Do they develop the topic sentence sufficiently?	
Summary sentence	Does it reflect the main theme?	

If you are finding it difficult to write paragraphs, try following the outline below.

Sentence type	Your sentence
Transition sentence	
Topic sentence	
Supporting sentences (c. 3–5)	
Summary sentence	
Transition sentence	

F Extension

Step 43 looks at punctuation, a key component of **coherence** in paragraphs.

Appendix 1, Step 18, Documents 5 and 6 are photocopiable versions of the documents presented in part E.

Appendix 3, Step 18 provides examples of good paragraphs from academic articles in a range of disciplines.

What should be included in my introduction?

> 'The first impression is the last impression.'
>
> **Nepalese proverb**

A Reflection

Using the skills learnt in Step 14, brainstorm everything you know about introductions in academic writing.

```
should be c. 5–10%
of the essay length.          [                ]              [                ]


                    ┌──────────────────────┐
                    │ Academic introductions │
                    └──────────────────────┘
                                                  [                ]
```

B Contextualization

The following is an introduction from an essay entitled 'What are the characteristics of good academic writing?' Several important components of the introduction have been highlighted. Label them accordingly.

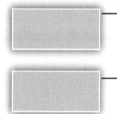

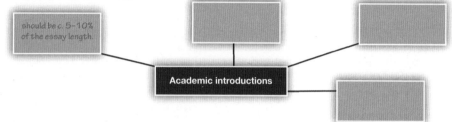

The question of good writing is one of crucial importance to anyone involved in academia. According to one recent survey, 55% of overseas students stated that they find academic writing difficult (Jones, 2008) – a term which is defined, for the purposes of this essay, as referring to all disciplines from the Bachelor's level and beyond. This finding is supported by Fitzpatrick (2003: 208), who maintains that academic writing is 'one of the biggest challenges that overseas students face, and yet there is little support provided to them'; this viewpoint echoes the general trend of the literature (e.g., Kenyon, 2007; Clarke and Wood, 2009). This essay uses both reports from the literature as well as data from both EAP teachers and students, although it confines itself to the humanities and social sciences. It argues that to be a successful academic writer, competence must be developed at the macro-, meso- and micro-level. As such, section 1 focuses on macro-level issues of academic writing, such as structure, section 2 concentrates on academic writing at the paragraph level, and section 3 considers the unit level of the sentence.

Analysis

What is the general purpose of an introduction?

It may be said that an introduction has three key functions, also know as 'the 3Ms'.

A Map	A Microcosm	A Marketing tool
To guide the reader through your essay, and show them the direction you will be going.	To give an overview of the main points of the essay and an indication of some of the main conclusions.	To 'sell' yourself to potential readers, showing them that your essay is interesting and worth reading.

What are the key components of an introduction?

The following list identifies the major components which your introduction *may* include. Depending on the length, type and focus of your essay, however, it may not include *all* of the aspects outlined below.

Interesting opening statement

The question of good writing is one of crucial importance to anyone involved in academia.
An interesting fact, statement or anecdote will both gain the reader's interest and indicate that you have something interesting to say.

TOP TIP: A short, powerful, dynamic sentence (rather than a long, detailed one) can often be highly effective in stimulating interest – think of it like the trailer for a film.

Attention-grabbing data

… 55% of overseas students stated that they find academic writing difficult (Jones, 2008).
A well-chosen and interesting number or statistic can sometimes say more than a hundred words of text.

TOP TIP: Do not just use a random number that you find: choose the data carefully, otherwise it will not have the desired effect.

Definition of terms

… a term which is defined, for the purposes of this essay, as …
If you are using specific terms which may be unfamiliar to the reader, or if your essay contains a number of complex technical terms, then it is best to define these at an early opportunity.
TOP TIP: Use a subject-specific dictionary for definitions rather than a general dictionary.

Relevant and interesting quotation

… Fitzpatrick (2003: 208) … maintains that academic writing is 'one of the biggest challenges that overseas students face, and yet there is little support provided to them' …
A well-chosen and appropriate quotation can give focus and clarity to the specific question you wish to address.

> **When to write your introduction**
> Although it may seem strange to say so, the introduction is not necessarily the best place to start writing. Many people find it is actually easier to write the introduction when they know more about the essay.

TOP TIP: Any quotation that you use should be better than what you could say yourself, otherwise there is no point in using it.

Background information

… this viewpoint echoes the general trend of the literature (e.g., Kenyon, 2007; Clarke and Wood, 2009).

Identify major scholars who have written on the subject before and why their work is important.

TOP TIP: Be brief – you can go into the detailed background information in the second paragraph (and beyond). You should just give an overview in the introductory paragraph.

Methodology

… reports from the literature as well as data from both EAP teachers and students …

This is important, particularly if your essay is research-based. You do not need to go into detailed analysis at this point, but an overview may be useful.

TOP TIP: This may be more relevant for science/social science students.

Limitations

… although it confines itself to the humanities and social sciences.

If there are any major restrictions to your investigations, you may want to outline them in the introduction.

TOP TIP: It is not a sign of weakness to present your limitations – it is better to tell the reader at the beginning.

Thesis statement

It argues that to be a successful academic writer, competence must be developed at the macro-, meso- and micro-level.

It is important to tell the reader what the main purpose/central argument of your essay is.

TOP TIP: Ideally, there should be no ambiguity; your idea should be clearly, precisely expressed.

Outline of sections

… section 1 focuses on … section 2 concentrates on … section 3 considers …

Present what you will be looking at in the rest of the essay to show the reader the direction in which you are going.

TOP TIP: It is important to use a range of verbs here, and it is common to use the present simple tense.

How does the introduction differ from the conclusion?

Students often confuse these two components of the essay, resulting in repetition of both content and language. The key distinction between these two parts of the essay is as follows:

- The focus of an introduction is to indicate to the reader *what you are going to say*.
- The focus of a conclusion is to remind the reader *what you have said*.

Conclusions are the specific focus of Step 20.

D Activation

Which sentence (a) or (b) is the better example of each component of an introduction?

1. **Interesting opening statement**

   a) The introduction represents the beginning of every academic essay, and is therefore important.

   b) Introductions are the backbone to every academic essay.

2. **Attention-grabbing data**

   a) 17% of students stated that they write their introductions after they have written the rest of their essay.

   b) 85% of tutors reported that their first impression of a student's essay was 'very important'.

3. **Relevant and interesting quotation**

   a) 'Introductions … stimulate interest, indicate direction and provide necessary support for the reader.'

   b) 'Introductions, it can be said, raise readers' interest levels, show them in which general direction the essay is heading, and give them the information they need.'

4. **Outline of sections**

   a) Part 1 will focus on the structure of introductions. Part 2 will focus on the content of introductions. Part 3 will focus on the language of introductions.

   b) Part 1 analyzes the structure of introductions while part 2 examines their content. Part 3, meanwhile, considers the cross-cutting importance of language.

E Personalization

Read the introductions to your previous essays. Do they contain the 3Ms?

- *Map*: Is it clear where it's going?
- *Microcosm*: Is the main focus of your essay clear?
- *Marketing tool*: Is the reader going to be interested?

If not, identify what components are required, and rewrite.

Consider the introduction for your next essay. If you lack confidence in writing it, create a blank table (use relevant components of the table below), and write it on a sentence-by-sentence basis. It will then be easier to put together as a whole.

Interesting opening statement	
Definition of terms	
Quotation	
Thesis statement	
Outline of sections	

F Extension

Step 15 focuses on writing a **thesis statement**, one of the key components of an introduction.

Step 20 analyzes **conclusions**, wherein you can compare them with introductions.

Appendix 1, Step 19, Document 7 is a photocopiable version of the table presented in part E.

Appendix 3, Step 19 presents sample introductions from different academic disciplines.

What should be included in my conclusion?

'All stories ... begin with the end.'

John Berger

A Reflection

Tick the statements which are true for you.

- [ ] My conclusions are extremely detailed.
- [ ] My conclusions do not use a range of LINKING DEVICES.
- [ ] My conclusions repeat what I have said in the introduction.
- [ ] My conclusions use exactly the same language as other parts of my essay.
- [ ] My conclusions sound different from the rest of my essay.

B Contextualization

The following conclusion is directly related to the essay discussed in Step 19:
'What are the characteristics of good academic writing?'

- *From this model, identify as many key characteristics of a conclusion as you can.*

> In short, it can be seen that there are four major characteristics of good academic writing: it is objective, complex, has a formal structure and uses good referencing. A good writer has to be competent at every level – macro (i.e., overall structure), meso (i.e., paragraphs) and micro (i.e., sentence). If just one of these areas is weak, the whole essay will be weakened as a result. Although this essay has only focused on academic writing in certain subject areas, the study has been wide-ranging enough to identify characteristics which are generally applicable. It is hoped that some of these recommendations may be used at the classroom level.

Characteristic 1: _____

Characteristic 2: _____

Characteristic 3: _____

Characteristic 4: _____

Characteristic 5: _____

C Analysis

What are five key characteristics of a conclusion?

A conclusion can have a number of different purposes, depending on the content, audience, type and function of the piece of writing. In certain subjects, your essays may not have a conclusion (they may have a DISCUSSION SECTION instead), or else the conclusion may be very brief. The following list identifies five features which are commonly found in conclusions. You do not necessarily need to cover all these features in every conclusion but, as indicated below, the first two aspects are extremely important.

Your conclusion must answer the question.

...there are four major characteristics of good academic writing: it is objective, complex, has a formal structure and uses good referencing.

The most important function of your conclusion is to demonstrate that you have fully understood and responded to the question. A full and detailed understanding of the title (see **Step** 13) is necessary. Ensure, therefore, that you are clear about *exactly* what the title is asking you to do.

> This essay/paper/dissertation has argued that ...
> has investigated ...
> has demonstrated ...
> has explained ...

The most common way of answering the question is to provide a summary of the key points. Your essay has a number of places which represent its 'skeleton', and these should be closely referred to when writing a conclusion. They are:

- your introduction (presents a general overview of the essay)
- your THESIS STATEMENT (identifies your specific focus/area of investigation)
- your topic sentences (provide an overview of the focus of each paragraph)

The summary approach is a particularly useful strategy in a longer piece of writing, where it is necessary to remind the reader of the points you have made. In a shorter piece of writing (and specifically in exam essays) you should keep your conclusion brief and focused.

Your conclusion must link back to your introduction.

A good writer has to be competent at every level – macro (i.e., overall structure), meso (i.e., paragraphs) and micro (i.e., sentence). If just one of these areas is weak, the whole essay will be weakened as a result.

The THESIS STATEMENT (see Step 15) in your introduction sets out the main focus of your essay. It is important that in your conclusion, you refer back to it. You need to demonstrate to the reader that you have done what you said you were going to do. In addition, this can create a satisfying 'full circle' effect.

> The focus of this essay was ...
> The purpose of this study was ...
> Returning to the question asked at the beginning, it is possible to argue ...

Your conclusion should leave the reader with a positive impression.

In practical terms, the impact of a conclusion can be very significant. A well-written conclusion can turn an average essay into a good essay, or indeed a good essay into an excellent one. The conclusion is the last thing which the marker will read; if it is well written, he or she may think it deserves a good mark. When writing your conclusion you should ask yourself: *if there is one thing I want the reader to understand from reading this essay, what is it?* Build your conclusion around this idea.

Your conclusion may refer to the practical application of your work.

It is hoped that some of these recommendations may be used at the classroom level.
Depending on the type of essay which you have written (see Step 16), there may be practical applications for some of your findings and you may wish to identify these.

> The results of this research suggest that ...
> The findings indicate a need for ...

Your conclusion may acknowledge limitations or make recommendations for future study.

Although this essay has only focused on academic writing in certain subject areas, the study has been wide-ranging enough to identify characteristics which are generally applicable.
As has been noted elsewhere, it is not a sign of failure to admit

> This investigation was limited by ...
> One source of weakness was ...
> A further study would ...
> It is recommended that ...

it if your essay has certain limitations. It is much better to highlight these weaknesses and answer any potential criticism, rather than to ignore them (see Step 25). Additionally, you may want to identify areas where further study and investigation would be beneficial.

What are five common problems associated with conclusions?

As the statements in part A indicate, there are certain things which a conclusion should *not* do:

Your conclusion should not go into too much detail.

Similar to an introduction, a conclusion tends to be c. 5–10% of the overall essay length. So, in a typical 1,500-word essay, this equates to around 75–150 words. The main body of your essay is the place to introduce and discuss issues, not your conclusion. The main purpose of the conclusion is to answer the initial question rather than to add new ones.

Your conclusion should use a range of linking devices.

Many conclusions use *therefore* several times. It is better to use a range of linking devices, such as: *in conclusion, to conclude, on the whole*, *altogether*, *in all*, *to sum up*, *on balance* and *thus*.

Your conclusion should not repeat what you said in your introduction.

As noted, your conclusion should refer back to your introduction. However, these parts of the essay have a different function. The introduction *predicts*; the conclusion *summarizes*; the introduction *analyzes* the question; the conclusion *answers* the question.

Your conclusion should not use exactly the same language as other parts of the essay.

You should not simply copy and paste phrases from other parts of your essay. However, paraphrasing or summarizing what you have written elsewhere is good practice.

Your conclusion should not sound different from the rest of your essay.

Your conclusion should be the natural end point of the essay – it should not feel different from what has come before. It should be written in clear, simple, direct language, and be full of CONTENT words (like the rest of your essay).

Activation

Write a conclusion based on the following essay. Certain key information is provided for you.

Essay title (length) ——— **'The English language no longer belongs to the English.' Do you agree with George Lamming's assertion?** (1,500 words)

Thesis statement ——— **This essay strongly argues that 'English' English no longer exists, and that it is now an international language; this phenomenon has been caused primarily by the rapid advance of globalization.**

Topic sentences

Para 1. The rise of English as the global lingua franca now seems unstoppable.

Para 2. In the modern world, it is impossible to say who 'owns' English; a system of 'protection', as attempted by the French government, would be impractical.

Para 3. Since the majority of people use English to talk to other non-native speakers, these questions of accuracy and standardization are unimportant.

Para 4. English is the global language of business.

Para 5. The globalization of culture has lead to English-language TV programmes, films and books being distributed throughout the world.

Para 6. Although globalization is not a new phenomenon, the electronic revolution has rapidly increased the rate of change.

E Personalization

■ **Examine one of your conclusions from a recent essay.**

- Go through the five key characteristics of a conclusion in part C and decide whether you are meeting these goals.
- See how long it is: is it 5–10% of the essay, or considerably more or less? If shorter, what could you add; if longer, what could you delete?

■ **Compare the introduction and conclusion from a recent essay.**

- Are they just paraphrases of each other, or do they have their own identity?
- Are they linked together?

■ **Read conclusions from texts in your subject area and analyze how they are written.**

F Extension

 Step 18 considers the elements of the paragraph, including the **topic sentences**. Since topic sentences for each paragraph together provide an overview of the essay as a whole (a 'skeleton'), they can be useful when you want to summarize the main points of your essay.

■ Step 19 focuses on key aspects of the **introduction**, which many students confuse with the conclusion.

■ Step 49 tells you what should be included in the **abstract**, a text which has many similarities to a conclusion.

■ Appendix 3, Step 20 provides sample conclusions from different academic disciplines. These conclusions come from the same source as the introductions in the previous step.

How can I make my essays more formal?

'High thoughts must have high language.'

Aristophanes

A Reflection

Which of these three sentences would be most appropriate in an essay?

1. Informal language is a load of rubbish you should avoid as much as you possibly can.
2. Informal language is abysmal contumely which it is imperative to eschew wherever feasible.
3. Informal language is a negative concept which should be avoided wherever possible.

B Contextualization

Fill in the blank spaces in the table below, which emphasizes specific differences between informal and formal English.

Informal English	Formal English	Rule
you can see from this graph that …	this graph shows that …	Pronouns – especially first- and second-person pronouns – are associated with less formal English.
a bit; a lot of		Formal language should be more precise and of an appropriate academic REGISTER.
! –	;	
not many		Often there is a more formal negative expression which can be used.
kids	children	
don't; there's		Full forms, rather than contractions, are used in academic writing.
do again; look into		
A1	excellent, first-rate	
Why did this happen? [question expecting an answer]	Why, therefore, did this happen? [no answer expected]	
at the end of the day		Clichés should be avoided in academic writing.

c Analysis

What are students' major problems with informality?

The idea of formality is one of the key features of academic English. This said, it is also important to note that while informality in academic English should be avoided, so should *over*-formality. In part A, just as sentence 1 is too informal for academic writing, sentence 2 is too formal. Sentence 3 has a good balance and is appropriate.

Whereas other steps have looked at macro-level issues, such as academic style (see **Step 2**), this step concentrates on the micro-level – at language and grammar choices. The list below identifies ten common areas where students face difficulties. As you read, tick the box which says 'this applies to me' if informality has been a problem for you in your previous essays.

Pronouns   ✓ this graph shows that   ✗ you can see from this graph that

Pronouns are relatively uncommon in academic English. Both the second-person pronoun *you* and the first-person *I* (discussed in more detail in **Step 22**) are seldom used. Third-person pronouns (especially *it*) are used occasionally.

This applies to me. ☐

Unspecific language   ✓ somewhat; considerable/significant   ✗ a bit; a lot of

Precision is a key aspect of academic writing. Words which are very general, and which can have many different meanings, should not be used. Other expressions which should be avoided include *stuff*, *thing* and *sort of*. **Step 37** focuses on vague and redundant language in more detail.

This applies to me. ☐

Punctuation   ✓ ; [ ]   ✗ ! –

There are some punctuation marks which are considered to be more informal (e.g., the exclamation mark (!) and the dash (–)), and these are generally not used in academic English. Certain punctuation marks (e.g., the semicolon (;) or square brackets ([ ])) are, however, used more frequently. See **Step 43** for full details.

This applies to me. ☐

Negative forms   ✓ few   ✗ not many

Other informal negative forms include *not much* (a more formal equivalent would be *little*) and *not any* ('no'). It is generally better to use the construction positive verb + negative adjective rather than negative verb + positive adjective e.g., *is bad* (rather than *is not good*) or *has been unrealistic* (as opposed to *has not been realistic*).

This applies to me. ☐

Slang words   ✓ children   ✗ kids

SLANG words are words which are not considered 'standard' in a language, or are considered more typical in the spoken form of a language. Such words, as well as TEXT ENGLISH (see **Step 2**), should be avoided in academic writing.

This applies to me. ☐

Slang	Formal
etc.	and so on
really	extremely
more and more	increasingly
nowadays	currently
like	such as

Contractions   ✓ do not/there is   ✗ don't/there's

Contracted forms (where apostrophes are used to show that sounds and letters have been omitted) are not appropriate in academic writing. Full forms should always be used.

This applies to me. ☐

Multi-part verbs   ✓ repeat/examine   ✗ do again/look into

Multi-part verbs (often known as **PHRASAL VERBS**) are generally a feature of speech or non-academic writing. In almost every instance, a one-word verb equivalent exists. Some examples are presented in the table on the right (with many more available in **Appendix 3, Step 21**). Similarly, many students often use the construction *do/make* + noun instead of a one-word verb (e.g., *do an evaluation* rather than *evaluate*).

This applies to me. ☐

Multi-part verb	One-word verb
take away	remove
give back	return
go down	decrease
go up	increase
look up to	admire
break up	split

Idioms   ✓ excellent, first-rate   ✗ A1

As with **SLANG**, an idiom is a **FIGURATIVE** word or phrase – i.e., its literal meaning can be difficult to understand from its components. The idiom which is most overused in academic writing is perhaps *on the one hand … on the other hand*. Since one of the main goals of academic writing is to avoid **AMBIGUITY**, idioms should not be used.

This applies to me. ☐

Direct questions   ✓ Why, therefore, did this happen?   ✗ Why did this happen?

Direct questions should be avoided in academic writing (except in your title). A **RHETORICAL QUESTION**, meanwhile, may be used. This type of question does not expect an answer, and tends to be used in order to raise awareness of a particular issue. In some subjects, however (especially sciences), **RHETORICAL QUESTIONS** may be viewed as being informal, and they should therefore be avoided.

This applies to me. ☐

Clichés   ✓ in conclusion   ✗ at the end of the day

A cliché is a word or expression which has been used so much that it has lost its original meaning. Often a cliché is also an **IDIOM**. According to the *Oxford English Corpus*, the following are the most commonly used clichés in English:

back on track	*the fact of the matter*	*in the final analysis*
few and far between	*a level playing field*	*when all is said and done*
in this day and age	*to all intents and purposes*	

This applies to me. ☐

D Activation

The following passage contains several instances of informal language. Rewrite it in a more formal, academic style.

> You might think that the sort of words you use in academic writing is not important. But nowadays, it's becoming really important for you to choose your language and grammar carefully. The fact of the matter is that many students are influenced by the writing style of mags and papers! They just do the same.

_____

_____

_____

_____

_____

_____

_____

E Personalization

 Ensure that you have checked through the ten problem areas in part C and ticked the ones that apply to you. Consider the relevant strategies for solving these problems.

Look through your last piece of writing and highlight any informal grammar or language which you used.
  - How could you resolve these issues?

Think about academic style in your home university system, focusing particularly on the categories in part C. There will probably be a number of similar areas.

F Extension

Step 1 looks at **the difference between writing and speaking** (which is more informal); similarly, Step 2 focuses on **the difference between standard writing and academic writing**. Step 37 analyzes ways in which you can avoid using **vague and unnecessary words**, the use of which is informal.

Step 43 focuses on **punctuation**, in particular the kind of formal punctuation which is used in academic writing.

Appendix 3, Step 21 lists commonly used phrasal verbs alongside their single-verb, more academic equivalents.

Should I use *I* in my writing?

'*Of all the words in all languages I know, the greatest concentration is in the English word "I".*'

Elias Canetti

A Reflection

Answer the following questions about the use of *I* in academic writing.

- How often do you use *I* in your academic writing?
- Do you know of any rules for using *I* in your particular subject area?
- Is it acceptable to use *I* in academic writing in your mother tongue?

B Contextualization

Look at the following uses of first-person pronouns in academic writing.

- *Decide whether you think they are acceptable or unacceptable. Justify your answer.*

Sentence	Acceptable?	Explanation
I argue there are four main areas that distinguish academic writing from other types of writing.	✓	*I* is sometimes used in thesis statements in order to express the main focus of your essay.
I argue in favour of Sowton (2012) in my essay.		
In the lecture, I was particularly interested in the section on academic writing.		
I interviewed 48 students to understand where they had most problems.		
I think Sowton (2012) is wrong for three main reasons.		
In particular, I would like to thank my tutor, who helped me so much.		
I and others consider the arguments of Sowton (2012) to be unclear.		
I will now look at the issue of structure.		
From this, we can therefore understand Sowton's main argument.		

c Analysis

> ### Why, in general, should *I* or *we* be avoided in academic writing?

Generally speaking, first-person pronouns (*I* or *we*, and their related forms such as *me* and *us*) are not used in academic writing. This is because good academic writing is based on what you can *demonstrate* rather than what you *believe*; it tends to be *objective* rather than *subjective*. When using *I* especially, one danger is that your writing is based on personal experience rather than on academic evidence.

In my country, academic writing does not follow these principles. Therefore, the argument is false.

First-person pronouns tend to be used more in certain academic subjects than in others. It is generally accepted that the first person is used less frequently in science subjects than any other.

> **First-person pronouns**
> Singular: I / me / my / myself
> Plural: we / us / our / ourselves

For those situations where you need to avoid using the first person, there are a range of grammatical structures and phrases which can be used. Examples of 'subjective' sentences from part B are presented below, alongside appropriate rewrites.

The passive voice

English verbs can appear in either the active or the passive voice. The active voice is most commonly used in English, and it follows the usual **SUBJECT–VERB–OBJECT** structure. The passive voice can be used when you want to remove the subject, which can be extremely useful when the subject is *I* or *we*.

Original: I and others consider the arguments of Sowton (2012) to be unclear.

Depersonalized: Sowton (2012) is generally considered unclear.

Using an abstract term

One of the reasons why the first person is often not suitable in academic writing is because it is considered too direct. Instead of using *I* or *we* as a subject, an abstract term can be used instead.

> This paper / article / essay ...
> The researcher ...
> This author / writer ...
> The / this data ...

Original: I argue in favour of Sowton (2012) in my essay.

Depersonalized: This article argues in favour of Sowton (2012).

Impersonal expressions

A number of phrases exist in English whose function is simply to introduce other ideas. They have no meaning by themselves; their role is as a 'platform' for other language.

> There is / There are ...
> It is ...
> One can ...

Original: I think Sowton (2012) is wrong for three main reasons.

Depersonalized: There are three main reasons why Sowton (2012) is wrong.

In what circumstances can the first person be used in academic writing?

There are a number of situations in which it is generally acceptable to use *I* or *we* in academic writing.

Thesis statement

I argue there are four main areas that distinguish academic writing from other types of writing.

As noted in Step 15, the first-person singular may be used in your thesis statement. Related to this, for longer pieces of writing, you may also use the first-person singular to establish your NICHE.

Communicating with the reader

By this, we can therefore understand Sowton's main argument.

An important principle of academic writing is that the reader should feel interested and engaged in your text. One of the ways in which this can be achieved is to communicate directly with the reader by using the first person, often in the plural, whereby the writer and reader are joined together in a shared understanding of the subject matter.

Transition between ideas

I will now look at the issue of structure.

This may be particularly useful in a piece of writing which has long sections (e.g., a dissertation or thesis) where you want to clearly signal to the reader that the essay is about to focus on a new topic.

To discuss your research

I interviewed 48 students to understand where they had most problems.

It is common to use the first-person singular when discussing research which you have actually done yourself. It sounds strange (and slightly old-fashioned) to use depersonalized phrases, e.g., 'The interviewees responded …'

Reflective writing

In the lecture, I was particularly interested in the section on academic writing.

As outlined in Step 16, REFLECTIVE WRITING is a kind of writing which you do only for yourself, in order to develop your own knowledge or to process information. In such a text, which is only for your own use, the use of the first-person singular is perfectly acceptable.

Acknowledgements

In particular, I would like to thank my tutor, who helped me so much.

In longer pieces of writing (particularly dissertations and theses), it is normal practice to thank those people who have helped you.

Step
22

Activation

None of the following sentences should use the first person. Rewrite them using some of the structures outlined in part C. Try to use as many different structures as possible.

1. I discuss the advantages and disadvantages of depersonalization in academic writing.

   _____

2. From this, we can understand more about the nature of academic writing.

   _____

3. I have clearly argued that academic writing uses *I* at certain times.

   _____

4. I have previously referred to this issue.

   _____

5. Following analysis of the data, I have clearly identified the main theme.

   _____

6. My data clearly demonstrate that academic writing is considered challenging.

   _____

E Personalization

■ **Establish whether *I* is commonly used in your specific subject area.**

- Ask the teachers in your department about when it is appropriate to use *I* in writing in your subject.
- Look carefully at your source material to see when *I* is used.

■ **Search your writing for first-person pronouns. Each time you find one, ask yourself:**

- is it an appropriate use? If not, how would you rewrite those sentences?

F Extension

■ Step 15 looks at THESIS STATEMENTS, where *I* is commonly used.

■ Step 16 focuses on different types of academic writing, including REFLECTIVE WRITING.

When should I use cautious or tentative language?

'The cautious seldom make mistakes.'

Confucius (adapted)

A Reflection

What is the difference between the following sentences? Rank them in order of strongest to weakest, where 6 is the most emphatic and 1 the least.

a) International aid probably contributes to solving world poverty.

b) International aid is the key to solving world poverty.

c) There are many who believe that international aid contributes to solving world poverty.

d) It is claimed that international aid contributes to solving world poverty.

e) It is possible that international aid might be a small factor that contributes to solving world poverty.

f) International aid contributes to solving world poverty.

B Contextualization

Which of the following sentences are examples of good writing? Justify your decision.

1. There is a clear and simple explanation for the use of cautious language in academic writing. — *This statement is too direct.*

2. Hedging is probably one of the most effective ways in which you can create distance between yourself and the text. — *This is appropriate 'hedging' – the adverb* probably *creates more distance between the writer and the text.*

3. Generally speaking, it is believed that there is a tendency for some students to overuse hedging language.

4. The data seem to prove the theory that using tentative language is a useful academic strategy.

5. Using tentative language may be a useful academic skill.

6. It is certainly true that misuse of hedging could lead to problems in academic writing.

7. There is a tendency to assume that cautious language is more common in scientific writing.

8. Hedging could be the solution to many of your academic writing problems.

UNIT E Making your writing more 'academic'

Step
23

c Analysis

What is the purpose of cautious language?

Cautious or tentative language – or **HEDGING LANGUAGE** – can have an important influence on how emphatic a sentence is. The sentences presented in part A demonstrate this clearly: whereas the tone of sentence (b) is extremely certain, the rest of the sentences have small and subtle changes (e.g., changing the verb, adding an adverb) which indicate that the writer has a different point of view. When ranked from strongest to weakest (b–f–a–c–d–e), these differences are very clear.

Hedging language is an important aspect of academic writing. It is particularly common when writing for the sciences. However, it is also commonly used in other subject areas. There are four main reasons why hedging is important in your academic writing:

- Professional writers frequently use hedging language to sound more 'professional'; it is important to use it.
- Hedging reduces the author's 'degree of liability' (Huebler, 1983: 18) – useful if you are not 100% sure about something.
- Hedging enables writers to 'use language with subtlety' and 'to mean precisely' what you want (Skelton, 1988: 107).
- Hedging makes your writing sound more polite – adding 'modesty and humility' (Hyland, 1994: 241) to your text.

What are some of the main difficulties in using cautious language?

Under-hedging

There is a clear and simple explanation for the use of cautious language in academic writing.

You should be extremely careful about making statements in your academic writing which are too strong and therefore cannot be justified (see Step 8). Of course, if you are 100% sure about something, or if the information can be considered 'common knowledge' (see Step 3), then hedging may not be required. However, as this example suggests, when discussing academic topics, there is seldom a clear and simple explanation.

> **Strong language**
> You should also be careful about using very strong language in your writing – words such as *clearly*, *obviously*, *certainly*, *undoubtedly*, *absolutely*, *always*, *never*, *every* and *all*.
> This does not mean that you cannot use this language, but you should consider whether it is acceptable.

Over-hedging

Using tentative language may be a useful academic skill.

Students often overuse hedging. You must be careful to use it only when necessary, according to the criteria listed above. If appropriate, do not be afraid just to use the verb *to be* – as in the example above.

Additionally, although compound hedges (see next page) are considered to be good practice, you should be careful about using too many next to each other. This may have the effect of weakening your argument to such an extent that it has virtually no meaning at all. For example:

Generally speaking, *it is believed* that there is *a tendency* for *some* students to overuse hedging language.

Unbalanced hedging

It is certainly true that misuse of hedging could lead to problems in academic writing.

Unbalanced hedging occurs when strong and weak forms are placed next to each other. The example above is typical – a strong phrase (*it is certainly true that*) mixed with a weak modal form (*could*). The tone of the sentence – and therefore the position of the writer – is unclear.

Compound hedge

There is a tendency to assume that cautious language is more common in scientific writing.

The combination of two (or sometimes more) of the above forms creates what is known as a 'compound hedge'. Such structures can be an effective way of using hedging, but be careful not to overdo it. Examples of some common compound hedges are:

- It **could** be **claimed** that ...
- The data **indicate** that the **probable** outcome is ...
- **Conceivably**, the **most likely** explanation is ...

What language can I use to hedge?

A range of different grammatical structures are used in hedging. The most common are outlined below.

Introductory verbs

The data seem to prove the theory that using tentative language is a useful academic strategy.

Other verbs in this category include: *tend to, assume, believe, indicate, suggest, appear to be.*

Modal verbs

Hedging could be the solution to many of your academic writing problems.

Other verbs in this category include: *will, may, might* and *would.*

Modal adverbs, adjectives and nouns

Hedging is probably one of the most effective ways in which you can create distance between yourself and the text.

Modal adverbs	Modal adjectives	Modal nouns
possibly, probably, sometimes, often, generally, perhaps, usually, commonly, conceivably, largely, apparently	*possible, probable, likely, (not) certain, (not) definite*	*possibility, probability, likelihood, assumption, tendency, trend, claim*

D Activation

Evaluate the following sentences and decide whether the hedging used is appropriate.

- *Correct the sentences accordingly.*

1. The Earth's diameter might be 12,756 kilometres.

   _____

2. The opinion polls prove that the Liberal Party will win the election.

   _____

3. One of the main functions of the pancreas is to produce hormones.

   _____

4. There is always a tendency for the graph to rise sharply.

   _____

5. The data seem to suggest that Sowton's argument is correct.

   _____

6. It is assumed that civil law and criminal law are different.

   _____

7. The USA's lies created disorder.

   _____

8. Undoubtedly, these problems may have begun last year.

   _____

E Personalization

 Read a text in your subject area and try to find as many examples of cautious language as you can. Try to find at least one example of the four types noted in part C.

Search recent pieces of your writing for examples of the type of strong language referred to in the box in part C.

Using the critical thinking skills learned in Step 8, are these statements justified, or do you need to use more caution?

For any of the language used in part C which you do not understand, look up the words in an ONLINE CORPUS so that you can see how they are used in context.

F Extension

Step 8 looks at **critical analysis** – a topic where hedging may often be needed in order to modify statements which are too direct.

Step 45 focuses on **adverbs**, a word class which is frequently used in hedging.

How can I make my writing more complex?

'Let us reserve the term "advanced" for those who deserve it.'

Robert Simpson

A Reflection

In what ways can writing be made complex in your mother tongue? Brainstorm your ideas.

* *Consider aspects such as sentence length, grammatical structures, language choice, punctuation.*

B Contextualization

Compare the passages below. The sentences on the left are written simply, whereas those on the right use a more complex structure.

* *Identify the major differences between the two sets of sentences.*

Simple	Complex
1. Complexity is an important issue in academic writing. Subordination is a key aspect of this.	**1.** When examining complexity in academic writing, subordination is an important issue.
2. Relative clauses make your writing more complex. They enable you to combine two sentences.	**2.** Relative clauses, which enable you to combine two sentences, make your writing more complex.
3. Stance adverbials can increase the complexity of your writing.	**3.** Interestingly, stance adverbials can increase the complexity of your writing.
4. The process of turning many words into one powerful noun is a useful academic strategy.	**4.** Nominalization is a useful academic strategy.
5. Punctuation is a strategy which can clarify texts. It is particularly important in academic writing. Therefore, careful attention should be given to it.	**5.** Punctuation (a skill used to clarify texts) is particularly important in academic writing; therefore, careful attention should be given to it.

1. _____

2. _____

3. _____

4. _____

5. _____

[c] Analysis

Complex writing: An overview

It is important to differentiate between *complex* and *complicated*. While these terms may have the same DENOTATION (basic meaning), they have a different CONNOTATION (secondary or suggested meaning). *Complicated* is a negative word, also implying 'difficult' and 'hard to understand'; complicated language should be avoided in academic writing if you want your reader to understand what you have written. *Complex*, however, is a more positive word, suggesting a structure which has many different components, all of which work together successfully.

In some circumstances, a simple, direct style may be appropriate. In others, a more complex style is necessary. This is because in academic writing you will often need to:

- discuss challenging ideas
- show the relationships between these ideas
- comment on these relationships

In such circumstances, a simple sentence structure is insufficient. A range of strategies for improving the complexity of your academic writing is presented below. The numbers used refer to the examples in part B. These strategies have been chosen using two criteria. Firstly, their frequency in academic writing: they are all common structures which you would regularly find in academic writing. Secondly, the language and grammar which they use is relatively straightforward, meaning that you should be able to incorporate them into your writing.

Strategy 1: Complex sentences

The basic structure of the sentence in English is SUBJECT–VERB–OBJECT. A piece of writing which is composed only of this kind of sentence would be grammatically accurate, but it would not necessarily be the most suitable or effective style for academic writing. This topic is explored in more detail in Step 26. Cleft sentences, already outlined in Step 17, are another more complex form of the sentence.

Strategy 2: Relative clauses

The function of a relative clause is to provide more information about a noun. Relative clauses use relative pronouns such as *which*, *that* and *who* in their structure.

Often, a relative clause appears at the end of a sentence or, as in the example in part B, it can divide the subject and the complement. Relative clauses used in this second way are an effective way of using a new term and defining it.

Types of relative clause

Students frequently find it difficult to know whether to use a comma in relative clauses. The basic principle is as follows: where the information which follows is 'extra' or 'additional', then a comma should be used (see type 1 below). Where the information which follows is critical to understanding the noun, there is no comma (type 2):

Type 1: Commas, which are used in certain types of relative clauses, are useful pieces of punctuation.

Type 2: Commas which are placed around direct speech are sometimes known as 'inverted commas'.

Note: The word *that* can be substituted for *which* in type 2 relative clauses, but not for type 1.

Strategy 3: Stance adverbials

ADVERBS (or ADVERBIAL PHRASES) are often used at the beginning of sentences in academic English. There are a number of reasons why they may appear here:

- **Authorial comment** (known as 'stance') on a particular topic. This may include:
  Doubt (seemingly, apparently, arguably, presumably)
  Certainty (without doubt, undoubtedly, unquestionably, undeniably)
  Reality (in fact, actually, in truth)
  Expectation (predictably, inevitably)
  Reaction (interestingly, surprisingly, unexpectedly, as might be expected)
- **Cohesion/linking to previous idea** (similarly, likewise, in the same way, on the contrary)

Strategy 4: Nominalization and creation of phrases

In your academic writing, you should try to maximize the number of CONTENT WORDS. One way to do this is to increase the number of nouns or noun phrases which you use with NOMINALIZATION and creation of phrases.

A noun is only a single word. However, you can use phrases of two or more words which work together as a single unit. Such noun phrases can be extremely dense in their meaning, i.e., you can say a lot in few words. If you can do this on a regular basis in your academic writing, you will be a very successful writer. One type of phrase is adjective + noun.

> **Top tip:**
> It is, of course, difficult to learn such complex phrases. As you are reading, it is important that you identify phrases which may be particularly useful in your field. It is not possible to place as many nouns next to each other as we like. A general rule is that once there are three or more, it becomes difficult to understand the term.

- The author presented an argument which will challenge you.
  The author presented a challenging argument.

The juxtaposition (placing next to each other) and hyphenation of nouns is also an effective way of creating noun phrases:

- The organizations which compose the United Nations …
  The United Nations organizations …
- The insect which causes the disease …
  The disease-causing insect. …

Strategy 5: Punctuation

There are three types of punctuation mark which can enable greater complexity in your writing (see Step 43 for more detail):

- **Brackets**: to add additional information which is less important than the rest of the sentence.
- **Semicolon**: semicolons are a way of combining two sentences which have a close relationship into one.
- **Colon**: to provide a list of information – enabling you to include more information but still be clear.

Activation

The following passage is perfectly acceptable, although it is written in relatively simple language.

- *Using some of the strategies outlined above, rewrite the passage in more complex language.*

> Language which is written in a complex way is a challenge for many students. However, it is a normal expectation at British universities. It is important to note that many universities have responded to this problem by providing writing courses which occur during term-time. It is not surprising that many students attend one or two classes and then leave. Others do attend the whole course.

_____

_____

_____

_____

_____

 # Personalization

▣ **How complex is your own academic writing?**

- Look through your recent writing and evaluate its complexity using the criteria outlined above.
- If you find any sentences/passages which are too simple, attempt to rewrite them in a more complex fashion.

▣ **Consider how professional writers create complex text:**

- Try to find examples of complex writing and the strategies used in your current reading.
- Pinpoint your search by looking for particular grammatical features – e.g., *which* or *that* (leading you to relative clauses), *of* (guiding you to complex noun phrases) or *~ly* (directing you to adverbs).

Extension

▣ Step 26 looks at different **types of sentences**, specifically more complex types of sentences.

▣ Step 30 analyzes **linking devices**, which can be extremely useful in making your writing more complex.

▣ Step 43 focuses on **punctuation**, which can greatly add to the complexity of your writing.

▣ Step 45 develops your understanding of **adverbs**.

How can I strengthen my argument?

> 'Convincing yourself does not win an argument.'
>
> Robert Half

A Reflection

Read these arguments and decide which are true and which are false.

- *Justify your answer.*

Example 1
- I am a student.
- All students like English.
- Therefore, I like English.

☐ True/false & reason:

_____

_____

_____

Example 2
- I am a student.
- Students attend university.
- Thus, I attend university.

☐ True/false & reason:

_____

_____

_____

Example 3
- Students are clever.
- I am clever.
- Hence, I am a student.

☐ True/false & reason:

_____

_____

_____

B Contextualization

Based *only* on your reading of this passage, which of the following conclusions do you think are true?

> Arguments are a very important aspect of academic writing, and it is important that students understand how they work. Syllogisms are tools which can be used in making arguments. There are also other mechanisms, which are equally useful. The idea of the syllogism has ancient origins; Aristotle himself said an argument could be expressed as two premises and a conclusion, and he was never wrong. Proper analysis of the premises of your argument will lead to a suitable conclusion. Based on my teaching experience, it is clear that almost all students have difficulty using syllogisms – in the last class I taught, 7 out of 9 students found them difficult.

Conclusion	According to text		Explanation
	True	False	
Arguments are unimportant in daily life.			
Most students have difficulty using syllogisms.			
Without a good argument, you cannot write well.			
Syllogisms are the best tool for making arguments.			

C Analysis

What are the general principles of arguments in academic writing?

The word *argument* has a different meaning in an academic context compared with its meaning in day-to-day English, where it suggests a conversation in which people disagree (perhaps angrily). In academic writing, there is only one side (you) and the language tends to be less aggressive. Arguments in academic writing are complex. They must be analytical, thorough and persuasive. A good argument has two components: the PREMISE and the CONCLUSION.

Premise

The premise of an argument is the supporting information on which any claim or conclusion is based. Arguments generally have two premises, and for an argument to be true, all the premises must be true. If any of the premises are false, then the conclusion will be false and the argument invalid. Example 1 from part A is false for this reason:

- I am a student: A true statement.
- All students like English: A false statement. Not all students like English.
- Therefore, I like English: A false conclusion, because one of the premises is false.

In Example 2, however, there is a clear relationship between the ideas. There is a logical progression from the first premise (the 'major') to the second premise (the 'minor'), thus it is true.

Conclusion

An argument's conclusion (also known as a *statement* or *claim*) must be directly related to the premises. Unlike Example 2, Example 3 is not reasonable based on the premises. It is important to ensure that the combination of your argument's premises genuinely does lead to the conclusion (i.e., that A + B = C). The evidence which you choose should therefore be both *relevant* and *rational* (i.e., not based on emotion, superstition or cultural/national influences).

Persuasion

When using arguments, you are attempting to convince the reader of your position. This process, known as *persuasion*, is a central concept in academic writing. In order to maximize your ability to persuade others of your opinions, persuasive language should be used.

> Persuasive language
> *It is claimed …*
> *It can be seen that …*
> *The reason for this is …*
> *As a result of …*

Deduction and inference

The conclusion of many arguments is based on the principle of *deduction*, where there is a clear, logical relationship between the premises – i.e., A = B, B = C, therefore A = C. However, when reading academic texts, the conclusion is not always clear. In such circumstances you may need to *infer* meaning. For example, from part B it is possible to argue, with a reasonable degree of confidence, that the statement Without a good argument, you cannot write well is true, even though the text does not say this directly. This is supported by the general tone of the passage, as well as by specific language clues (e.g., *very important aspect*).

Note: while it is important to develop the skill of inference in order to understand academic reading, you should try to be as clear as possible in your own writing.

What are some of the common mistakes found in academic arguments?

Although the principles of good arguments are apparent, mistakes in academic writing are still relatively common. Whether in your own text or when reading other texts, it is important to be able to detect poor arguments.

Making a conclusion which is not supported by the premises

This kind of argument is known as a **LOGICAL FALLACY**. There are many different types of logical fallacies, some of which are easy to identify, others which are difficult. Three of the most common logical fallacies found in academic English are presented below. A more detailed list can be found in Appendix 3, Step 25.

- Arguments are unimportant in day-to-day life.

Fallacy of inversion: Where the conclusion to an argument contradicts another statement earlier in the text. In the example given, it is impossible to draw this conclusion based on the information in the text, namely 'Arguments are a very important aspect of academic writing'.

- … it is clear that almost all students have difficulty using syllogisms – in the last class I taught, 7 out of 9 students found them difficult.

Generalization: You should not make general statements based on specific examples. In this example, the sample information is extremely small, and yet the writer has presented an extremely strong general conclusion.

- Aristotle … was never wrong.

Defence of experts: As noted previously (e.g., Step 8), critical analysis is important in British universities. It is the content of an argument which is important rather than the person who said it, even if they are a well-known scholar or world-famous expert.

Using premises based on personal experience rather than proper sources of information

- Based on my teaching experience, it is clear that almost all students have difficulty in using syllogisms.

This conclusion is unreasonable because it is not based on sufficient evidence. It is only based on the writer's own experience (my … experience) and it uses vague language (almost all).

Presenting a strong conclusion with weak supporting evidence

- Syllogisms are the best tool for making arguments.

Generally speaking, the stronger or more complex your claim, the more evidence you need to justify it. In the example above, the evidence from the text is insufficient for the conclusion; it merely describes syllogisms as a tool (i.e., one of many). The subsequent sentence confirms this. A related danger is that the process of the argument is reversed – i.e., that the writer starts with the conclusion, and then works backwards to try to find suitable premises. This is *not* how good arguments are constructed.

> ### Facts vs arguments vs assertions
> An argument is very different from a fact or an assertion and you should be careful to distinguish between them. A 'fact' represents 'accepted knowledge' (see Step 3) – for example 'Water boils at 100°C'. An argument, however, may not be generally accepted, although over time it may become a fact (e.g., Galileo's argument that the Earth moves around the Sun …). An assertion, meanwhile, is a strong statement of belief, rather than an argument based on logical premises.

D Activation

The following statements were written by students.

- *What feedback would you give them to improve the quality of their arguments?*

1. I based my argument on the experiences of my friend John.

2. This essay has so many appendices and uses so much data that the argument must be correct.

3. My tutor wrote this book, therefore the arguments must be good.

4. In my opinion, the argument is very strong.

5. Since 52% of the respondents agreed that the plan was good, it should definitely be implemented.

E Personalization

■ **When checking your arguments, ask yourself the following questions:**
- Have you ignored any facts?
- Have you manipulated any facts?
- Do you have enough evidence to make your claims?
- Is your evidence of good enough quality?

■ **Use the technique of playing devil's advocate (see** Step 47**). Go through your essay and deliberately try to find problems with its logic.**

F Extension

■ Step 8 examines **critical thinking**, a skill which helps you not only to develop good arguments in your own writing, but to recognize bad arguments in the writing of others.

■ Step 9 helps you to develop your **reading skills**, important to identify the flaws in any arguments.

■ Step 32 examines the language of **cause and effect**, which is often used when presenting arguments.

■ Appendix 3, Step 25 develops your understanding of **logical fallacies**, presenting other high-frequency examples.

How can I write a good sentence?

'In my sentences, I go where no man has gone before.'

George W. Bush

A Reflection

Answer the following questions about sentences:

- What is a sentence? _____

- For an academic text, what is the ideal length of sentence?
  a) As long as possible.
  c) As long as it needs to be.
  b) At least 18 words.
  d) No fewer than eight words.

B Contextualization

Read the following passage. Identify:

a) which sentences represent the four types of English sentence

b) which sentences represent four major problems in using sentences

Sentences are the fundamental building blocks of a text[1]. Because sentences are important[2]. Although sentences in academic writing may be quite long, you do not necessarily need to imitate this yet[3]. Longer and more fully-formed sentences may be a goal, for they represent a more mature form of writing[4]. In addition, the issue of sentence variety is important but it is often not noticed by students or taught in classrooms and this is an error but one which is common and found throughout the world[5]. Sentence variety, which is absent from many student essays, can be achieved in a number of different ways and is an important aspect of academic writing[6]. It is often ignored[7]. One of these ways is to ensure that you use lots of different types of sentences another way is to use a range of different language[8].

Types of sentence	Sentence number/comment
Simple	1 – contains just one independent clause
Compound	
Complex	
Complex-compound	

Sentence problems	Sentence number/comment
Short sentence	
Overlong sentence	
Run-on sentence	
Sentence fragment	

c Analysis

What is a sentence?

A common myth about academic writing is that sentences have to be extremely long. This is simply not true. There is no specific or required length for a sentence: sentences should be as long as they need to be. The most important thing is that you are comfortable with the length of sentence you are writing. Problems can arise when people try to write sentences which are too long: one mistake can make the whole sentence difficult to understand.

Before analyzing what makes a *good* sentence, it may be useful to review what its core principles are. Grammatically speaking, a sentence contains at least one CLAUSE which contains both a subject and a verb. In addition, writing good sentences requires you to have a good understanding of WORD CLASS (see opposite). You will also need to know the basic rules of SYNTAX, the principles and rules which govern how a sentence is constructed. In English, some of these key principles are as follows:

- word order is SUBJECT–VERB–OBJECT
- adjectives precede nouns
- prepositions precede the words to which they refer
- adverbs can have a flexible position

> **Review: word class (see Step 17)**
> Noun: person, place or thing
> Verb: the action of a sentence
> Adjective: describes a noun
> Adverb: modifies a verb/adjective
> Pronoun: replaces a noun or noun phrase
> Conjunction: links sentences together
> Preposition: shows relationships between nouns in terms of space, time, movement, etc.

What different types of sentences are there in English?

Good texts tend to contain a mixture of different types of sentences. Variety is an extremely important aspect of academic writing. An outline of the four basic sentence types in English appears below.

Simple sentences

Sentences are the fundamental building blocks of a text.

Simple sentences are composed of a single independent clause (i.e., a subject and a verb). By definition, simple sentences tend to be relatively short. If you lack confidence in writing sentences, it is best to focus on using this type of sentence.

> **Other ways of categorizing sentences**
> Topic sentence: the sentence at the beginning of a paragraph which provides an overview of what follows.
> Supporting sentences: sentences in a paragraph which develop your argument and provide evidence.
> Concluding sentence: a sentence which may appear at the end of a paragraph and summarizes the main point.

Compound sentences

Longer and more fully-formed sentences may be a goal, for they represent a more mature form of writing.

Compound sentences are composed of two independent clauses joined together by a COORDINATING CONJUNCTION. Commonly used coordinating conjunctions include *for*, *and*, *but*, *not*, *or*, *yet* and *so*. Compound sentences can be particularly effective when you want to compare or contrast the relationship between two equally important pieces of information.

Complex sentences

Although sentences in academic writing may be quite long, you do not necessarily need to imitate this yet.

A complex sentence consists of both an independent and a SUBORDINATE CLAUSE. Complex sentences, which always contain either a SUBORDINATING CONJUNCTION (e.g., *because*, *although*) or a RELATIVE PRONOUN (e.g., *who*, *that*), are composed of an independent clause and a dependent clause.

Complex-compound sentences

Sentence variety, which is absent from many student essays, can be achieved in a number of different ways and is an important aspect of academic writing.

A complex-compound sentence mixes the previous two sentence types. As such, it consists of at least two independent clauses and at least one subordinate clause. While this type of sentence is common in academic English, such sentences can be challenging to write at first.

What sentence problems are common in English?

Short sentences

It is often ignored.

Too many short sentences can make your text sound immature. One important aspect of academic writing is to show clearly the relationship between different ideas; this is difficult to do on a regular basis by only using short sentences. A balance between different forms is, therefore, important.

Overlong sentences

In addition, the issue of sentence variety is important but it is often not noticed by students or taught in classrooms and this is an error but one which is common and found throughout the world.

This is not to say that long sentences are inherently bad. However, problems emerge when students write sentences which are longer than they are capable of writing. The SYNTAX may become extremely confusing and difficult to follow. One common problem is that a number of sentences are linked together by simple conjunctions such as *and* and *but*.

Run-on sentences

One of these ways is to ensure that you use lots of different types of sentences another way is to use a range of different language.

In an attempt to sound more 'academic', students may join sentences together with a comma (or even just place two sentences next to each other without any punctuation).

Sentence fragments

Because sentences are important.

Sentence fragments may just be a subordinate clause (not an independent clause). You can check if you have written a sentence fragment rather than a full sentence by asking three questions:

- *Is there a verb?* If not, add one.
- *Is there a subject?* If not, add one.
- *Is there a* SUBORDINATING CONJUNCTION? If so, delete it, or add a subordinate clause.

Activation

Write a paragraph in response to the following question: 'What different types of sentence are there in English?'

- *Ensure that you use each of the sentence types outlined in part B at least once.*

_____

_____

_____

_____

_____

_____

_____

_____

_____

E Personalization

■ **Read through your writing and identify what kind of sentences you tend to use.**

- Mark the relevant clues, such as INDEPENDENT CLAUSES, SUBORDINATE CLAUSES, COORDINATING CONJUNCTIONS, SUBORDINATING CONJUNCTIONS and RELATIVE PRONOUNS. If you find it difficult to do this, there may be fundamental problems with your structure and use of parts of speech.

- Do the same for texts in your subject area.

- Decide whether your writing adopts a similar style/balance of sentences as the 'professional' text. If not, identify those areas where you need to make changes.

■ **Practise writing each of the different types of sentence, gaining confidence in how they are structured.**

- It is best to start with simple sentences, and then move to the more challenging sentences.

F Extension

■ Step 17 contains more details about **parts of speech**, the building blocks of sentences.

■ Step 18 analyzes **paragraphs**, the building blocks of which are sentences.

■ Step 30 looks at **linking devices**, which are a key feature of complex, compound and complex-compound sentences.

■ Step 37 helps you minimize the problem of **vague and redundant language**, which can make sentences extremely difficult to read.

■ Step 43 focuses on **punctuation**, an important aspect of good sentence construction.

■ Appendix 4, Step 26 contains details of a useful website which can provide you with information about how complex/complicated your sentences are.

How can I make my writing more emphatic?

'True eloquence is emphasis.'

William Alger

A Reflection

Using a MINDMAP, brainstorm a list of ways in which you currently add emphasis to your writing.

Use an emphatic adverb

Emphasis in academic English

B Contextualization

Read the following sentences and state how particular emphasis is achieved in each case.

Emphatic form	How the emphasis is achieved
The sheep enterprise should also be changed to organic for three reasons: the higher prices that will be achieved for the meat, the increased benefit to the environment and also convenience.	
A key requirement of this system is that the public-key can be derived from the private-key easily but not vice-versa.	
Education is a right.	
Despite having different ribosomes and their own DNA, there is evidence to suggest that mitochondria and chloroplasts evolved from prokaryotes.	
Not all schooling is education nor all education, schooling.	
Most importantly, the death penalty should remain within the jurisdiction of a state.	

Analysis

Why is emphasis important in academic writing?

An assumption often exists that academic writing should somehow be boring and uninteresting. This, however, is not true. Academic writing should try to be attractive and attention-grabbing, and the ability to emphasize particular ideas, concepts or sentences is important.

When trying to make their writing more emphatic, students sometimes make it too emotive and subjective. You should be careful not to do this. You must still follow basic academic principles.

What strategies can be used to increase the emphasis of my writing?

Use a variety of structures

As Step 26 suggested, students often use exactly the same sentence type throughout their writing. As a result, the text can sound uninteresting. Using a variety of sentences is important and will keep the reader engaged.

'Rule of three'

The sheep enterprise should also be changed to organic for three reasons: the higher prices that will be achieved for the meat, the increased benefit to the environment and also convenience.

The 'rule of three' is a principle of English writing which states that presenting ideas in a set of three is more effective than any other number. The effect on the reader is likely to provoke interest and help the reader remember particular ideas more easily.

Using a word or phrase from another language

In a book about academic *English*, it may seem strange to discuss foreign languages. However, because English is a global language, it often absorbs useful terms from other languages. In academic English, these foreign words and phrases may sometimes be used (rather than a translation) in order to indicate a very specific meaning. Clearly, using a word in this very focused way creates more emphasis. Some of the most commonly used foreign phrases in academic English (with their rough translations in brackets) appear below. While some are subject-specific (e.g., *blitzkrieg* in international relations, or *laissez-faire* in economics), others can be used more generally.

- **French**: *fin-de-siècle* ('typical of the late 19th century; decadent'); *laissez-faire* ('the policy of letting private business develop without government control'); *vis-à-vis* ('with regard to'); *volte-face* ('a complete change of opinion or plan')
- **German**: *blitzkrieg* ('rapid attack'); *leitmotif* ('recurring theme'); *weltanschauung* ('philosophy, outlook on life'), *zeitgeist* ('spirit of the times')

> ### A note on bold, italics, underline, capitalization ... and humour
>
> Strategies which are often used by students to emphasize particular words are to make them **bold**, underline them, CAPITALIZE them or put them in *italics*. However, with the exception of the latter, these techniques are generally considered informal and inappropriate for academic writing. Italics may occasionally be used, for example, to indicate a word from another language, or a specific term you wish to define.
>
> Humour is another strategy which people try to use to add emphasis to their writing. This, however, should be completely avoided. When native speakers try to do this in academic writing, it seldom works and usually sounds contrived. When non-native speakers try it, it generally sounds even worse.

- **Italian**: *chiaroscuro* ('light and dark'); *cognoscenti* ('experts'); *lingua franca* ('common language')
- **Latin**: *a posteriori* ('derived by reasoning from observed facts'); *a priori* ('from what was before'); *et al.* ('and others', used in referencing); *status quo* ('situation which has not changed'); *vice versa* ('the other way around')

Emphatic adverbs

Most importantly, the death penalty should remain within the jurisdiction of a state.

Emphatic adverbs, often placed at the beginning of a sentence, can highlight particular areas. Such adverbs include: *especially*, *particularly*, *crucially*, *most importantly* and *above all*.

Information placement

Despite having different ribosomes and having their own DNA, there is also other evidence to suggest that mitochondria and chloroplasts evolved from prokaryotes.

As noted in other steps, the place in a sentence where information is prioritized is either the beginning or the end. Therefore, you should place the information you particularly want to emphasize in either of these two positions.

Rhetorical devices

Not all schooling is education nor all education schooling.

A key requirement of this system is that the public-key can be derived from the private-key easily but not vice-versa.

Although rhetorical devices are more commonly used in presentations, they can also have a role to play in academic writing. Certain devices, such as *alliteration* (where the same sound is repeated at the beginning of a word), are considered inappropriate. Others, meanwhile, can be highly effective. Such devices include:

- anaphora (the repetition of the same word or words at the beginning of successive phrases, clauses or sentences, e.g., *we shall not flag or fail … we shall go on to the end ... we shall fight in France …*)
- antimetabole (reversing the order of repeated words, often to show contrast, e.g., see the 'schooling' example above)
- antithesis (establishes a clear contrast between ideas by placing them next to each other, e.g., *to err is human; to forgive, divine*)
- parallelism (using either the **INFINITIVE** or **GERUND** form creates a nice 'echo effect' in your writing, as well as being a useful tool for comparing and contrasting different ideas, e.g., *she likes cooking, running and travelling*)

Short, powerful sentence

Education is a right.

Since the overwhelming majority of sentences in academic English are at least 12 words long, whenever a shorter sentence is used, the reader tends to take more notice. A short sentence, therefore, can be an effective way of highlighting a particularly important idea. In particular, using such a sentence at a paragraph's beginning (to present a concise overview of the paragraph) or at the end (to provide a very focused summary) can be very effective. A short sentence can also work well as the first or last sentence of the whole essay. This said, you should be careful not to overuse this device. If you do, your writing may sound 'breathless' and too simplistic.

Activation

Increase the emphasis of the following sentences using the strategy in brackets.

1. The purpose of this essay is to interpret the data clearly, concisely and in specific language. (parallelism)

    _____

    _____

2. English is the language which people can use to communicate with each other in India. (word in its original language)

    _____

    _____

3. Globalization is largely understood as the rapid shift of power from states to the market. (add an emphatic adverb)

    _____

    _____

4. The principle reason behind the decision was clear; namely, it related to the financial benefit which could be gained as a result. (short, powerful sentence)

    _____

    _____

 Personalization

Choose a selection of sentences from your most recent piece of writing which you think are uninteresting.

-   Rewrite them using one of the strategies listed above.
-   Compare the rewrites with the original and note the difference.

Extension

Step 17 examines the principles of **text organization**. These are important to understand if attempting to make your text more emphatic.

Steps 38 and 39 focus on **academic collocations** and **phrases**. Using good-quality, high-frequency academic language is another way of making your writing sound more emphatic.

Step 45 looks at the specific way in which **adverbs**, including emphatic adverbs, can be used in academic English.

Appendix 3, Step 27 presents a list of Latin words and phrases which are commonly used in academic English.

How can I make my writing more coherent?

'It is all in pieces, all coherence gone.'

John Donne

A Reflection

Answer the questions about text organization and paragraphing in academic English.

- *These two topics are important aspects of coherence. If you are unsure about these areas, review Steps 17 and 18.*

   1. What are the two main principles of text organization in English?

   _____

   2. What are the different components of a good paragraph?

   _____

B Contextualization

Evaluate the following sentences in terms of their coherence.

- *If appropriate, rewrite them in the third column.*

Sentence	Evaluation	Improved sentence
1. Although overly long sentences which contain significant amounts of information are common in student essays at university level, this does not necessarily mean that they are what you should try to implement on account of the fact they can be difficult to understand.	Too long and complicated.	Overlong sentences which contain significant amounts of information are common in student essays at university level. However, this does not necessarily mean they are a target because they can be difficult to understand.
2. Sentences in academic English which contain very detailed and focused noun phrases at the beginning should use the passive voice.		
3. The background to this point is universally known, and so will not be discussed here.		
4. In other words, reformulation can help improve the coherence of your academic writing.		

UNIT F Developing your writing style

Step
28

115

Analysis c

What does 'coherence' mean?

The areas of 'coherence' and 'cohesion' (see Steps 28 and 29) are closely related to each other. While *cohesion* generally refers to the way in which a text links together, *coherence* relates to the overall idea of logical development and whether your argument is consistent throughout. There are three key questions which can be asked in order to see if your text is coherent:

> **Time management: a review**
>
> Incoherent text is often the result of poor planning, organization and time management. It is important to follow each stage of writing an essay (i.e., brainstorming, outlining, writing and proofreading) so that your essay is coherent. Review Step 12 for more details.

- **Is it clear?**
  - Can the reader easily follow your line of argument?
  - Does the argument develop in a clear, logical, step-by-step fashion?
  - Have you chosen the correct overall structure for your essay?
  - Have you written good topic sentences which clearly outline each paragraph?

- **Is it consistent?**
  - Is your argument/position the same at the beginning as at the end?
  - Are you clear exactly what the title is asking you to do, and how you intend to answer it?

- **Is it concise?**
  - Does each paragraph contain only one main idea?

What makes academic writing incoherent?

The following list identifies four of the most common factors that may make academic writing incoherent, along with some potential solutions.

Sentence length

- **Problem:** Overlong sentences are a common feature of poor academic writing. Many non-native speakers write very long sentences, believing that such sentences are more 'academic'. This is not true. It is much better to write a sentence which is shorter and more accurate than one which is long and difficult to follow. Three of the best indicators that your sentence may be too long are that it has:
  - too many words (if more than 25, it should be checked carefully)
  - too many PREPOSITIONS (more than four can make it difficult to understand the meaning)
  - too many CONJUNCTIONS or RELATIVE PRONOUNS (more than three suggests that the sentence may be too complicated)

- **Solutions:**
  - Divide the sentence into two (using a full stop or semicolon).
  - Change the structure of the sentence.
  - Simplify the idea of the sentence – do not try to achieve too much.

The Fog Index

The Fog Index is a way of measuring a sentence's level of difficulty. The index indicates how many years of schooling it would typically require to understand a particular sentence.

For example, the Fog Index of the following sentence is 8, and can be considered too simple:

The Fog Index is a way of checking how clear your essay is.

This sentence, however, has a score of 19, which is too complicated and, potentially, hard to understand:

The Fog Index is a sophisticated mechanism for scrutinizing the intelligibility of your academic prose.

The aim should be a score of about 12–16:

The Fog Index is a useful device for analyzing the clarity of your text.

It is possible to check the Fog Index of your writing at several websites, including:

www.online-utility.org/english/readability_test_and_improve.jsp

Inappropriate grammar

Problem: Non-native speakers often try to use 'complicated' grammar which they do not fully understand. It is important to recognize that the grammar used in academic writing is actually relatively simple. A good understanding of a few key frequently occurring forms (e.g., the present simple, relative clauses and modal verbs) will make your text more coherent.

Solution: Use grammar which you are (a) confident with and (b) makes your writing as clear as it can be. For example, sentence 2 in part B is grammatically accurate, but it lacks coherence because of the very long subject. Replacing the active voice with the passive would create greater coherence:

The passive voice should be used for sentences in academic English which contain very detailed and focused noun phrases at the beginning.

Idea development

Problem: In academic English, your ideas should flow clearly and be developed step-by-step. In poorly written essays, the argument may be circular, or repeated within a paragraph.

Solutions:

- Do not analyze or expand upon an idea before you have defined it.
- Ensure that your text follows the rules of text organization and paragraph development (see Steps 17 and 18.)
- Do not omit any relevant details of your argument. Missing out a step can cause confusion. If the information is obvious or commonly known, this may be possible: you must judge your AUDIENCE carefully when making this decision. For example, sentence 3 in part B may or may not be acceptable, depending on the audience.

  The background to this point is universally known, and so will not be discussed here.

Reformulation

Problem: Some points you need to make will be complicated and difficult to understand. This is the nature of academic writing. Aim to make these points as coherent as possible.

Solutions:

- Provide an ongoing summary (e.g., towards the end of paragraph) if you feel this would help understanding.
- Use signposting language such as *in other words, to put it simply, in short, in brief*.

  In other words, reformulation can help improve the coherence of your academic writing.

D Activation

The following paragraph has been written in an incoherent way.

- *Identify three relevant problems.*
- *Rewrite it accordingly.*

> There are many and varied important academic skills which exist and coherence is one of the more important ones, although it is one which many people do not always know much about. The logical progression of your argument should occur on a step-by-step basis. An argument means the position you take with regard to the essay title. To concern arguments you need ensure that you have particularly been careful and that your position is consistent throughout.

Major problems	Rewritten paragraph
1.	
2.	
3.	

E Personalization

 Give a recent essay or piece of writing to someone who speaks a different language to you or studies a different subject.

Ask them whether they are able to follow and understand your argument.

Copy and paste a sample of your own writing into the Fog Index readability calculator on the website given in part C.

- What is your overall score? Is it appropriate? Too simple? Too complicated?
- Look at the specific sentences which were considered problematic. Rewrite them accordingly.

F Extension

Steps 8 and 25 analyze the components of a **strong argument** in more detail.

Step 12 focuses on the development of **time-management** skills. Poor time-management skills are a major cause of incoherence in academic writing.

Steps 17 and 18 look at aspects of **text organization** and **paragraphing**. A good understanding of these areas can lead to more coherent text.

Step 30 provides additional information about **linking devices**.

How can I make my writing more cohesive?

> 'We must all hang together ...
> or we shall all hang separately.'

Benjamin Franklin

A Reflection

Which of the following sentences best describes your current writing?

- My writing links together well and there is clear transition between the ideas.
- My writing does contain aspects of cohesion, but I only use a very narrow range of language.
- My writing jumps about and sometimes the sentences have no relationship to each other.

B Contextualization

Look at the following text, which contains several useful cohesive devices.

- *Complete the table with examples from the text.*

There are three major reasons why cohesion is such an important academic skill. Firstly, as Smith (2000) argues, cohesive texts are much easier to follow than pieces of writing which lack cohesion. He further states that articles which do not cohere can confuse a reader, whereas those which do cohere can assist them. The second reason is that linking your ideas cohesively ensures that your writing is not repetitive. Finally, increased cohesion makes your text more interesting; if it is more interesting, the understanding is likely to increase. In short, these strategies can help you attain a higher standard of writing. Further reasons for this are outlined below.

Aspect of cohesion	Examples
Enumerators	Three major reasons ... Firstly ... The second reason ... Finally ...
Word family	
Personal pronouns	
Synonyms	
Demonstrative pronouns	
Umbrella terms	
Definite article	
Linking devices	
Words referring backwards/forwards	
Academic punctuation	

Analysis

Why is cohesion important?

Cohesion is an important component of academic writing. It enables the reader to follow the line of your argument clearly and to understand your point of view. In addition, using this skill means that your text avoids repetition. More cohesive texts are also more interesting.

Many students find it difficult to make their writing cohesive. The result is that it can often sound disjointed, uninteresting and poorly argued. Using a range of the following strategies will hopefully enable you to write more cohesively.

> **Current practice**
> Although many students understand the importance of cohesion in their writing, they commonly lack the language and grammar to do it successfully. For example, enumerators such as *firstly … secondly … thirdly* and conjunctions such as *therefore* and *however* are overused.

What strategies can be used to increase cohesion?

Referring backwards

High-frequency **COLLOCATIONS** which can be used in your text to refer to information already referenced include *as noted above*, *as mentioned previously* and *as discussed earlier*. When using such phrases, ensure that the point is clear to the reader. In addition to this, there are several grammatical strategies which can be used to avoid repeating the same language. This is important, as otherwise your academic writing may lack variety and consequently be less interesting to the reader. Three particularly common and effective strategies are as follows:

■ **Personal pronouns** … as Smith (2000) argues … He further states that articles …

The grammatical job of a pronoun is to replace a noun phrase. Without pronouns, it would be necessary to repeat the same noun phrases again and again, which would make the text less interesting to read. In academic writing, third-person pronouns (*he/she/it/one/they*) are most commonly used, since first- and second-person pronouns (*I* and *you*) are considered subjective and informal.

■ **Demonstrative pronouns** He further states that articles which do not cohere can confuse a reader, whereas those which do cohere can assist them.

Using this category of word (*this/that/these/those*) enables the writer to refer to a particular idea or object. In the example above, *those* refers back to the word *articles*. *This* is particularly common in academic English; as discussed in more detail on page 121, it is often combined with an umbrella term.

■ **Definite article** … the understanding is likely to increase.

One of the main functions of the definite article is to indicate that the writer and the reader have a shared understanding of a particular term.

Referring forwards

Further reasons for this are outlined below.

There are a number of words and phrases which can be used in order to indicate to the reader that new information is coming. When a reader expects new information, transition between ideas is much easier. Such phrases include: *below*, *next*, *as follows*, *the following*, *subsequently* and *consequently*.

Word chain

A word chain is a sequence of words used in a piece of writing which have a close relationship to each other. Sometimes these words may be from the same word family, or be synonyms of each other, or indeed may be umbrella terms.

◾ **Word family** Cohesion … cohesive … cohere … cohesively

Repetition of the same word (or word ROOT) may be used as a mechanism for increasing the links between sentences. However, as Step 36 argues, frequent repetition of exactly the same word may cause the reader to lose interest, and it may be wise to use different word classes from the same root instead.

◾ **Synonyms** Texts … writing … articles

Word chains may also be achieved by using synonyms of the same word. This will enable the reader to make links, whether consciously or subconsciously, between the terms.

◾ **Umbrella terms** These strategies can help you attain a higher standard of writing.

A word chain may also use umbrella terms – broad, wide-ranging terms which can be used to refer to several different ideas at the same time. In the example above, the word *strategies* is a general way of referring to the three specific ideas mentioned previously. A list of useful umbrella terms appears in Step 33. Umbrella terms are often preceded by demonstrative pronouns or *such*.

Linking devices

Whereas … in short

Linking devices, such as conjunctions and adverbs, are an extremely effective way of increasing the cohesiveness of a text. Words such as *however*, *therefore* and *moreover*, for example, indicate contrast, conclusion and addition. Indeed, linking devices are such an important aspect of cohesion that the next step is entirely focused on them.

Punctuation

Finally, increased cohesion makes your text more interesting; if it is more interesting, the understanding is likely to increase.

Although punctuation is often something which is feared by students, it can help considerably in creating cohesion. In the academic context, there are specific punctuation marks which are frequently used in order to do this:

- the colon : which indicates a list, or that the information which follows is important
- the semicolon ; which indicates a close thematic link between two sentences
- brackets ( ) which can be used to demonstrate that certain information is relatively less important

D Activation

Look at the following information about the English language. Rewrite this information as a single cohesive paragraph.

Use as many of the mechanisms identified in part C as you can.

- English is an important world language.
- English is the international language of business. Can bring economic development.
- The role of English: developing relationships and diplomacy improvements. English is one of the official languages of the United Nations.
- English is important in culture.

_____

_____

_____

_____

_____

_____

_____

_____

_____

_____

_____

E Personalization

Take a sample of your own writing and do the following:

- Look at the cohesion strategies outlined in part C.
- Highlight all those which you have used. Evaluate whether you have used them successfully or not.
- Rewrite the passage using either (a) a greater number or (b) a greater variety of cohesion devices.

F Extension

- Step 28 looks at **coherence** in academic writing, a topic which is directly linked to that of cohesion.
- Step 30 examines **linking devices**, a particularly useful strategy for increasing cohesion in your writing.
- Step 43 looks at **punctuation** which, if used well, can greatly add to the cohesion of your writing.

What kind of linking devices can I use in my academic writing?

> *'If a link is broken, the whole chain breaks.'*
> Old proverb

A Reflection

Read through the following list of words and underline those which you *understand*.

- *Then tick those which you regularly use in your academic writing.*

accordingly	but	in conclusion	otherwise
after	consequently	in contrast	similarly
alternatively	conversely	in fact	since
although	even though	in other words	subsequently
and	finally	in summary	then again
apart from	first of all	in the same way	therefore
as	firstly/secondly/thirdly	in this case	thus
as a result	for example	indeed	to begin with
as noted above	for instance	likewise	to conclude
as stated previously	for this reason	meanwhile	to illustrate this
as well as	furthermore	moreover	to sum up
at first	hence	nevertheless	until
because	however	on the contrary	when
before	in addition	on the other hand	whereas
besides	in brief	on the whole	while

B Contextualization

Read through the following passage and identify the function of the LINKING DEVICES, which appear in bold.

Linking devices have a number of specific language functions, such as sequencing, summarizing and referencing. **In addition**, linking devices enable writers to express their ideas naturally. **Although** linking devices can be extremely useful, it is important not to overuse them, **otherwise** your writing may sound too verbose. **In contrast**, not using them enough will make your writing sound simplistic. **Finally**, be sure that you use a suitable range of linking devices.

c Analysis

What is the purpose of linking devices?

Function

LINKING DEVICES (LDs) are a common feature of academic writing. There are three main ways in which they can improve the quality of your academic writing:

- LDs increase the cohesion of your academic writing, showing the relationship between your different ideas.
- LDs add shape and clarity to your academic writing, enabling you to express exactly what you want to say.
- LDs make your academic writing sound more professional.

To demonstrate this, compare the passage in part B with the one below. They are identical, except that the LDs have been deleted in the examples below.

Linking devices have a number of specific language functions, such as sequencing, summarizing and referencing. Linking devices enable writers to express their ideas naturally. Linking devices can be extremely useful, it is important not to overuse them, your writing may sound too verbose. Not using them enough will make your writing sound simplistic. Be sure that you use a suitable range of linking devices.

Common problems

Since LDs are so common in both spoken and written English, students can normally understand a considerable number of them. They are part of your PASSIVE VOCABULARY but not necessarily your ACTIVE VOCABULARY. As a result, it is common to either (a) not use enough LDs or (b) continually use 'old favourites' such as *however*, *therefore*, *although* and *on the other hand* in your writing. The problem with using the same LDs all the time is that your writing will lack variety, specificity and sophistication.

In addition, there is a third problem which some students face: the *overuse* of LDs. When LDs are overused, they tend to lose their impact, and your writing may become repetitive and vague. This example of TAUTOLOGY is demonstrated below, by adding an unnecessary LD to two sentences from the text:

...Furthermore, ~~in addition,~~ linking devices enable writers to express their ideas naturally.
...In contrast, ~~on the other hand,~~ not using them enough will make your writing sound simplistic.

Grammar

Grammatically speaking, an LD can either join a sentence to a previous sentence, or else link a SUBORDINATE CLAUSE to an INDEPENDENT CLAUSE. When an LD joins a new sentence to a previous sentence, it is followed by a comma. However, for the sake of emphasis/variety, it may also appear later in the sentence, where it is surrounded by commas:

In contrast, not using them enough will make your writing sound simplistic.
Not using them enough, in contrast, will make your writing sound simplistic.

However, when an LD joins two clauses, it precedes the subordinate clause, and is *not* followed by a comma. Since the subordinate clause can usually appear either before or after the main clause, the LD may therefore also appear in the middle of a sentence:

Although linking devices can be extremely useful, it is important not to overuse them.
It is important not to overuse linking devices, although they can be extremely useful.

What is the function of linking devices?

This list also includes examples of signposting language – language such as as *noted previously* – which can be used by the reader to navigate through a text. In addition, some of the expressions below must be followed by a noun to make sense (e.g., *besides*). The 'X' indicates where this is the case.

Function	Sentence to previous sentence	Subordinate clause to main clause
To add information	furthermore, in addition, moreover, besides X, apart from X	and, as well as
To show cause and effect	therefore, thus, hence, consequently, as a result, for this reason, accordingly	because, since, as, otherwise
To contrast/contradict information	in contrast, on the other hand, conversely, however, nevertheless, meanwhile, on the contrary	whereas, while, although, even though, but
To emphasize/highlight	in fact, indeed	–
To equate/show similarity	in the same way, similarly, likewise	–
To refer back	as noted above, as stated previously	–
To present alternatives	alternatively, on the other hand, then again	–
To provide supporting information	for example, for instance, in this case, to illustrate this	–
To show a sequence	finally, subsequently, first of all, to begin with, at first, firstly, secondly, thirdly, etc.	after, before, when, while, as, until
To summarize/simplify	on the whole, in brief, to conclude, in conclusion, in summary, to sum up, in other words	–

Note: Many of the words within the same table cell have *similar* rather than *identical* meanings. Check them in context to see how they work.

D Activation

In the following passage, written by a student, the teacher has identified a number of mistakes related to linking devices.

- *Complete the table which follows with appropriate feedback for the student.*

> Some call these kinds of words linking devices. Others[1] call them transitional devices. Because[2] students do not have a sufficient range of linking devices, they tend to overuse the same ones. Students could benefit significantly by learning 15 to 20 key linking devices, but they do not want to take the time to learn them[3]. As a result[4] they seldom improve and the problem remains. Therefore, in conclusion[5], teachers should provide more support in this important area.

Teacher feedback
1. *These two sentences could be more cohesive if a contrastive linking device such as* while *or* whereas *was used.*
2.
3.
4.
5.

E Personalization

- ▣ Look at a three-paragraph sample of your own academic writing.
- ▣ Underline/highlight all the linking devices which you can find.
- ▣ Evaluate your writing – i.e., *Do I overuse the same LDs? Do I use too many? Too few?* Compare with published academic writing.
- ▣ Identify strategies to solve your problems. For example:
  - Same LDs: *ban yourself from using those LDs you overuse.*
  - Too many LDs: *limit yourself to a maximum of one LD per sentence.*
  - Too few LDs: *learn a small number (e.g., 10–15) of LDs which you can use accurately and effectively.*

F Extension

- ▣ Step 17 looks at the issue of how text should be **organized**.
- ▣ Steps 24 and 29 focus on wider strategies to make your academic writing more **complex** and **cohesive**.
- ▣ Step 32 examines, in detail, the language of **cause and effect**.

What is the best way of reporting others' words?

'The foolish and the dead alone never change their opinions.'

James Russell Lowell

A Reflection

Why, in academic writing, is it important to report what others have said?

• *Review* Steps 3–6 *for further information.*

B Contextualization

Look at these sentences and identify the ways in which the views of other writers are expressed.

Sciences

1. The vitamins contained in beer … seem to be responsible for this reduced level of homocysteine in alcohol-dependents who consume this type of beverage (Denke, 2000; Sakuta et al., 2007).

2. This has been verified when the effectiveness of the association of psychotherapeutic with pharmacologic anti-craving therapy is demonstrated in different trials (Ansoms et al., 2000).

3. … scientific research on this subject has shown methodologic flaws (Klatsky et al., 2003).

> **Baltieri, D., Daró, F. R., Ribeiro, P. L. and De Andrade, A. G. (2009). The role of alcoholic beverage preference in the severity of alcohol dependence and adherence to treatment.** *Alcohol,* **43, 185–195.**

Humanities

4. Hesmondhaulgh's article (2002) demonstrates that a number of factors were involved: rising prosperity in the global North, increasing leisure time … and so on.

5. Nicholas Garnham, a major player in this development in his role as a consultant at the GLC in the early 1980s, analyzes this moment of cultural industries policy in his article in this special issue.

6. While some commentators have hailed creative industries policy as a genuine and promising attempt to marry access and excellence (e.g., Hughson and Inglis, 2001), others have been more sceptical.

> **Hesmondhalgh, D. and Pratt, A. (2005). Cultural industries and cultural policy.** *International Journal of Cultural Policy,* **11, 1: 1–13.**

Law

7. … methods which according to Kusanagi (2004) were used with *Sho-nen* A.

8. Takamura and Noda (2000: 254) criticize the response of the school officials.

9. In the essays collected in Pratt et al. (2005), several of which discuss the 'new punitiveness' as a supposedly global phenomenon, Japan is never mentioned.

> **Smith, D. and Sueda, K. (2008). The killing of children by children as a symptom of national crisis: Reactions in Britain and Japan.** *Criminology and Criminal Justice,* **8, 5–25.**

UNIT G Using functional language in your writing

Step
31

c | Analysis

What is the purpose of reporting what others have written?

Reporting what others have written or said about a particular issue is an extremely important component of your writing. In particular pieces of academic writing, e.g., a literature review (in a dissertation or thesis), the entire focus is on what other people have written.

- It shows that you have read, analyzed and synthesized a range of sources, thereby demonstrating that you have a broad understanding of the subject area.

- It shows that you have considered these sources critically, i.e., in an *analytical* way, rather than just *descriptive*. In particular, your choice of reporting verb enables you to add AUTHORIAL COMMENT.

- It shows that you are academically responsible: that you are not plagiarizing, and that you are trying to represent others' views fairly.

When you report on what other people have written, the importance of critical reading skills (see Step 9) cannot be underestimated. When reading academic texts, it is often necessary to go beneath the surface to identify what a writer really thinks about a subject.

Specific language which may be used to report what others have said includes the phrase *according to X*, which is very commonly used in academic writing, e.g., (7) according to Kusanagi (2004). However, this phrase is often overused and alternatives should be used, such as For X, … and In X's opinion/view. Another common strategy is to use the author's name followed by a relevant noun, such as X's article/paper/research' e.g., (4) (Hesmondhalgh's article (2002) demonstrates that). A more advanced and extremely effective strategy is to contrast the view of two different authors (or sets of authors) in one sentence by using an appropriate linking device. Sentence (6) does this:

While some commentators have hailed creative industries policy as a genuine and promising attempt to marry access and excellence (e.g., Hughson and Inglis, 2001), others have been more sceptical.

However, by far the most prevalent way to report what other people have said is to use reporting verbs. Examples from part B include verify (2), show (3), analyze (5), criticize (8) and discuss (9). The next section looks at these verbs in more detail.

How can reporting verbs be used?

One of the major difficulties faced by native and non-native speakers alike is knowing the differences between reporting verbs. The differences can be very subtle and not immediately obvious. In order to fully understand how a reporting verb can be used, it is important to consider three aspects:

- The verb's DENOTATION: the core meaning of the verb.

- The verb's CONNOTATION: the secondary, suggested (or implied) meaning of the verb.

- The verb's **strength**: is the verb particularly strong (emphatic), neutral or weak?

The following table outlines some of the most commonly used reporting verbs in academic English.

Reporting verbs to avoid

Say, mention, come up with, reckon, guess, feel may all be considered informal and should thus be avoided.
Point out is sometimes used, but it is a phrasal verb and there are many who would consider it informal.
Write is vague and unsophisticated; many alternatives exist.
State is a perfectly acceptable reporting verb, but is often used too much. Variety (as well as accuracy) is important.

Verb	Denotation	Connotation	Strength
add	Provide extra information	May be considered informal	Neutral
advocate	Strongly support/recommend	Formal	Neutral/strong
affirm	Declare positively	Useful when comparing the views of two or more authors	Strong
agree	Share the opinion	–	Neutral
analyze	Examine closely' (compare *examine*)	–	Neutral/strong
calculate	Determine mathematically	Often used with quantitative data	Neutral
challenge	Present a contradictory view to	–	Strong
claim*	Make an argument for	Can imply criticism/lack of data	Neutral/weak
comment*	Express an opinion about	–	Neutral/weak
conjecture	Suggest an idea/theory	Can imply criticism/lack of data	Weak
describe	Say what something is like	–	Neutral
discuss	Talk about	Quite general	Neutral
establish	Create a strong position	–	Strong
highlight	Focus on a specific point (compare *underline*)	–	Strong
hypothesize	Present a hypothesis	The idea is being tested	Varies
illustrate	Demonstrate with an example	–	Neutral
imply	Indicate indirectly	–	Weak
insist*	Emphasize (compare *assert*, *maintain*)	Can imply criticism/lack of data	Strong
investigate	Examine to discover the truth	Detailed lengthy process	Neutral
measure	Gather information about	Often in a scientific context	Neutral
misinterpret	Draw an incorrect conclusion	Very critical	Strong
observe*	Notice, record	Quite general	Neutral/weak
overlook	Ignore	Critical	Neutral
posit	Propose an explanation	Very formal	Neutral/strong
postulate	Strongly argue	Very formal	Strong
predict	State what may happen	May be quite vague	Neutral
propose*	Put forward an argument	May be tentative	Weak
prove	Demonstrate using evidence (compare *reveal*)	–	Strong
quantify	Demonstrate using numbers/data	–	Neutral
show	Provide information about	Weaker than *prove*	Neutral/strong
speculate	Predict with limited evidence/reason	Very critical	Strong
state*	Report what has been said (compare *argue**)	–	Neutral
suggest*	Provide an explanation for	May suggest slight authorial criticism	Neutral/weak

*Typically followed by a *that*-clause

Step
31

D Activation

Read the following passage and choose the correct word(s) in each case (it may be possible for two words to be correct).

Sowton (2012) (1) (*argues/conjectures/illustrates*) _____ that reporting verbs are a common feature of academic discourse. His specific (2) (*analysis/examination/ explanation*) _____ of the topic is, however, (3) (*advocated/challenged/ described*) _____ by Otaqui (2011). Matthewman (2011) (4) (*affirms/ misinterprets/proves*) _____ this viewpoint when she (5) (*notes/reveals/suggests*) _____ that Sowton's data might be incorrect.

E Personalization

 Read through a recent essay and identify how you report other people's writing.

- Is it satisfactory?
- Are you fairly representing other writers' viewpoints?
- Is there any language which you overuse (e.g., *state, according to*)?

Identify 5–10 verbs from the previous page which are unfamiliar.

- Using an ONLINE CORPUS, see how they are used in your particular subject area.
- Learn and practise using them until you are confident.

F Extension

- Steps 3–6 focus on the closely related topics of **plagiarism**, **referencing** and **using academic sources**.
- Step 23 focuses on **cautious** or **tentative language**, which may be used when referring to other writers' views.
- Step 36 concentrates on the issue of **repeated language**, looking in particular at the issue of denotation and connotation.
- Step 45 examines the specific use of **adverbs**, which are often combined with reporting verbs.
- Appendix 4, Step 31 provides additional information on **reporting verbs** in context from **corpora**.

How can I show cause and effect?

'Great events do not necessarily have great causes.'

A. J. P. Taylor

A Reflection

What are the possible causes of the following effect?

• *Brainstorm as many ideas as you can.*

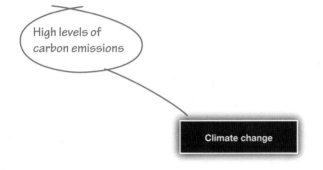

High levels of carbon emissions

Climate change

B Contextualization

Read the following text and identify any language which can be used to express cause and effect.

• *What other language do you know which indicates cause and effect relationships?*

Increased use of cause and effect language results in better academic writing. On account of this, academic writing uses a range of different structures to show these relationships. Therefore, it is important for students to become familiar with as many of these terms as possible, since a good understanding of how they are used will inevitably improve the quality of your academic writing. In short, the message is clear: if you use cause and effect language, your writing will be more sophisticated. The reasons for this will become clearer the more you read academic articles and see how frequently professional writers use this type of language.

Analysis

Why is cause and effect language useful in academic writing?

The idea of cause and effect is at the very heart of academic writing. Conclusions ('effects') which are not supported by reasons ('causes') may be considered poor arguments (see Step 25). Likewise, it is bad practice to list lots of information without presenting what conclusions can be drawn. This kind of writing is more descriptive than analytical, which is usually not the aim of academic writing (see Step 25). Good academic writing is about *why* and *how*, not just *where*, *when* and *what.* As per the patterns of organization in academic writing outlined in Step 17, the cause normally precedes the effect:

High levels of carbon emissions have caused climate change.

Of course, it is possible to swap the sentence round ('passivize' it) if the result needs to be emphasized.

What grammatical devices can be used to express cause and effect?

A range of grammatical devices can be used to express cause and effect. It is important to become familiar with the strategies outlined below so that your writing has variety.

Strategy 1: Using conjunctions to indicate causes

On account of this, academic writing uses a range of different structures to show these relationships.

Probably the most common way to express cause and effect is through **CONJUNCTIONS (LINKING DEVICES)**. In this respect, *because* is the most commonly used in academic English. In fact, at times, it may be overused. Synonyms also include *due to*, *owing to* and *as a result of*. All three are considered formal, and therefore acceptable to use in academic English.

> **A note on *because***
> Note: *because* should not generally be used at the beginning of a sentence. This is considered poor style.

As and *since* have a similar meaning and often appear at the beginning of a sentence. If you use these conjunctions, it is important to ensure that the sentences contain both a cause and an effect. A common mistake is to only include one or the other.

Strategy 2: Using conjunctions to indicate effects

Several conjunctions can be used at the beginning of sentences to indicate an effect or result. As these conjunctions are 'sentence-to-sentence' linkers, they should be followed by a comma. The most commonly used conjunction to indicate effect in academic writing is *therefore*:

Therefore, it is important for students to become familiar with as many of these terms as possible …

Other examples include: *consequently*, *so*, *thus*, *hence*, *because of this*, *for this reason*.

Strategy 3: Using verb phrases

Increased use of cause and effect language results in better academic writing.

A number of verb phrases can indicate cause and effect. These are near-exact synonyms, i.e., there is not much difference in either **DENOTATION** or **CONNOTATION**. The following substitution table presents those verb phrases which are most appropriate in the academic context.

Cause	Verb phrase	Effect
High levels of carbon emissions	lead to/result in	climate change.
	cause/are the cause of	
	produce	
	give rise to	

As noted, the usual word order of English is **SUBJECT–VERB–OBJECT**. However, if you wish to emphasize the effect (conclusion) rather than the cause (reason), you can use the passive and swap subject and object, e.g., Climate change is caused by high levels of carbon emissions.

Strategy 4: Using noun phrases

The reasons for this will become clearer the more you read academic articles …

Some high-frequency language in this category includes:

Explaining causes	Explaining effects
The reason/explanation/cause for this is …	The consequence/result is therefore …
The grounds/basis for this are as follows:	The effect of this is …
The source/foundation for this claim is …	The outcome is …

Strategy 5: Using conditionals

… if you use cause and effect language, your writing will be more sophisticated.

The zero or first conditional can be used to talk about possible causes and effects, the second and third conditionals for causes and effects which are unlikely or impossible.

Zero conditional
If + *present simple* + *present simple*
If climate change worsens, humans are to blame.

First conditional
If + *present simple* + *future simple*
If carbon emissions increase, sea levels will rise.

Second conditional
If + *past simple* + would + *infinitive*
If governments agreed on a strategy, climate change would slow down.

Third conditional
If + *past perfect* + would have + *simple past participle*
If the Kyoto Protocol had been followed, carbon emissions would have decreased.

Hedging and cause and effect

When you are not entirely certain of the relationship between a cause and an effect, it is common practice to use **HEDGING LANGUAGE** (see Steps 22 and 23).

Impersonal expression: **It is possible that** high levels of carbon emissions lead to climate change.

Modal verb: High levels of carbon emissions **could** lead to climate change.

Introductory verbs: High levels of carbon emissions **appear to lead to** climate change.

Distancing phrase: **It is generally believed that** high levels of carbon emissions lead to climate change.

D Activation

Look at the flow chart below and write a short paragraph describing the processes involved.

- *Use as much of the language from part C as possible.*

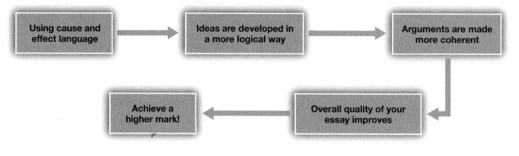

_____

_____

_____

_____

_____

_____

_____

_____

_____

_____

_____

E Personalization

 **Go through a recent essay and identify the cause and effect language used.**

- Do you use a good range of devices?
- Are you using them all correctly?

Look up any of the grammatical devices from part C that you are not familiar with in online corpora to see how they function.

F Extension

Steps 8 and 25 discuss the issues of critical thinking and arguments, both of which require a range of cause and effect language.

Step 23 focuses on cautious or tentative language.

Step 30 details the use of linking devices in academic writing.

How should I define unfamiliar words and phrases?

> *'I wish he would explain his explanation.'*
>
> Lord Byron

A Reflection

How would you explain the meaning of the following terms?

- *Try to write definitions for each term using no more than 15 words.*
- *What problems do you envisage there might be in defining these terms?*

Democracy _____

Beauty _____

Courage _____

Justice _____

Criticize _____

B Contextualization

Look at the following essay titles and decide which of the terms used would require definition.

1. Explain the difference between civil law and common law. (*Law*)
2. What is palaeography, and what are its applications in the modern world? (*Humanities*)
3. In what way can game theory be used to understand the concept of 'perfect competition'? (*Business*)
4. To what extent should the state fund universities? (*Humanities*)
5. What is Keynes' theory of full employment? (*Economics*)

Look at the following definitions of the term *state* and explain the differences between them.

- *Consider where these definitions may have come from.*

   Definition 1: A nation, or country.

   Definition 2: A distinct set of political institutions whose specific concern is with the organization of domination, in the name of the common interest, within a delimited territory.

   Definition 3: That organization that successfully claims a monopoly on the legitimate use of physical force within a given territory.

c Analysis

Why do I need to define certain words and phrases?

Reasons for defining

Academic writing regularly uses language which needs to be defined and explained to the reader. There are three main reasons for this:

- Some words have a different meaning in academic English than in general English (e.g., criticize).

- **ABSTRACT NOUNS** which, as their name suggests, do not have a universally agreed meaning, are used on a fairly frequent basis (e.g., democracy, beauty).

- Some terms may be unfamiliar to your audience and therefore need explaining so that the essay can be fully understood. This is particularly important for **KEYWORDS**.

Many of the words that require definition will be found in your title. When given an essay question, one of the first jobs you need to do is decide which terms require definition. From the example questions in part B, it is likely that the following words would need to be defined. These definitions should appear in either the introduction or the second paragraph.

1. civil law/common law
2. palaeography
3. game theory/perfect competition

4. state
5. full employment

Different purposes

When defining or explaining a term, it is important to know *why* you are doing so. The language you use, and the focus you have, will differ according to your purpose. The table below indicates three different ways the term *euthanasia* may be defined or explained, according to different requirements.

Purpose	Example definition/explanation
To explain its basic meaning (denotation)	*Euthanasia is a process which enables someone to end their life prematurely.*
To state its relevance	*Euthanasia is a topic which has been discussed at length in the media over the past few years.*
To indicate something interesting about it	*As its controversial nature suggests, euthanasia is an issue which divides opinion sharply.*

Level of commitment to a statement

It may be necessary to indicate your level of commitment to a statement. On the spectrum below, statements towards the right are more certain, whereas those to the left are less certain.

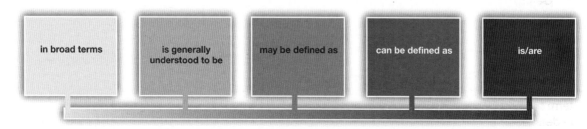

| in broad terms | is generally understood to be | may be defined as | can be defined as | is/are |

Three-part definition: introduction

A range of **LANGUAGE FRAMES** can be used to define words. The most common – and the easiest to use – is the three-part definition, with a **VERB PHRASE**, **UMBRELLA TERM** and a **RELATIVE CLAUSE**. Three-part definitions for some of the words in part B are:

Common law describes a branch of law in which the decisions of judges are most important.

In simple terms, palaeography can be defined as a discipline which focuses on the study of ancient writing.

Full employment can be described as the state in which all the economic resources of a country are fully utilized.

> **Introductory language**
> When defining a term, there may be introductory language you can use. Examples include:
> *Although there is no universal definition of X …*
> *In this essay/paper/article …*
> *The term X is used to refer to …*
> *… are used interchangeably …*
> *According to X …*
> *By this we mean …*

Three-part definition: analysis of the component parts

1. **Verb phrase** Useful verbs include *define*, *describe*, *classify*, *characterize*, *label*, *explain* and *clarify*.

2. **Umbrella term** An umbrella term is a broad, wide-ranging term related to the term being defined. *Institution*, for example, would be an umbrella term for *university*, as well as *school*, *prison*, *hospital*. A selection of useful umbrella terms appears in the box on the right.

3. **Relative clause** As outlined elsewhere, a relative clause is a grammatical structure which provides additional information about a noun. Ensure that you go into sufficient detail to distinguish the term from any other. The type of relative clauses used will be *defining*, so no comma is required.

> **Useful umbrella terms**
> **Organization:** *institution/body/association*
> **Words:** *term/expression*
> **Idea:** *concept/notion*
> **Process:** *system/method/mechanism*
> **Academic field:** *subject/discipline/area*
> **Subject:** *topic/issue/matter*
> **General terms:** *branch/type/example/illustration/model/state*

Using dictionaries

It is generally inappropriate to use a general dictionary of English in an academic essay. It is better to use either a subject-specific dictionary or a direct quotation or paraphrase by a well-known writer in the field. Notice the difference in emphasis of the definitions of *state* in part B:

- Definition 1 comes from the *Macmillan Essential Dictionary for Learners of English* and provides only a very basic explanation, which is unsuitable for an academic essay.

- Definition 2 comes from the *Oxford Concise Dictionary of Politics* and offers a more focused, detailed, academic description.

- Definition 3 is the view of a specific scholar in the field (Max Weber). His definition represents his own attitude towards the term.

Style and formatting

There is no universal agreement on the styling of terms that require definition. This said, quotation marks are often used around terms where there is ambiguity (particularly if the term has a meaning in general as well as academic English), e.g., 'state'. Italics are often used in definitions of foreign-language terms, e.g., *zeitgeist*.

UNIT G Using functional language in your writing

Step 33

137

D Activation

Write definitions for these terms.

1. Economics _____

_____

2. Malaria _____

_____

3. Cirrhosis _____

_____

4. Photosynthesis _____

_____

5. Modern history _____

_____

6. Duty of care _____

_____

E Personalization

Identify terms in your field which are either controversial or difficult to define.

- Write your own definition for these terms, practising the language identified in part C.
- Show your definitions to a friend/colleague on the same course and ask them to identify the word you are describing.
- Check your definitions against those provided in a subject-specific dictionary.

Look at your recent essays:

- Decide whether the definitions you wrote were suitable. If not, why not?
- Decide whether you defined all the words you should have.

F Extension

Step 19 focuses on the **introduction** to an essay, where a definition is likely to appear.

Step 23 looks at **cautious** or **tentative language**, which may be used when defining.

Step 31 analyzes **strategies for reporting others' words**, which may be helpful when referring to a particular scholar's definition of a key term.

Step 37 suggests strategies for avoiding **vague** and **unnecessary words**.

Appendix 2, Step 33, Activity 3 presents a list of more words to define, with a range of sample definitions.

How can I compare and contrast different ideas?

> *'We are so made that we can derive intense enjoyment from a contrast.'*
>
> **Sigmund Freud**

A Reflection

Using the mind map below, brainstorm the situations in which you would need to use the language of comparison and contrast.

Describing different processes

Language of comparison and contrast

B Contextualization

Look at these sentences and identify the language which is used for comparison and contrast.

- Able (2001) and Cole (2004) adopt contradictory positions over the issue of nuclear weapons. Whereas Able argues that an increase in the number of weapons leads to increased security, Cole suggests the opposite.

- There are close parallels between the characters of Hamlet and Othello: they are both outsiders and find interaction with other people difficult. In contrast, Othello can be viewed as a man of action, whereas Hamlet is a man who thinks, and does nothing.

- In the United Kingdom, both government and privately run schools must be inspected by the government. By the same token, students tend to take the same exams at 16 and 18, namely GCSEs and A-levels. However, many argue that there is a significant disparity in the quality of education offered by both types of institution, although exam results for the best-performing schools are quite similar.

- Economics today is a considerably more interesting subject than it was 150 years ago. Back then, it was known as the 'dismal science'. The recent publication of books such as *Freakonomics* has created a more positive impression of the subject, although many are still suspicious.

Step 34

Analysis

What is the importance of comparing and contrasting?

Comparing and contrasting ideas is an important academic writing skill which is required in all subject areas. Indeed, such is its importance that some essays (so-called 'evaluative' essays) have this idea of comparison and contrast at their very core (see Step 16). Many students tend to use the same language whenever comparing or contrasting different ideas. This language includes vague comparative adjectives (e.g., *better than*), overused nouns (e.g., *similarity*) and conjunctions (e.g., *on the other hand*). However, a wide range of language exists to perform this function. A good knowledge of these forms, outlined below, can not only add variety to your language but also improve accuracy and specificity.

> **Review: evaluative essays**
> The purpose of this type of essay is to compare and contrast the different views on a topic. It may support one side or another, or else take a balanced overview.

How can I identify similarities and differences?

At times, it can be difficult to identify exactly what the similarities and differences are. One technique which can help you is the Venn diagram.

Stage 1: Draw two circles which intersect with each other.

Stage 2: Label each of the circles, using the terms which you are comparing (e.g., *academic writing/standard writing*).

Stage 3: Brainstorm ideas connected with each topic and place them in the appropriate part of the Venn diagram (e.g., *use of referencing* is related only to academic writing because it is not a feature of standard writing; *rules of syntax*, however, is important in both types of writing and therefore appears in the middle).

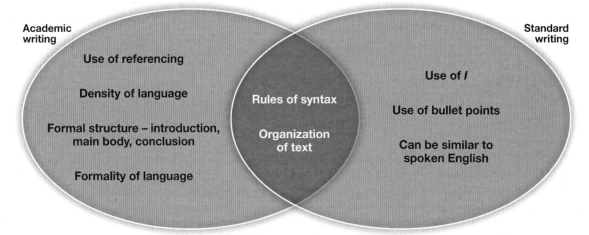

By analyzing this diagram, the following example sentences can be made:

- **Both** academic writing **and** standard writing have the same text organization; namely, 'topic before comment' and 'old before new'.
- Standard writing **differs from** academic writing in its use of *I* and bullet points.
- **One key distinction between** the two types of writing is the way that text is organized.

What specific language can be used?

Comparative and superlative adjectives

Both of these forms are commonly used in comparing and contrasting ideas.
The basic rules which govern their usage are:

	One- or two-syllable words	Other words
Comparative	Add ~*er* to the adjective, add *than*	Precede the adjective with *more*
Superlative	Add ~*est* to the adjective, add *the*	Precede the adjective with *the most*

To provide additional details in the comparative, the adjective can be preceded by an adverb:
- to strengthen the comparison: *considerably, significantly, rather, somewhat*
- to weaken the comparison: *slightly, scarcely, hardly, barely*

Conjunctions and linking devices

A number of linking devices can be used to compare and contrast, e.g., *both … and, neither … nor, whereas, while, however, nevertheless, although, even though, despite*; see Step 30.

Nouns, verbs, adjectives and adverbs

Comparison (nouns)	Contrast (nouns)
similarity, comparison, likeness, correspondence, parallel, connection, relationship	*difference, dissimilarity, disparity, distinction, divergence, variation, discrepancy, opposition*

Note: Adjectives to intensify the meaning which can be used with both sets of nouns include *important, relevant, specific* and *apposite*. Additionally, for contrast nouns such as *distinct, discrete, clear, clear-cut, well-defined* and *marked* can be used. For comparison, *close* and *strong* perform the same function.

Comparison (verbs)	Contrast (verbs)
compare, relate, equate, link	*contrast, differ, vary, change, diverge*

Note: Comparison verbs are often used in the passive voice with a modal verb (e.g., *X and Y can be compared*).

Comparison (adjectives)	Contrast (adjectives)
similar, like, alike, comparable, parallel, analogous, related, akin	*dissimilar, unlike, unrelated, divergent, unalike, contradictory, opposite*

Comparison (adverbs/adverbial phrases)	Contrast (adverbs/adverbial phrases)
Sentence–sentence linking: *similarly, equally, likewise, correspondingly, by the same token* Main–subordinate clause: *just as, in the same way*	*conversely, on the contrary*

Notes on comparing and contrasting:

1. A number of hedging adverbial phrases can be combined with some of the forms above, e.g., *in a number of respects, to some extent, in part, to a degree* and *in some measure*.
2. Impersonal expressions (see Step 22) are often used to introduce comparisons and contrasts, e.g., *there is, it is possible to see, one can identify*.
3. Confusion often exists over how to use prepositions when comparing and contrasting. For example, there is a subtle difference between *compared to* and *compared with*. Note: *compared to* is preferred when the similarity between two things is the point of comparison; *compared with* suggests that the differences are as important, or more important, than the similarities, *different from* and *in contrast* are more common than *different to* and *by contrast*; and *similar* is often followed by *to*.

Activation

Compare and/or contrast the following.

Learning English and learning another foreign language

_____

_____

Your country and the United Kingdom

_____

_____

Any two famous thinkers

_____

_____

Two writers/scholars in your subject area who have contradictory views

_____

_____

Personalization

- **Consider the words and phrases used on the previous page and identify any which are unfamiliar.**
  - Look them up in a dictionary or in an online corpus so that you understand how they are used.
  - Ensure that you are clear about the small differences in meaning, noting that synonyms are not exactly the same as each other, only similar (see Step 36).
  - Using the online corpus, identify if there are any particular words with which they form a strong COLLOCATION.
  - Read through articles in your subject area. Look in particular for combinations of the forms and see how they contribute to the overall effect of the text.
- **Search your writing and identify how you compare and contrast ideas at the moment. Focus on:**
  - any forms which you frequently repeat
  - any vague or unspecific language which you use

Extension

- Step 16 focuses on **different types of academic essay**, including the evaluative essay, which has the notion of comparison and contrast at its centre.
- Step 30 analyzes the **use of linking devices** in English.
- Step 31 looks at **reporting verbs**, which are used to compare and contrast what different writers think about a particular subject.
- Step 35 includes reference to comparison and contrast language in its focus on **interpreting information from tables and graphs.**

What language should I use to interpret tables and graphs?

A Reflection

Analyze this graph and write three sentences which highlight the *main* results.

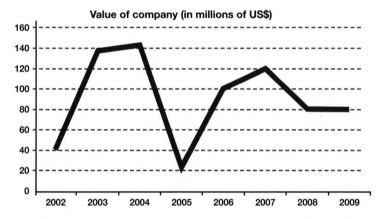

Value of company (in millions of US$)

Example: There was a slight increase in the value of the company between 2006 and 2007.

1. _____

_____

2. _____

_____

3. _____

_____

B Contextualization

Match the words in bold with their definitions in the column on the right.

• *All sentences are taken from an academic* ONLINE CORPUS.

The loss of status as many nations reserve currency may cause the dollar to **plummet** even further.	have the same value (negative connotation)
The White Army reached a **peak** of 100,000, compared with the Red Army, which had over three and a half million members in 1920.	fall quickly
As shown in table 3, in the distribution sector as a whole, output **stagnated** in the interwar period.	gradual increase over a period of time
After exercise, the pulse rate shot up to 110 but the SpO_2 level **remained constant** at 98.	significant (possibly exponential) rise
Not only has the population increased, but so has China's economy, which has seen a **steady rise** between 1978 and 2006.	high point, maximum value
The strain within the gel **increased dramatically** to ≈ 40,000%.	have the same value (neutral positive connotation)

c Analysis

What information should I analyze in a table or graph?

Tables and graphs are a core component of many essays, especially those in the sciences or social sciences. These tables and graphs may either be cited from books and articles, or they may have emerged from your own EMPIRICAL RESEARCH.

When interpreting tables and graphs, it is important to identify the *main* results and relate these to the reader. Poor essays will often describe everything, even minor, unimportant points. Detailed description of a table or graph may, at times, be necessary; however, good academic writing will tend to analyze tables and graphs to focus on either meaningful issues or overall patterns and trends.

Meaningful issues (e.g., high point, low point, significant differences, surprising similarities)
- The company's value was highest in 2004.
- There was a sharp drop in the company's value between 2004 and 2005.

Overall patterns and trends (e.g., trends over time, long-term analysis)
- The value of the company fluctuated significantly between 2002 and 2006.
- The company price has stabilized somewhat since 2006.

Ten top tips for using tables and graphs successfully
- Ensure that you use the appropriate type of graph, i.e., the graph which will most clearly show the main points you will focus on. Graphs used frequently in academic writing are line graphs, pie charts, bar graphs and histograms.
- Label your graphs clearly and appropriately (especially the axes and the legend), otherwise the information will mean nothing to the reader.
- Give an appropriate title to the table or graph. It should be brief and concise, and does not necessarily have to be grammatically 'perfect' (e.g., often no verb will be included).
- Provide a caption/label for the graph so that it can be easily referenced in the text (e.g., 'graph 1' or 'table 2').
- Include raw data in an appendix if you feel that it might be useful or interesting to the reader.
- Compare two or more graphs/tables for effective analysis.
- Use a range of appropriate reporting verbs to interpret the graphs/tables.
- Scan in tables and graphs from original sources carefully. Poor-quality images will not be clear to the reader. If the original source is poor quality, it may be necessary to create the table or graph yourself electronically.
- Learn more about this topic by assessing the way in which professional writers interpret tables and graphs.
- Remember that the connotations of the language you use are very important (see below).

What language can be used to interpret tables and graphs?

The idea of CONNOTATION is very important when interpreting tables and graphs. For example, while stagnate and remain constant may be synonyms, the former has a negative connotation whereas the latter has a neutral one. It is therefore important to check the specific meaning of these words in a dictionary or, better still, an ONLINE CORPUS.

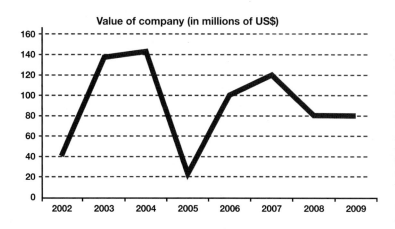

Value of company (in millions of US$)

Language notes

Words which discuss extremes cannot generally be intensified (e.g., you cannot say ~~complete apex~~ or ~~absolute nadir~~). These would be TAUTOLOGIES.

Choose adjectives and adverbs carefully. While they can add detail, accuracy and analysis to your writing, they can also be unnecessary.

COLLOCATION is a particularly important issue in this field.

What grammar can be used to interpret tables and graphs?

The following aspects of grammar are commonly used when interpreting tables and graphs:

- the PASSIVE VOICE (see Step 41), especially with expressions using as (e.g., as can be seen/as is shown)
- COMPARATIVE and SUPERLATIVE forms (see Step 34)
- impersonal expressions (see Step 22)
- the present perfect and past simple verb forms (see Step 41)

Interpretation of graph

1. The company's value rose sharply/markedly/dramatically/suddenly/considerably between 2002 and 2003.
2. The company's value increased slightly between 2003 and 2004.
3. The company's value reached its zenith/summit/highest point/apex/peak in 2004.
4. There was a sharp/significant fall in the company's value between 2004 and 2005. Its price tumbled/collapsed/plummeted.
5. The company's nadir/lowest point/all-time low was in 2005.
6. The company experienced gradual/steady/moderate growth between 2006 and 2007.
7. The company's value stagnated/flatlined between 2008 and 2009.

Prepositions which are commonly used

Since time is one of the key components of tables and graphs, prepositions of time are important:

1. *Between 1999 and 2001/from 1999 to 2001:* gap between two points in time
2. *In 2008:* months/years/long period of time
3. *At 20:00:* specific time
4. *After/before:* time following/preceding
5. *Since 2004:* from a point in time
6. *For 12 years:* for a length of time

Activation

Write five sentences to describe the data in the following table.

Number of undergraduate students in England, analyzed by place of origin

Year	UK	Other EU countries	Non-EU countries
2008–9	1,403,755	56,340	96,430
2007–8	1,360,015	53,915	91,090
2006–7	1,636,200	64,235	102,990
2005–6	1,349,865	45,290	86,830
2004–5	1,320,440	41,650	86,290

Source: Higher Education Statistics Agency

1. _____

2. _____

3. _____

4. _____

5. _____

Personalization

- Consider how important this topic is in your subject area. For different subjects it will have a higher or lower importance.

- Check using an online corpus to see how the language noted above is used in your subject area.

- Evaluate your previous use of language in this area against the model presented in part C.

Extension

- Step 23 examines **cautious** or **tentative language**, while Step 42 looks at **modal verbs**. There may be occasions where you are not 100% certain how a table or graph should be explained. In such circumstances, this language may be useful.

- Step 31 discusses different ways in which other people's ideas can be reported – a skill which is often used when analyzing data presented in tables and graphs.

- Step 34 focuses on different strategies for **comparing** or **contrasting**. The language presented in this step is useful for analyzing two or more graphs.

- Step 38 analyzes **collocations**, which are particularly relevant in this topic area.

How can I stop repeating the same language?

'Those who do not learn from history are doomed to repeat it.'

George Santayana

A Reflection

Look at the following groups of words, which are considered synonyms.

- *What is the difference between the words in each group?*
- 1. colleague; mate; acquaintance; comrade; ally
- 2. handicapped; crippled; person with a disability; disabled; differently abled
- 3. fat; ample; plump; portly; obese; overweight
- 4. slender; skinny; anorexic; slim; lean
- 5. sick; under the weather; ailing; nauseous

B Contextualization

Read through these sentences, each of which includes a synonym for the word *research*.

- *In each case, identify the problem with the synonym the student has used.*

Sentence	Problem/Reason
Stoddart's **investigation** into the matter was extremely thorough.	_____
The 2004 **forensic analysis** by Sowton is considered the first major paper on the subject.	_____
Her **legwork** into this topic is extremely detailed and accurate.	_____
The **seek** was generally well-received, although some criticize its methodology.	_____
It was an extremely successful piece of **study** which sent shockwaves through the establishment.	_____
Thein's **exploration** of the topic was particularly interesting.	_____

C Analysis

What is the problem with using the same language?

The main reason why students use the same language again and again in their writing is simple: their range of language is smaller than that of a native speaker, and they prefer to use words which are familiar to them. However, to be a successful academic writer, you need to be able to use a range of language. There are three main reasons for this:

- A repetitive style makes your essays less interesting and more difficult to read. Variety is important to keep the reader interested.
- In academic writing, the ability to be precise and state *exactly* what you mean is key.
- Frequently using the same words may give the marker the impression that you have only a narrow and limited vocabulary. Such poor language may be (wrongly) equated with a poor knowledge of content.

What strategies can increase your range of language?

Strategy 1: Using synonyms

The word *synonym* is frequently misunderstood. *Synonym* does not mean 'having exactly the same meaning' but 'having a similar meaning'. This difference is extremely important. You cannot simply delete one word from your text and insert another and think they have an identical meaning. Although words may have the same DENOTATION (core meaning), they will almost certainly have a different CONNOTATION (secondary, suggested or implied meaning). For example, all these words have the same denotation, i.e., *friend*, but the connotation is very different:

- **colleague:** 'someone who you work with'
- **mate:** informal term for 'friend'
- **acquaintance:** 'someone you have met (often a "friend of a friend") but do not know that well'
- **comrade:** 'a member of the same communist or socialist political party; fellow-soldier'
- **ally:** 'a country that has agreed to help another country, especially in a war; a person who supports someone in a difficult situation, especially a politician'

A similar pattern may be seen for the other synonyms, outlined in part A. Check the specific meaning of these words using a dictionary or an ONLINE CORPUS.

When deciding how similar one word is to another, there are four criteria which should be considered. These criteria are outlined below, alongside the examples from part B.

1. **Context**: when and with whom you would use the word, e.g., is it a word in general use or is it a piece of JARGON?
   Investigation: suggests a piece of work done by the police.
2. **Formality**: is the word formal or informal?
   Legwork: this is quite informal, and more appropriate in a spoken context.
   Forensic analysis: conversely, this is too formal for the context.
3. **Value judgement**: does the word have any bias or additional meaning (e.g., criticism)?
   Exploration: whereas *research* is a neutral word, *exploration* is more positive in tone, implying a wide range and focus.
4. **Collocation**: are there any particular words which go together to consider?
   Piece of study: although *study* and *research* have very similar meanings, *study* does not collocate with *piece of*.

In addition, a common mistake is to substitute a word with one from the wrong word class. *Research*, for example, is both a noun and a verb. The student has used seek – a synonym for the verb only.

Strategy 2: Change word class

As noted in Step 4, changing the word class can help avoid unnecessary repetition. Although you might be using the same ROOT, it won't be identical. Typically, this involves nouns and verbs since they are the two major types of CONTENT WORDS, which are commonly used in academic writing. For example:

- changing the word class can be a useful strategy
- strategically, a change of word classification can be of use

When doing this, it is important not to invent English words which you think might or should exist. For example, not every adjective can be made into an adverb by adding ~*ly*. If you try changing word class, it is important to check that the word does actually exist.

Strategy 3: Learn from others

When you are reading articles, books and so on, you should be reading for two main purposes. First and foremost, you are reading for content – to understand the information which the text contains. Secondly, however, you should also be reading to develop your academic style and your knowledge of academic vocabulary.

What resources can help me acquire new language?

There are a number of ways in which you can acquire new language. The strategies which you use will depend on many factors, such as your PERSONAL LEARNING STYLE. Whatever mechanisms you use, you should be aware of their respective strengths and weaknesses. These are presented below.

English-only dictionary

Advantages: Reading the definition of a word in context (and in the TARGET LANGUAGE), makes it more likely to be remembered in the future.

Disadvantages: Definitions can be difficult to understand; it is not always clear what you need to look up.

Electronic/online dictionaries

Advantages: They are quick and easy to use.

Disadvantages: Students can become overreliant on them. They may also simply insert the longest/most complicated word they find, rather than the word which is most appropriate.

Online corpora

Advantages: Can help you check to see if the word is commonly used in academic English.

Disadvantages: Can be challenging to use if you are unfamiliar with them.

D Activation

Using some of the strategies outlined in part C, rewrite the following passage using less repetition of the same language.

> Reusing identical language in academic writing is considered bad style by most academics. Reusing identical language gives the impression that your knowledge of the subject is also poor, whereas you might actually know quite a lot. A range of language will make your academic writing sound more professional and interesting.

_____

_____

_____

_____

_____

_____

_____

_____

_____

_____

E Personalization

■ Consider how much time you spend using an electronic dictionary, and whether you should employ other methods.

■ Read through a recent essay and ask yourself whether there are any words you do not understand.

■ Try to identify your idiosyncrasies – those words which you overuse.

• Search for synonyms for these words.

F Extension

■ Step 31 focuses on reporting what other people have written, looking at the small but important differences contained in reporting verbs. Appendix 4, Step 31 refers you to online corpora.

■ Step 37 analyzes **vague and unnecessary language**, a closely related topic.

How can I avoid using vague and unnecessary words?

> 'Good prose is like a window pane.'
>
> **George Orwell**

A Reflection

Look at these statements and decide if you agree or disagree.

1. I think that longer phrases sound more 'academic'.   Agree / Disagree
2. I use lots of extra words in order to reach the word count.   Agree / Disagree
3. I often translate phrases into English word-for-word.   Agree / Disagree
4. Sometimes I do not know the word I need, so I use a vague word   Agree / Disagree
   instead (e.g., *thing*).

B Contextualization

Read through the following passage.

- *Underline any language which you think is vague or unnecessary. An example has been done for you.*
- *Rewrite the passage accordingly.*

> Thus, <u>with regard to</u> introductions, the general consensus of opinion is that a number of factors have to be included. Questions still remain, however, as to what the appropriate length of an introduction should be. Yet, taking all this into account, despite the fact that students are often able to use language well, until such a point in time as they are able to avoid using an excessive number of words, they will in no way be able to write good introductions.

Thus, regarding introductions, ...

_____

_____

_____

_____

_____

c Analysis

Why is vague and unnecessary language used?

Many student essays are weakened by the use of vague language which has little meaning, or by unnecessary phrases which do not add anything to the content of their work.

The passage below represents an improved version of the paragraph on the previous page. By reducing the vague and unnecessary language, the passage has been reduced from 82 words to 50. This process makes the passage clearer, more concise, and easier to follow and understand.

Thus, ~~with regard to~~ regarding introductions, the ~~general~~ consensus ~~of opinion~~ is that ~~a number of~~ several factors have to be included. Questions ~~still~~ remain, however, as to ~~what the appropriate length of~~ how long an introduction should be. Yet, ~~taking all this into account~~ considering all this, ~~despite the fact that~~ although students can often use language well, until ~~such a point in time as~~ they ~~are able to avoid using an excessive number of words~~ can use fewer words, they will not ~~in no way~~ be able to write good introductions.

There are four main reasons why vague and unnecessary language is often used in academic English.

It is thought that longer phrases sound more 'academic'.

As this book suggests, academic writing does not have to be long and complicated in order to be good. Often there is an assumption that the longer and more complex your language, the more intelligent you appear. This is simply not true. A short phrase can be extremely powerful. As Step 39 indicates, the overwhelming majority of commonly used academic phrases are only two or three words long. Do not equate length with quality.

Long phrases (whether needed or not) help to reach the word count.

Sometimes there are far more practical reasons why students use longer phrases: they help to increase the word count. While this approach may be understandable, it will not help you become a more successful student. The focus of academic writing should be quality, not quantity. Generally speaking, the quality of your essays will increase the more CONTENT WORDS you use (as opposed to structure words). By definition, vague and unnecessary words are structure words. Better time management and planning would help with this process.

Phrases are often translated directly from my mother tongue.

Languages have their own separate identities, using their vocabulary and grammar in different ways. Therefore, simply translating a phrase from your mother tongue into English will often result in a phrase which would not be considered English. One solution is to use ONLINE CORPORA (web-based collections of well-written academic English). By inputting your phrase into the corpus, you can check whether it is commonly used (or indeed used at all) in academic English.

Sometimes I do not know the word I need, so I use a vague word instead (e.g., *thing*).

Since these words can have such a broad meaning, they end up meaning nothing. Vague nouns which should not be used include *thing(s)* and *stuff*; vague adjectives include *good*, *bad* and *nice*.

How can vague and unnecessary language be categorized?

Problems here can be placed in three categories. Examples from part B are presented.

Too many words

- until such a point in time as → until
- will in no way be able to → will not be able to

Such phrases may occasionally be used for emphasis, but generally add little to the meaning. They represent an unnecessary use of words. A common error of this type is to use *make/do/get* + noun rather than a simple verb (e.g., *do an evaluation* rather than *evaluate*).

Too complicated

- with regard to → regarding
- despite the fact that → although

Such phrases are not wrong, but usually a shorter, more concise equivalent is available. The longer form may be used at times to clarify a specific meaning.

Too repetitive

- general consensus of opinion → consensus
- still remain → remain

Many phrases use words which are completely unnecessary, because the meaning is already present, e.g., the word *consensus* already contains the ideas of *general* and *opinion* within it. Such mistakes, TAUTOLOGIES, are often made by native speakers.

What common redundancies and tautologies exist in academic English?

The tables below indicate common redundancies (left) and tautologies (right). A more extensive list is available at Appendix 3, Step 37. Appropriate alternatives are provided.

Redundancy	Improved version	Tautology	Improved version
ahead of schedule	*early*	a total of three reasons	*three reasons*
almost all	*most, the majority*	brief in duration	*brief*
along the lines of	*similar to*	completely destroyed	*destroyed*
as well as	*also, and*	current status	*status*
at all times	*always*	end result	*result*
conduct a review of	*review*	first began	*began*
give consideration to	*consider*	mutual agreement	*agreement*
in advance of	*before*	potentially dangerous	*dangerous*
in possession of	*have/has*	shorter in length	*shorter*
is able to	*can*	true fact	*fact*
with a view to	*for*	usual habit	*habit*

D Activation

Rewrite the following piece of text, removing any vague or redundant language.

> Following the completion of their first draft, overseas students from abroad often choose not to recognize the fact that their essay is in possession of an excessive number of words. For many, their usual habit is to avoid carrying out an evaluation of their work. The honest truth of the matter is that the majority of students do not proofread properly. Proofreading, on most occasions, is too brief in duration. Students do not want to edit their work in case they need to make their essay longer in length.

_____

_____

_____

_____

_____

_____

_____

_____

_____

_____

E Personalization

- Read a piece of your writing. Try to identify any vague and unnecessary language, and understand why you made the mistake.
- Create a 'hit list' of your language problems (redundant phrases and tautologies that you use frequently) so you are less likely to make them in the future.

F Extension

- Step 11 focuses on MOTHER-TONGUE INFLUENCE in your English – one of the key causes of vague language.
- Step 39 highlights **high-frequency academic phrases** which can be learnt and used as an alternative to mother-tongue translation.
- Appendix 3, Step 37 lists common redundancies and tautologies in academic writing.

What are collocations and how can I use them?

'You shall know a word by the company it keeps.'

John Firth

A Reflection

Look at these pairs of words. Circle the phrase which you think is most commonly used in English.

- fast car / quick car
- fast shower / quick shower
- smoke fatly / smoke heavily
- make homework / do homework

- fully recognize / completely recognize
- fully broken / completely broken
- cause problems / provide problems
- have a job / work a job

The word *education* has many collocations. Think of as many as you can.

_____ _____ _____ _____

_____ _____ _____ _____

_____ _____ _____ _____

B Contextualization

Read through the following passage, identify any COLLOCATIONS and complete the table. An example has been done for you.

Collocations are <u>particularly useful</u> in academic English, and indeed when students are taught about the topic, their interest levels are generally high. At least, this is what the research indicates. Reading critically is a good way of developing your understanding of collocations. One of the key criteria in using collocations is identifying the frequency with which they appear together.

Verb + noun	
Verb + adverb	
Noun + verb	
Noun + noun	
Adjective + noun	
Adverb + adverb	
Adverb + adjective	*particularly useful*

c Analysis

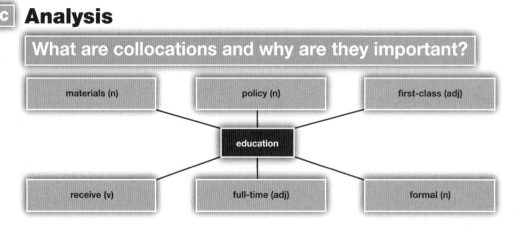

What are collocations and why are they important?

materials (n) — policy (n) — first-class (adj)

education

receive (v) — full-time (adj) — formal (n)

A collocation is a series of words that will often appear together. Collocations exist in all languages. Although they are an important part of the language, they can be very difficult to use correctly. There is often no apparent logical reason why one particular word goes with another. For example, in English we always say *fast car* and *quick shower*, even though the two adjectives are close synonyms of each other. Although one could understand what is meant by *quick car* and *fast shower*, a native speaker would never say either. An additional problem is that collocations are often not transferable between languages. For example, in English students *do homework*, but in many other languages they *make homework*.

Much language teaching research literature identifies a strong link between knowledge of collocations and good academic writing skills. Generally speaking, text which contains collocations:

- sounds more professional and closer to that of a native speaker
- is richer, and consequently more interesting to the reader
- appears more precise, enabling you to express your meaning as clearly as possible (e.g., avoiding general language which has no real meaning)

Collocational strength

Strong collocations are those in which one of the components can only appear with a very limited number of other words. An example is *auspicious*, an adjective which can only precede a very small group of nouns, i.e., *day*, *occasion*, *moment* and *event*. Weak collocations can collocate with many other words. *Tall*, for example, can appear alongside many other words (*tree*, *man*, *latte* and *story*). In your academic writing, the majority of collocations will be towards the medium/strong end of the scale.

Types of collocation

There are a number of grammatical structures which can form collocations. Some of the most common combinations appear in part B.

> **Note**
> It is important to distinguish academic collocations from idioms. Idioms (such as *up to the minute* or *figure something out*) tend to be more informal, and therefore are not much used in academic English. Phrasal verbs may also be categorized as collocations, but these are generally considered too informal for academic writing as well.

> **Developing your knowledge of collocations**
> Learn them as whole pieces of vocabulary rather than by their component parts (i.e., *do homework* rather than *do + homework*). This will help to minimize mistakes.
> When learning new words, ensure that you learn which words they collocate with as well as their meaning.
> Use a collocation dictionary (e.g., the *Oxford Collocations Dictionary*) and online corpora to develop your knowledge.

Which common collocations exist in English?

The following table provides a list of useful collocations used generally in academic language. These collocations are all CONTENT WORD focused. Step 39 provides examples of collocations which contain more STRUCTURE WORDS.

Verb + noun

- develop + an understanding/a framework/ a plan
- do business/an experiment/homework
- find an answer/a solution/time
- follow advice/an example/a procedure
- give a definition/a description/ an explanation
- make an attempt/a criticism/ a reference/an effort
- reach an agreement/a conclusion/ a decision
- submit an application/an essay/ your resignation
- take an opportunity

Verb + adverb

- reading critically/carefully/with interest
- strongly suggest/argue
- dramatically increase/change
- fundamentally change/disagree
- recently develop/arrive/start

Noun + verb

- the research indicates/shows/ demonstrates
- X's argument illustrates/justifies/supports
- the figure shows/reveals

Noun + noun

- sample size
- data set
- control group
- quality assurance/control

Adjective + noun

- key criteria/reason/idea
- major problem/issue/challenge
- detailed/in-depth/ground-breaking research
- significant differences
- specific argument/reason
- present/current study
- previous studies

Adverb + adverb

- much more/less
- almost certainly/entirely
- very interestingly/importantly/noticeably
- interestingly enough

Adverb + adjective

- particularly useful/challenging/important
- significantly higher/different/changed
- relatively interesting/important/high

Note: Collocations may be combined in order to create 'high-density', extremely powerful academic writing. For example: *This ground-breaking research demonstrates the particularly challenging issue of heart disease.*

Activation

Using a collocation dictionary and/or the corpus-based collocation website
http://www.collins.co.uk/Corpus/CorpusSearch.aspx, identify which content words
collocate with the following; and in what order.

Word	Collocates
development (D) (noun)	economic D, early D, rapid D, industrial D, child D, language D, research and D, D grant, facilitate D
significant (adjective)	
completely (adverb)	
confidence (noun)	
indicate (verb)	

 Personalization

- Consider the use of collocations in your mother tongue and compare this with English.
  - Are collocations common? Are there any particular structures which occur frequently?
  - Do you know any which are the same as or different to English?
- Look again at a recent article which you have read, and try to identify any two- or three-word collocations.
- Search the Internet for lists of collocations which may be relevant to your subject area. There are a number of academic articles which have these. Learn them.

Extension

- Step 39 focuses on the related area of LEXICAL BUNDLES – collocations which use more STRUCTURE WORDS.
- Collocations dictionaries can be a useful study aid. One of the most well-known is the *Oxford Collocations Dictionary*.

What phrases are commonly used in academic writing?

'After people have repeated a phrase a great number of times, they begin to realize it has meaning.'

H. G. Wells

A Reflection

In what circumstances would you use the following phrases in academic writing?

1. The structure of the: <u>Description (e.g., the structure of the double helix is as follows)</u>

2. The role of the: _____

3. One of the most: _____

4. At the beginning of: _____

5. In contrast to: _____

6. In the next section: _____

B Contextualization

Read the following passage and identify any academic phrases which are frequently used in academic writing. An example has been done for you.

Academic phrases, <u>also known as</u> 'lexical bundles', are an important feature of academic discourse. One of the most important reasons that you should use these short, formulaic phrases is that they are a common feature of academic writing. As well as this, academic phrases can lessen certain grammatical problems which you might face. It should be noted that academic phrases are not a complete solution to grammatical problems; at the same time, they may offer a partial solution. As a result, it is clear that a good understanding of these three-, four- and five-word phrases is one of the key ways you can make your writing sound more 'academic'.

An academic phrase may be defined as a group of three, four or five words which often appear together. They may be considered as a kind of COLLOCATION.

c Analysis

Why are phrases important in academic English?

As noted in the previous step, collocations are a particularly important aspect of academic English. While many collocations contain strong content words and can be used in specific subject areas, there are also others which contain more structural words and which have a more general application in academic English. These three-, four- or five-word phrases are found in all subject areas, and their importance may be summarized as follows:

1. They enable you to sound more professional and part of the ACADEMIC COMMUNITY, since they are a common feature of academic writing.

2. They can be used for a number of academic purposes and functions, such as description and quantification (see below).

3. They minimize problems in terms of using prepositions, articles and other types of STRUCTURE WORDS, particularly if they can be remembered as single pieces of language (i.e., *the role of the*) rather than as individual pieces of grammar (i.e., *the + role + of + the*).

4. They can also help with your academic reading. For example, as noted in Step 9, one way to increase the efficiency and effectiveness of your reading is to read in phrases.

According to Hyland (2008: 13–14), these academic phrases can be used for a range of important functions in academic writing. These include:

- **Description** (e.g., *the structure of the*)
- **Procedure** (e.g., *the role of the*)
- **Quantification** (e.g., *one of the most*)
- **Time/place** (e.g., *at the beginning of*)
- **Transition** (e.g., *in contrast to*)
- **Structuring** (e.g., *in the next section*)

What common lexical bundles are there in academic English?

The table opposite presents some of the general academic phrases which appear most frequently in academic English. This information is taken from Hyland, K. (2008). As can be seen: Lexical bundles and disciplinary variation. *English for Specific Purposes*, 27, 1: 4–21.

Note that some of the four- and five-word phrases are merely extensions of the three-word phrases.

> **Common problems**
> Students will often know a handful of academic phrases (e.g., *first of all*) which they then overuse in their writing. Students may also have problems with mother-tongue influence. Many academic phrases which exist in your mother tongue do not exist in English (e.g., *as I know*).
> Be careful not to overuse these academic phrases. Although they can be highly effective when used in conjunction with content words, using too many academic phrases will mean that your text contains too many structure words.

Common lexical bundles

Three-word	Four-word	Five-word
in order to	on the other hand	on the other hand the
in terms of	at the same time	at the end of the
one of the	in the case of	it should be noted that
the use of	the end of the	it can be seen that
as well as	as well as the	due to the fact that
the number of	at the end of	at the beginning of the
due to the	in terms of the	may be due to the
on the other	on the basis of	it was found that the
based on the	in the present study	to the fact that the
the other hand	is one of the	there are a number of
in this study	in the form of	in the case of the
a number of	the nature of the	as a result of the
the fact that	the results of the	at the same time the
most of the	the fact that the	is one of the most
there is a	as a result of	it is possible that the
according to the	in relation to the	one of the most important
the present study	at the beginning of	play an important role in
part of the	with respect to the	can be seen as a/the
the end of	the other hand the	the results of this study
the relationship between	the relationship between the	from the point of view
in the following	in the context of	the point of view of
the role of	can be used to	it can be observed that
some of the	to the fact that	this may be due to
as a result	as shown in figure	an important role in the
it can be	it was found that	in the form of a

D Activation

Complete these sentences using a suitable academic phrase.

- *Note: these sentences have all been taken from sentences in published academic essays.*

1. Ranke came to his conclusion _____ earlier research.

2. It thereby recognizes _____ psychology in determining the origins of social behaviour.

3. This could also be linked to _____ many have a lack of language skills and familiarity with British institutions.

4. The gradual increase before the peak is _____ the general effect of increasing temperature.

5. _____ books of the Enlightenment era was undoubtedly Adam Smith's *The Wealth of Nations*.

6. *Theory of International Politics* was written by Waltz _____ the pluralist challenge to classical realism.

E Personalization

- Use ONLINE CORPORA to search for these phrases in your subject area in order really to understand how they are used.

- Check the use of these phrases in your writing to ensure you are using them correctly.

- When you read, look out for other academic phrases which may be useful. The list presented on the previous page is only an indication of those used most frequently. Many others also exist.

F Extension

- Step 28 analyzes the issue of **coherence**: the accurate use of academic phrases can improve this aspect of your writing.

- Step 38 focuses on **collocations**, of which academic phrases are an example.

- Unit J looks at **proofreading strategies**, which may be important when checking you have used the phrases correctly.

How can I use prepositions effectively?

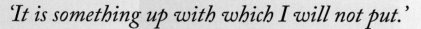

'It is something up with which I will not put.'

Winston Churchill

A Reflection

What prepositions do you know in English?

* *Preposition: Word or group of words used before a noun or pronoun to show place, position, time or method.*

at   in   on

B Contextualization

There are many verbs and nouns in academic English which form strong collocations with prepositions. Complete the table below with suitable prepositions.

Preposition	Commonly associated verbs	Commonly associated nouns
against	act; check	arguments; case
	consider; define	–
	account; allow	basis; case
	benefit; suffer	distance; results
	divide; engage	changes; decrease
	divide; enter	insight; investigation
	approve; compose	basis; complexity
	base; concentrate	demand; effect
	adapt; add	approach; attention
	agree; associate	case; comparison

Analysis

What is a preposition?

A preposition is a word or group of words used before a noun or pronoun to show place, position, time or method. The importance of prepositions can be seen by the frequency with which they occur in English. Of the top 25 most commonly used words in writing, at least a third are prepositions. The words in the box are the most common.

When used alone, their specific focus is on factors such as **time** (e.g., in 2004), **place** (e.g., under the table) and **direction** (e.g., towards the back). However, their particular importance can be seen in the way in which they can be combined with words of other classes (especially nouns and verbs) to form **noun collocations**, PHRASAL VERBS and PREPOSITIONAL PHRASES.

MOTHER-TONGUE INFLUENCE is a major reason why students find prepositions so difficult. Some languages place prepositions *after* the word they refer to (English generally places them *before*); others change the form of the word itself (especially the ending), as with INFLECTION, to perform the same task. Moreover, different languages may use different prepositions to express the same idea – e.g., where English might use *on*, another language may use the equivalent of 'in'.

> ### Commonly used prepositions in English
> about; above; across; after; against; along; among; around; as; at; before; behind; below; beneath; beside; between; beyond; but; by; despite; down; during; except; for; from; in; inside; into; like; near; of; off; on; onto; out; outside; over; past; since; through; throughout; till; to; toward; under; underneath; until; up; upon; versus; with; within; without.

Which prepositions collocate with which nouns/verbs?

In academic writing, nouns and verbs often form strong collocations with specific prepositions. For example, the PHRASAL VERB account for is relatively common (not ~~account from~~ or ~~account in~~), as is the noun COLLOCATION research into (not ~~research as~~ or ~~research with~~). The table below indicates high-frequency verbs and nouns in academic English and the prepositions they are normally associated with.

Preposition	Commonly associated verbs	Commonly associated nouns
against	act; check; compare; decide; direct; protest; vote; warn	arguments; case; decisions; struggle
as	consider*; define*; know*; regard*; see*	–
for	account*; allow*; apply*; argue; ask; look; prepare; require*; stand; vote	basis; case; evidence; need; opportunity; reason; precedent; preference; quest; stimulus
from	benefit; suffer; come; derive*; differ; exclude*; subtract*	distance; results; transition
in	divide*; engage*; express*; include*; involve*; participate; result; see*; specialize; succeed	changes; decrease; differences; error; increase; reduction; rise; shift
into	divide*; enter; incorporate*; segment*	insight; investigation; research
of	approve; compose*; conceive*; consist; convince*; dispose; know; made*; think	basis; complexity; exploration; extent; idea; lack; means; number; part; role; significance

Preposition	Commonly associated verbs	Commonly associated nouns
on	base*; concentrate; decide; depend; expand; experiment; insist; occur; operate; rely; work	demand; effect; emphasis; influence; law; reliance; research; pressure; section; work
to	adapt; add*; adjust*; assign*; belong; consent; lead; react; refer; relate*; respond; turn	approach; attention; key; response; relation; right; shift
with	agree; associate*; compare*; connect*; couple*; deal; equip*; involve	case; comparison; ease; obsession; problem

* These verbs generally or frequently appear in the passive voice.

What prepositional phrases are common in academic English?

PREPOSITIONAL PHRASES are relatively common in academic English. They comprise a preposition and a NOUN PHRASE. Prepositional phrases can add richness to your academic writing, and knowledge of them can aid your academic reading. Recognizing these two- to four-word phrases can help you break the text into meaningful units, increasing your reading efficiency. The following prepositional phrases are some of the most common in academic English.

against
against the backdrop of

as
as far as
as a result of
as the representative
as well as

at
at an advantage
at any rate
at a disadvantage
at the expense of
at first
at the latest
at least
at most
at times
at risk

by
by accident
by means of
by the time of
by then

for
for example
for instance
for the moment
for the sake of
for use in

in
in accordance with
in addition to
in case of
in compliance with
in conjunction with
in contrast to
in the face of
in lieu of
in line with
in order to
in need of
in place of
in search of
in the short/long term
in spite of
in view of

into
into line with

on
on account of
on behalf of
on the basis of
on the grounds of
on purpose
on the side of
on the verge of

out
out of hand
out of touch with

over
over a period of

through
through the use of

under
under consideration
under the control of
under discussion
under duress
under the impression

upon
upon the basis of

up to
up to the value of

with
with the exception of
with regard to
with respect to
with the development of
with the threat of

within
within the framework of

without
without exception
without success
without the support of

Note: It is sometimes said that you should never end a sentence with a preposition. Few people follow this old-fashioned view, but ending a sentence with a preposition is generally more informal in style.

D Activation

Complete these sentences using a preposition and a commonly associated verb from the table in part C.

- *Ensure that you use the right tense and voice.*

1. The appendices should _____ as necessary.
2. These proposals _____ research undertaken by Dyer (2007).
3. The delegates _____ the candidate they wish to take control.
4. Many scholars _____ the need for further research.
5. It is hoped that this paper _____ practical implementation in the appropriate sectors.
6. This setback should not _____ the excellent achievements of the project.
7. Both engines __ _____ a particular type of flywheel.
8. Despite overwhelming support, the government _____ supporting the project.
9. This feedback _____ the overall report.
10. She _____ one of the finest scholars of her generation.

E Personalization

- Search for high-frequency prepositions in your writing to see whether you are using them correctly.
- Search an ONLINE CORPUS to see how the words presented in part C are used.

F Extension

- Steps 28 and 29 analyze **coherence** and **cohesion**. Overuse or misuse of prepositions may lead to problems in both of these areas.
- Step 30 looks at **linking devices** and Step 39 at **common academic phrases**. Much of this language involves prepositions.
- Step 38 examines **collocations**, a closely-related topic.

What tenses should I use in academic writing?

'I see the past, present and future existing all at once before me.'

William Blake

A Reflection

Write explanations for the following terms, all of which are related to verbs.

• *Use a dictionary if you are unsure.*

Tense	An element of the verb which relates mainly to time
Aspect	
Voice	
Mood	

How do the same categories work in your mother tongue? Is 'time' seen in the same way as in English?

B Contextualization

Look at the verb forms in the following passage and complete the table which follows.

Verbs **are**[1] a difficult and challenging aspect of language for students. In academic writing, it **is** generally **accepted**[2] that certain verb forms, such as the present simple, appear more frequently than others, such as the present continuous. This difference **has been noted**[3] by many scholars in the field. Moreover, due to technical advances in the way that texts **can be analyzed**[4], the detailed study of verbs in academic writing **is becoming**[5] more popular. These advances have made it easier for those academics who **have been analyzing**[6] such texts manually over the past few years. Thus, important discoveries **have been**[7] **made** by a number of linguists working in the academic fields of verbs and verb phrases.

Verb form	What is being described	Verb form
1. are	State in the present, generally true	Present simple/active
2. is accepted		
3. has been noted		
4. can be analyzed		
5. is becoming		
6. have been analyzing		
7. have been made		

c Analysis

How does the English verb system work?

Verbs provoke considerable argument and debate. Rather than enter this debate, this step presents information about verbs which will hopefully clarify how they work, what features to consider when using them and the forms which are common in academic English. There are four key components which should be considered when using a verb: tense, aspect, voice and mood.

Tense

There are three tenses in English: the **past**, **present** and **future**. Past tenses describe events, states and activities which have already finished while future tenses predict what will happen in time to come. Present tenses have a connection to the present, whether in a general long-term way (e.g., *I wait for the bus every day*) or a specific, short-term manner (e.g., *I am waiting for the bus now*).

Aspect

Aspect is the form of a verb that shows, for example, whether the action is completed or still continuing. There are four aspects in the English verb system: the **continuous**, **simple**, **perfect** and **perfect continuous**. The elements used to show aspect in English are often misunderstood, or ignored, because students think they have no meaning. However, aspect indicates very important information about the verb. These four aspects are explained below, accompanied by an example.

> The **continuous** aspect is used to describe **unfinished activity**.
> … the detailed study of verbs in academic writing **is becoming** more popular.

> The **simple** aspect is used to describe **states** and **events**.
> Verbs **are** a difficult and challenging aspect of language for students.

> The **perfect** aspect is used to describe **what happens before a point in time**.
> This difference **has been noted** by many scholars in the field.

> The **perfect continuous** aspect is used to describe **unfinished activity before a point in time**.
> These advances have made it easier for those academics who **have been analyzing** such texts manually …

Note: Regardless of whether they are in the past, present or future, each aspect has the same function: the past continuous refers to past unfinished activity, the present continuous to present unfinished activity and the future continuous to future unfinished activity.

Voice

VOICE is the form of a verb that shows whether the subject of a sentence performs the action, or is affected by it. There are two voices in English. Verbs usually appear in the ACTIVE VOICE, meaning that they appear in a SUBJECT–VERB–OBJECT pattern. In academic English, the PASSIVE VOICE is used in several different scenarios:

Common academic verb forms

The actual range of verb forms in common academic usage is probably smaller than you might think. Of the 12 possible verb forms, there are four which are extremely common, namely:

- Present simple (*This represents …*)
- Past simple (*This represented …*)
- Future simple (*This will represent …*)
- Present perfect (*This has represented …*)

The continuous aspect (see left) is rarely used in academic English. It is estimated that the present simple is ten times more common in academic discourse than the present continuous. With its focus on the temporary, the continuous tends to be more common in spoken language.

- When the subject of the sentence is either absent, unknown or unimportant.

  ... it **is** generally **accepted** that certain verb forms ... appear more frequently than others ...

- When you want to emphasize the object of the sentence.

  This difference **has been noted** by many scholars in the field.

- When there is a very long subject.

  Thus, important discoveries **have been made** by a number of linguists working in the academic fields of verbs and verb phrases.

The passive is used in academic English much more frequently than in standard English. This is because in academic writing, *who* does something is less important than *what* happens. For this reason, the passive voice is, for example, commonly used in the methodology section of a research paper. This said, it is important not to overuse the passive voice, as your text may sound dry and uninteresting.

Mood

The mood of a verb identifies the degree to which a verb is factual or non-factual. There are three moods in English.

1. **Indicative**: a factual mood, which is used for the overwhelming majority of verbs in both standard and academic English (e.g., *she goes*).

2. **Subjunctive**: a non-factual mood, rarely used, which refers to hypothetical and conditional situations (e.g., *If I were you, I would go.*).

3. **Imperative**: a non-factual mood relating to requests or commands (e.g., *go/be gone*).

Five top tips for using verbs

- Ensure that the auxiliary verbs are being correctly used (i.e., *do/be/have*).
- The present simple is extremely common in academic writing; it is far more common than you might think. It should be your default option if you are unsure which verb form to use.
- Verify additional information about the verb, such as whether it is regular or irregular, transitive or intransitive.
- Do not be afraid of using the verb *to be*: it is not 'unacademic' as some think, but common in academic English.
- Check that your verbs are in grammatical agreement (i.e., singular/plural).

How can 'time' expressions be used?

'Time' expressions are an important accompaniment to verbs and are frequently used in academic English. Generally speaking, 'time' expressions are either adverbs (e.g., *historically*), adverbial phrases (e.g., *in the past*) or prepositions (e.g., *at*). The table below indicates some common academic time words, categorized according to the verb form they most frequently appear with.

Past perfect	Past simple	Past continuous
after; before; already ... by; until	historically; in the past; yesterday; last year; X years ago	between X and Y; from X to Y; when; while
Present perfect	**Present simple**	**Present continuous**
since; for; until now; just; in the last year; recently; lately; already	every day; regularly; always; never	at the moment; now; currently
Future perfect	**Future simple**	**Future continuous**
by; by the time; within	tomorrow; in X years' time	[see future simple]

Note: Although *year* has been used in the examples above, other measures of time could be used instead.

D Activation

Read the following passage and insert an appropriate verb form in the space provided.

- *Note 1: In some cases an adverb is needed, which you must place in the correct position.*
- *Note 2: All sentences have been taken from the* British Academic Written English (BAWE) *corpus.*

> 1. It was therefore precisely in those areas where it (*develop*) _____ a unique function … that the structure of the court (*make*) _____ it chronically inefficient.
>
> 2. The World Health Organization (*predict*) _____ that by 2020, depression (*be*) _____ the second leading contributor to the global burden of disease.
>
> 3. Historically, thrombelastography (*use, first*) _____ clinically for haemostatic monitoring during liver transplantation.
>
> 4. The potential in developing countries also correlates with the high population growth (*experience, currently*) _____ .
>
> 5. At that time, the Third Roman Legion (*station*) _____ in Syria before (*transfer*) _____ to Moesia.

E Personalization

 Look at an article (or several articles) in your subject area.

- Highlight every verb form and try to understand what verb form is being used *and why*.
- Work out the frequency of each verb form in order to understand which forms are most prevalent in your discipline.
- Compare and contrast this information with your own usage.

Compare the way in which verbs are used in your mother tongue with how they are used in English.

- Where are the areas of similarity, which can help you understand English verbs better?
- Where are the areas of difference, which may impede your ability to understand?

F Extension

Step 11 examines **mother-tongue influence**, which may be particularly evident when using verbs.

Step 40 looks at **prepositions**, which often combine with verbs to create VERB PHRASES.

Step 42 focuses on **modal verbs**, a particular type of auxiliary verb which is commonly used in English.

Step 45 provides additional information about **adverbs**, including the position they take in sentences.

Unit J discusses the importance of **proofreading**. Since verbs are such a common aspect of writing, it is likely that you will make mistakes in their use.

How can I use modal verbs correctly?

> *'It depends on what the meaning of the word "is" is.'*
>
> **Bill Clinton**

A Reflection

Look at these statements about modal verbs. Choose true or false.

1. Modal verbs can be used without a main verb.   True / False
2. Modal verbs can have more than one meaning.   True / False
3. Modal verbs can change form.   True / False
4. Modal verbs can be placed next to each other.   True / False
5. Modal verbs are a common feature of academic English.   True / False

B Contextualization

Match the following groups of modal verbs with their specific function.

can/could/may/might   ability

may/could/might   probability

must not/should not/should/must   requests/permission

can/could   conditionality

will/shall   possibility

will/would   necessity/obligation

Add any additional information about these modal verbs that you know.

In requests, *can/could/may/might* indicate different degrees of formality, with *can* being the least

formal, and *might* the most formal.

Analysis

How are modal verbs used in English?

General principles of modal verbs

Modal verbs are a kind of AUXILIARY VERB, meaning that they appear before a main verb. Their main function is to modify the meaning of the main verb in some way. English is quite unusual in using modal verbs – many languages use different strategies (e.g., changing the verb ending or using a piece of vocabulary). At a very general level, there are two major reasons why we use modal verbs to:

- identify whether it is possible, or necessary, to do something
- identify whether something is true or not

These two 'umbrella' functions of modal verbs are more commonly identified with a list of specific uses. These can be categorized as follows: **requests/permission**, **possibility**, **necessity/obligation**, **ability**, **probability** and **conditionality**.

> ### Modal verbs in English
> Although many grammar specialists argue over the exact number of modal verbs in English, it is generally thought that there are nine in use: *can*, *may*, *might*, *could*, *would*, *will*, *shall*, *must* and *should*. In addition, *ought to* and *used to* act like modals and have many of the same qualities.

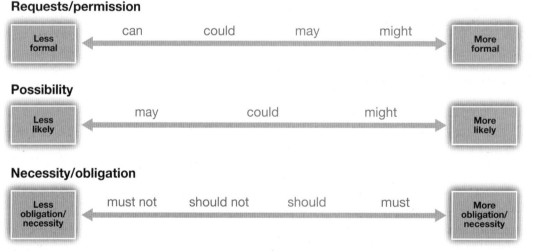

Requests/permission

| Less formal | can | could | may | might | More formal |

Possibility

| Less likely | may | could | might | More likely |

Necessity/obligation

| Less obligation/ necessity | must not | should not | should | must | More obligation/ necessity |

Note: *Ought to* (*ought not to*) can be used as a synonym of *should* (*should not*).

Ability

Can refers to present ability, whereas *could* refers to past ability.

Probability

Will/shall refer to things which are more definite in the future, whereas *would* refers to a situation where the speaker might want to do something but is unable to.

Conditionality

Will is used in the first conditional, to talk about a situation which will happen if a condition is fulfilled.

Would is used in the second conditional to talk about situations that are less likely and less real.

How are modal verbs used in academic English?

Modal verbs are a relatively common feature of academic writing. It is estimated that they comprise one to two per cent of academic text. In addition to the items noted on the previous page, there are a number of specific academic purposes for which modal verbs can be used.

- To express caution (i.e., hedging): *this may be because ...; The reason could be ...; it can be argued that ...*
- To predict risk: *this may result in ...; this will create ...*
- To identify expectation: *this should yield the following results ...*
- To state use and function: *this can be used as ...*
- To provide recommendations: *future studies should examine ...*
- To emphasize importance: *this research must be used otherwise ...*

What are the grammatical rules with regard to modal verbs?

There are several rules regarding the use of modal verbs.

Modal verbs cannot be used without a main verb.

In other words, a modal must appear in conjunction with a main verb. Main verbs are always found in the INFINITIVE (whether continuous, perfect or passive), without *to*. For example:

- *Continuous infinitive*: At present, the data may be indicating the following ...
- *Perfect infinitive*: The data may have indicated the following ...
- *Passive infinitive*: The following may be indicated by the data ...

Modal verbs can have more than one meaning.

The majority of modal verbs have more than one meaning. As such, when reading you must be sure to look carefully at the context; when writing you must be sure to avoid ambiguity. *Could* is an example of one such modal verb.

- Could you help me with my experiment? **(request)**
- I could do the experiment myself, but I value your input. **(ability)**
- If the experiment is successful, it could represent a significant breakthrough. **(possibility)**

Modal verbs cannot change form.

This should be remembered particularly when using the third-person singular and past simple. Therefore:

- This can be seen from the following example. (not ~~This cans~~)
- The experiment could have yielded further useful results if more time had been allowed. (not ~~coulded~~)

Modal verbs cannot be placed next to each other.

However, in standard English it is possible to have more than one modal verb in a sentence.

D Activation

The following passage contains no modal verbs. Identify places where modals could improve it.

- *Note: you may also need to change the main verb.*

> Students use modal verbs to make the meaning of their texts more specific. It is common to find whole essays where modal verbs are not used, even though they are better if modal verbs were used on a relatively frequent basis. As a result of mother-tongue influence, it is argued that a lack of confidence in how they are used is the main reason for this. If students take the time to learn the specific functions of modal verbs, their essay improves. It is concluded, therefore, that modal verbs are an important aspect of academic writing.

E Personalization

- **Look at a sample of your writing and check your use of modal verbs.**
  - Are you using them appropriately?
  - How often do you use them? Too little? Too much?
  - Are you using them when you should just be using forms of *to be*?

- **Does your mother tongue have modal verbs, or does it show things like 'possibility' another way?**
  - Consider this in relation to English in order to identify areas where you might make mistakes.

F Extension

- Step 23 focuses on **cautious** or **tentative language** and provides more details about the use of modal verbs (as well as modal nouns, adjectives and adverbs) for hedging purposes.

- Step 32 examines **cause and effect**, often indicated using modal verbs.

- Steps 47 and 48 look at **proofreading skills** and **strategies**. Since modal verbs are an area where mistakes are relatively common, it is important to check their usage carefully.

- Appendix 2, Step 42, Activity 4 offers an opportunity to develop your understanding of modal verbs with a gap-fill exercise taken from an academic **online corpus**.

How can I punctuate properly?

'The older I grow, the less important the comma becomes. Let the reader catch his own breath.'

Elizabeth Clarkson Zwart

A Reflection

Answer the following questions:

- *What is the purpose of punctuation?*
- *How is punctuation used in your mother tongue? Is it the same as or different from English?*

B Contextualization

What different kinds of punctuation marks exist?

- *Using the passage below as a guide, complete the table.*

As Sowton (2012) argued, 'Academic writing is a multi-faceted idea … it is complex yet simple, confusing yet surprisingly easy to understand the basic concepts'. It is something very different from text messages or e-mail; however, it is surprising how often phrases of the type 'LOL!' or 'Hi – wot ru doin l8r – me x' find their way into essays. Sowton's argument can be divided into three main areas: language, grammar and structure.

Punctuation mark	Name	Function(s) of punctuation mark
	apostrophe	
( ) [ ]		
		To introduce a series, example or explanation.
	comma	
		To represent a break in thought or idea.
	ellipsis	
!		
		To mark the end of a sentence.
	hyphen	
		To indicate that a question is being asked.
' ' and " "		
	semi-colon	

c Analysis

What is the purpose of punctuation?

In speech, features such as intonation, pitch and pauses can be used to clarify meaning. In writing, punctuation performs this function. Punctuation enables the writer to say exactly what they want to say and therefore minimize misunderstanding. It is therefore extremely important in academic writing. The following table identifies the most commonly used punctuation marks in English and their functions. You should refer back to the text on the previous page to see the punctuation in context.

Punctuation mark	Name	Function(s) of punctuation mark
'	apostrophe	1 To designate possession (with nouns). 2 To replace deleted letters in words (contraction).
( ) [ ]	brackets	1 To add information which is important, but not directly relevant to the sentence. 2 To indicate authorship when referencing.
:	colon	1 To introduce a series, example or explanation. 2 To separate the year and page (in referencing).
,	comma	To divide the sentence into smaller units of meaning (e.g., RELATIVE CLAUSES, SUBORDINATE CLAUSES, lists). See below for further details.
– abc –	dashes	To represent a break in thought or idea.
…	ellipsis	To show where words/sentences have been deleted in a longer passage of writing.
!	exclamation mark	To indicate extreme emotion, e.g., surprise, amazement or happiness.
.	full stop/period	To mark the end of a sentence.
-	hyphen	To join separate words together to form COMPOUND WORDS.
?	question mark	To indicate that a question is being asked.
' ' and " "	quotation marks	To make it explicit that an author's exact words are being used.
;	semicolon	1 To specify a close thematic relationship between two clauses within a sentence. 2 To divide a list of bullet points.

- In lists: Commas can be used to separate items in lists, for introductory adverbs and for APPOSITION.
- Separating clauses: If a SUBORDINATE CLAUSE precedes an INDEPENDENT CLAUSE, a comma can be used.
- Certain relative clauses: Non-defining relative clauses, which add information, need commas.
- APPOSITION: a way of defining nouns by using commas is an effective academic tool.

A note on commas

Commas are a very important piece of punctuation which have a number of different functions. Many languages (especially European) have them, but their usage can be quite varied. Therefore, a more detailed analysis of their use in academic English is presented on the left.

- Before quotations: According to Sowton (2012), 'Commas are ... very important'.
- Before introductory adverbs: Clearly, commas can be effectively used after introductory adverbs.

Note: they should *not* be used to link sentences together. This 'comma splicing' is a common error. A full stop or, if the sentences are closely related, a semicolon should be used instead.

What punctuation is/is not used in an academic context?

Punctuation which does not generally occur in academic writing

Certain punctuation is generally considered informal, and is not commonly used in academic writing. In the table below, acceptable academic alternatives are provided.

Punctuation mark	Alternative
exclamation mark	• Stance adverbials (e.g., *controversially*, *importantly*) • Emphatic adjectives (e.g., *revolutionary work*, *groundbreaking paper*, *radical thesis*)
dashes	• Brackets • Relative clauses • Prepositions (e.g., 12 to 15 not 12–15)
apostrophes (for contraction)	Full forms (e.g., *cannot*, *do not*, *will not*, *it is*, *they are*)

Punctuation which does generally occur in academic writing

In contrast, the following punctuation marks are commonly used in academic English. The reasons for this, or the particular context in which these marks may be used, are explained in the right-hand column.

Punctuation mark	Rationale
semicolon	• Aids cohesion between complex ideas • Helps break up long sentences
colon	• Enables clarity when listing and can add greater emphasis to the information which follows the colon
brackets	• Round brackets – ( ) – divide crucial information related to your argument from that which is supplementary • Square brackets – [ ] – may be used within direct quotations to clarify exactly what is meant, e.g., when a pronoun is used and it is impossible to understand what it means from the context (e.g., it was argued that 'She [the Prime Minister] was angry'.)
ellipsis	• Allows you to follow good academic style and quote only the *exact* words necessary (e.g., 'She [the Prime Minister] was angry because ... of indiscipline').
quotation marks	• Single quotation marks are generally preferred in academic English
hyphen	• COMPOUND ADJECTIVES are frequently used, and they are often created using a hyphen (e.g., *first-class, well-known*)

D Activation

In terms of their punctuation/capitalization, how would you improve each of the following sentences?

1. It is important to be able to distinguish important from less important information particularly in academic writing otherwise sentences look extremely long and are difficult to follow.

2. According to Otaqui (2000), 'punctuation is considered, as noted previously, by the overwhelming majority of professors to be a critical factor in high-quality academic writing.'

3. Comma splicing is a serious problem in academic writing, proofreading is a good strategy for eliminating this problem.

4. capital letters should be used for proper names, the first word of a sentence and, as stoddart (2001: 208) argues in his book *guide to punctuation*, 'at the beginning of direct quotations'.

5. In addition to their use in references, there are three main areas where colons can be used, which are series, examples and explanations.

E Personalization

Consider how punctuation is used in your mother tongue. Make a note of any specific differences between it and English.

Read through a passage of your writing and focus only on the punctuation.

- Identify any specific weaknesses you have, and focus on improving these.

F Extension

Step 1 examines the differences between **speech** and **writing**, of which punctuation is a major part.

Steps 4 and 5 focus on **referencing**, wherein the specific uses of punctuation (e.g., brackets, ellipses, colons) are outlined.

Step 30 looks at when commas are used with **linking devices**.

Step 48 looks at high-frequency mistakes to identify when **proofreading**, many of which are related to punctuation.

How can I use articles?

> *'We should have the art rather than the article.'*
>
> **Winston Churchill**

Reflection

Answer the following questions about articles:

- *What ARTICLES are used in English?*
- *Does your mother tongue use articles?*
- *What percentage of academic writing do you think is composed of ARTICLES?*

B Contextualization

How are ARTICLES used in English? Read through these sentences and explain the usage.

Sentence	How article is used
The subject is complicated.	*The* is used when we know which particular thing is meant – i.e., here it is clear from the context that the subject is the article system in English.
The article system in English is generally considered to be difficult by students.	
Articles are used thousands of times **a day** by English native speakers.	
An is **a form** of the indefinite article.	
Articles help a text flow. **The text** is improved because of the additional cohesion they provide.	
Chinese, **an Asian language**, has no article system.	
The is **the definite article**.	
For many students, articles are **the hardest aspect** of grammar to understand.	

Why are articles not used in the following examples?

Sentence	Why no article is used
Many languages do not have an article system.	
Articles are often not taught well **at school**, which is why students find them difficult.	
Articles are not used in **Japan** and **Korea**, but they are in the United Kingdom.	
Articles help your text to breathe, just like **oxygen**.	

c Analysis

What are articles and why does English use them?

Nouns are frequently preceded by a DETERMINER. A determiner is a word which explains whether a noun is definite (e.g., *the/this/your*) or indefinite (e.g., *a/some/many*). Articles are the most commonly used type of determiner in English; other kinds include POSSESSIVE PRONOUNS (e.g., *my*, *our*), DEMONSTRATIVES (e.g., *this*, *that*) and QUANTITY WORDS (e.g., *any*, *either*).

Some languages have no articles (e.g., Russian, Japanese, Chinese), some have a definite article but no indefinite article (e.g., Arabic), whereas others have a complex system of articles reflecting gender, number, person and/or case (e.g., French, German). English has only two articles: the definite article (*the*) and indefinite article (*a* or *an*).

Articles are extremely important in academic English. *The* is the most commonly used word in English, and around ten per cent of all the words used in any piece of academic writing are articles. The importance of accurate usage, therefore, cannot be underestimated. In a 2,000-word essay, articles will be used around 200 times. If you are consistently misusing articles, the quality of your writing is going to be severely affected.

The explanations which follow focus on the most important uses of articles in academic English.

> **Checking for mistakes**
> One of the best ways to check for article mistakes is to read your work aloud. When reading the text in your head, it is easy to skip over these problems. It is much easier to hear your mistakes than read them.

Main uses of the definite article

■ **The** is used when we refer to something specific which has already been established/mentioned.
  Articles help a text flow. The text is improved because of the additional cohesion they provide.
  A is used to introduce text for the first time – but *the* is used subsequently.

■ **The** is used when we refer to a definite, concrete idea (often involving POSTMODIFICATION).
  The article system in English is generally considered to be difficult by students.
  The phrase *in English* after the first noun phrase defines which particular article system is meant.

■ **The** is used when we know which particular thing is meant.
  The subject is complicated.
  The subject here is clear because of the content – i.e., the English article system.

■ **The** is used for unique objects – when there is only one thing that the speaker could be talking about.
  The is the definite article.
  There is only one definite article in English.

■ **The** is used usually with superlatives.
  For many students, articles are the hardest aspect of grammar to understand.
  Note that comparatives – e.g., *harder* – are not usually preceded by *the*. the ... the ... is a comparative structure used to say that things change or vary together – e.g., *The older* I get, *the happier* I am.

Main uses of the indefinite article

▣ ***A/an*** are used to introduce something for the first time – where it is not known (or does not matter) which one is meant.
An is a form of the indefinite article.
There is more than one form of the indefinite article – *a* being the other.

▣ ***A/an*** can be used when defining a noun as being part of a group.
Chinese, an Asian language, has no article system.

▣ ***A/an*** are often used in phrases related to frequency or numbers.
Articles are used thousands of times a day by English native speakers.

Main instances when no article is used

▣ No articles are needed when discussing 'things in general' (i.e., when making a general, wide-ranging point about something).
Many languages do not have an article system.

▣ Articles do not precede FIXED PHRASES AND EXPRESSIONS.
Articles are often not taught well at school, which is why students find them difficult.

▣ Generally speaking, country names do not contain articles (except those which have a countable noun as part of their name).
Articles are not used in Japan and Korea, but they are in the United Kingdom.
Other examples are countries with *states* or *republic* in their name.

▣ UNCOUNTABLE NOUNS (especially substances and masses) and ABSTRACT NOUNS tend not to contain articles.
Articles help your text to breathe, just like oxygen.

Compare and contrast the use of articles
The following example sentences all use the same noun – *university* – but in each case the article use is slightly different.
- Universities are places for learning. / A university is a place for learning.
  = in general, that is the function of a university.
- We went to the university last week.
  = the writer and reader have a shared understanding of which university is meant.
- I was at university in the 1990s.
  = *at university* is a fixed phrase, and therefore no article is needed.
- I studied at York University.
  = *York University* is a proper noun and therefore does not take an article.
- The York University which I remember was very different.
  = In this example, however – which involves postmodification – a specific, concrete idea is being referenced (notice the relative clause after the noun); therefore, the definite article is required.

Activation

Read through the following passage and correct any article mistakes which you find.

> The articles are the very important part of English language. This is demonstrated most clearly by the fact that *the* is a most frequently used word in English. *A* and *an* are also in very common use, as can be demonstrated by listening to the any conversation in the Britain.

Personalization

☐ If your mother tongue does contain articles, compare their use with that of articles in English. It is the small differences between them which will commonly cause you problems in your academic English.

- If you are not sure how the article system works in your language, look it up on the Internet or in a language book.

☐ If your mother tongue does not contain articles, consider how it indicates differences between 'definite' and 'indefinite' ideas. This may be where you make mistakes.

☐ Give a sample passage from your writing to a native speaker and ask her or him to read through it – this may help you focus on your specific mistakes.

☐ To see how frequently articles are used in academic English, search for *the* and *a* in an electronic article.

Extension

☐ Step 11 analyzes the influence of your **mother tongue** on your English. Your mother tongue can be particularly influential in this area of grammar.

☐ Steps 46, 47 and 48 all focus on the issue of **proofreading**. Proofreading skills are especially important for checking the use of articles, since they are (a) used so frequently and (b) so easy to get wrong.

☐ Appendix 3, Step 44 contains additional information about determiners.

How can I use adverbs effectively and accurately?

'I adore adverbs. They are the only qualifications I really much respect.'

Henry James

A Reflection

Using the mind map below, list the adverbs which you commonly use in your academic writing.

- *Refer to a previous essay if necessary.*

My use of adverbs in academic English

B Contextualization

Read these sentences and identify the function of the highlighted adverb.

Sentence	Function
Finally, be sure that you use a suitable range of linking devices.	Adverbs can be used to link sentences or clauses together.
Hedging is **probably** one of the most effective ways in which you can create distance between you and the text.	
The evidence indicates that the frequency of adverbs in academic writing is **actually** increasing.	
Evidently, essays in the humanities contain more adverbs than those in the sciences.	
Typically, good academic texts will contain a number of adverbs.	
From Dodsworth's perspective, adverbial phrases are a crucial feature of academic discourse.	
Inevitably, essays which do not contain adverbs will sound less authentic.	

c Analysis

What are the advantages of using adverbs in academic writing?

Used well, adverbs can add meaning to an academic text. Used poorly, they can reduce the quality and impact of your writing. A general rule is: use adverbs when they genuinely add value to your writing. When they do not, delete them.

Adverbs can be divided into five main types:

■ **Place**: *where* something happens (e.g., *there*, *here*, *downstairs*)

■ **Time**: *when* something happens (e.g., *recently*, *afterwards*, *tomorrow*)

■ **Manner**: *how* something happens (e.g., *well*, *quickly*, *accurately*)

■ **Degree**: *to what extent* something happens (e.g., *very*, *really*, *so*)

■ **Frequency**: *how often* something happens (e.g., *sometimes*, *generally*, *always*)

> **Adverbs: a review**
> * Adverbs modify verbs, adjectives and, sometimes, other adverbs.
> * Adverbs are a relatively common feature of academic writing since they add purpose, sophistication and accuracy.
> * Adverbial phrases (groups of two or more words which work together like an adverb) are also a common feature of academic English.

The first three types tend to appear in end position in the sentence, the last two in mid-position. In academic English, adverbs can have other specific functions, outlined below. The first two have already been outlined in Step 23 and Step 30, respectively.

Expressing doubt/certainty regarding a statement

■ Hedging is probably one of the most effective ways in which you can create distance between you and the text.

* Related adverbs/adverbial phrases: *arguably*, *decidedly*, *definitely*, *incontestably*, *incontrovertibly*, *most likely*, *very likely*, *quite likely*, *probably*
* Position: initial position

Linking clauses and sentences

■ Finally, be sure that you use a suitable range of linking devices.

* Related adverbs/adverbial phrases: *subsequently*, *similarly*
* Position: initial or mid-position

Actuality and reality

■ The evidence indicates that the frequency of adverbs in academic writing is actually increasing.

* Purpose: to comment on how true a statement is seen to be
* Related adverbs/adverbial phrases: *in fact*, *truly*
* Position: mid-position

Source of knowledge

■ Evidently, essays in the humanities contain more adverbs than those in the sciences.

* Purpose: to show where the information is from and the writer's attitude to the source
* Related adverbs/adverbial phrases: *apparently*, *reportedly*, *reputedly*, *according to*
* Position: very often found in initial position but can also be mid-position

Limitation

◼ Typically, good academic texts will contain a number of adverbs.

- Purpose: to mark the limitation of a proposition
- Related adverbs/adverbial phrases: *generally*, *largely*, *in general*, *in most cases*
- Position: initial or mid-position

Viewpoint or perspective

◼ From Dodsworth's perspective, adverbial phrases are a crucial feature of academic discourse.

- Purpose: to indicate from which perspective a proposition is true
- Related adverbs/adverbial phrases: *in X's view/opinion*
- Position: initial position

Attitude

◼ Inevitably, essays which do not contain adverbs will sound less authentic.

- Purpose: to convey directly the writer's/speaker's attitude toward the proposition, typically conveying an evaluation, value judgement or assessment of expectations
- Related adverbs/adverbial phrases: *as might be expected*, *conveniently*, *disturbingly*
- Position: initial position

In what position should adverbs appear in a sentence?

Knowing where to place an adverb in a sentence can be a difficult task. There are three general positions in which they can appear: initial position, mid-position and end position.

Initial position

Adverbs occur at the beginning of the sentence far more frequently in academic writing than in other forms of English. Often, these adverbs will be followed by a comma. An adverb in initial position can be described as a STANCE ADVERBIAL: it affects the meaning of the whole sentence.

Note: adverbs which modify adjectives (e.g., *always right*) or other adverbs (e.g., *very quickly*) always come first. The exception to this rule is the adverb *enough* (e.g., *early enough*).

Mid-position

There are three points to note about adverbs appearing in mid-position, namely:

◼ Generally speaking, these adverbs appear between the subject and verb.
- *I also finished my essay last night.*

◼ When AUXILIARY VERBS are used, these adverbs are placed between them and the main verb.
- *I have also finished my essay.*

◼ When the verb *to be* is the main verb, the adverb comes directly after it.
- *My essay is also interesting.*

End position

Many of the adverbs which would normally be placed in end position may be moved to initial position for the sake of emphasis. For example:

◼ I will finish my essay tomorrow.

◼ Tomorrow, I will finish my essay.

D **Activation**

Use each of the adverbs below to write a sentence relevant to your subject area.

1. Seldom _____

_____

2. In most cases _____

_____

3. In fact _____

_____

4. Unfortunately _____

_____

5. Additionally _____

_____

6. Last week _____

_____

7. Even _____

_____

 E **Personalization**

■ **To decide whether your use of adverbs is sufficient:**
  - Identify sentences in your essay where you have used no adverbs.
  - Decide whether they could be improved by using an adverb outlined in part C.

■ **To identify whether you are using adverbs in the correct place:**
  - Go through your essay and identify where you have used adverbs (top tip: searching for ~*ly* may speed up your search, since the majority of adverbs in English end with these letters).
  - Check their usage according to the rules outlined above.

F **Extension**

■ Step 17 focuses, in part, on the **different parts of speech** used in English.

■ Step 23 discusses the use of **cautious and tentative language**, where the use of adverbs can be an extremely useful strategy.

■ Step 30 looks at **linking devices**, where adverbs and adverbial phrases play an important role.

Why is proofreading important?

> *'No passion in the world is equal to the passion to alter someone else's draft.'*
>
> H. G. Wells

A Reflection

Consider your current practice in terms of proofreading your essays.

- *Look at the following spectrums and place a cross at the appropriate place.*

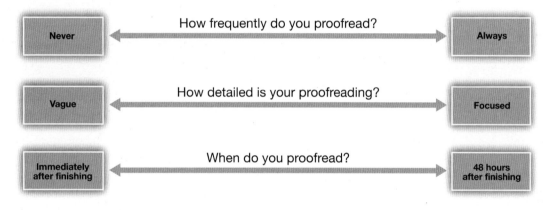

Never ←————— How frequently do you proofread? —————→ Always

Vague ←————— How detailed is your proofreading? —————→ Focused

Immediately after finishing ←————— When do you proofread? —————→ 48 hours after finishing

B Contextualization

The following passage has not been proofread. Read through it and identify areas which need to be improved.

Texts witch are not proofread often repeat teh same information. Proofreading, can also help identify sentences which are too long as this is a common problem which students face because they thinking that longer sentences are by definition a better thing when actually they can be very difficult to follow and you often end up repeating the same information. You also need to check if your sentences make. You often find that you repeat yourself. As Sowton 2012 argues, 'proofreading is as important as planning'. Technical, bespoke jargon mixed with words which are really slangy is something else which should be avoided. We can conclude, therefore, that proofreading is important.

c Analysis

What is the purpose of proofreading?

Proofreading is an important academic skill, yet many essays do not get proofread. The main reasons for this are:

- Students do not see the point of proofreading, so do not proofread.
- Students lack the technique and knowledge of how to proofread, so do it poorly.
- Students run out of time to proofread and are unable to do it.

The aim of this step is to identify why proofreading is important. Steps 47 and 48 look at specific strategies which can be developed to improve your proofreading skills, and identify the kind of problems which you should be looking for.

In brief, writing which has not been proofread can appear:

Difficult to understand

Taking time to proofread your essay can significantly improve the reader's ability to understand the content. Specific problems to target include:

- **Overly long sentences**. Break them down into smaller sentences which can be more easily understood.
  - Proofreading, can also help identify sentences which are too long as this is a common problem which students face because they thinking that longer sentences are by definition a better thing when actually they can be very difficult to follow and you often end up repeating the same information.
- **Lack of cohesion**. Is it clear what all pronouns refer to? Is there a 'chain' through your writing? Have you used linking devices appropriately?

Unprofessional

If a student does not take pride in his or her work, this will create a very negative impression on the person marking the essay. The marker may think that this carelessness is reflected in the content.

- **Typos**. Is everything spelt correctly? Have you made any silly, unnecessary mistakes?
  - Texts witch are not proofread often repeat teh same information.
- **Poor punctuation**. Have you used full stops/commas/semicolons correctly? Have you used capital letters in the right way? Is any of the punctuation informal?
  - Proofreading, can also help identify sentences which are too long as …
- **Poor formatting**. Have you paragraphed appropriately? Have you used the same font throughout?
  - You often find that you repeat yourself.
- **Weak structure**. Are all your sentences complete? Is there a subject and verb in all of them?
  - You also need to check if your sentences make ⬭.

> ### Proofreading: an activity that two can enjoy!
>
> It is very useful to proofread your work with a friend. As well as making the process more interesting (and possibly fun), there are good academic reasons for doing this. As the quotation at the beginning of this step suggests, it is much easier to see the mistakes in someone else's writing than in your own. In addition, it may be useful to work with a friend whose mother tongue is different from yours, since he or she might be able to identify mistakes which you cannot.

Unbalanced

Proofreading can help smooth out an essay and ensure you are consistent.

- ■ **Inconsistent position.** Is your argument the same throughout the essay? Do you contradict yourself at any point?
- ■ **Repetition.** Have the confidence to state something once and well. Do not repeat the same information.
  - You often find that you repeat yourself.

Non-academic

Your essay should follow the generally agreed academic conventions.

- ■ **Inappropriate language.** Have you used the right level of formality – not too informal but also not overly formal?
  - Technical, bespoke jargon mixed with words which are really slangy is something else which should be avoided.
- ■ **Referencing conventions.** Have you followed the recommended conventions? Are they consistent? Have you sourced where you found all your ideas?
  - As Sowton 2012 argues, 'proofreading is as important as planning'.
- ■ **Lack of supporting evidence.** Have you ensured that the arguments/conclusions which you are making are supported?
  - We can conclude, therefore, that proofreading is important.

  This conclusion cannot be made based on the supporting evidence which precedes it.

How should I proofread?

For your proofreading to be successful, it is recommended that your answers in part A should be towards the right-hand side of the spectrums. The reasons for this are:

- ■ **How frequently?**
  As indicated by the reasons above, you should *always* proofread. Good time-management skills are important, to ensure you include proofreading in your essay planning.

- ■ **How detailed?**
  There is no point in proofreading your essays unless you do it in a *focused* way. Proper proofreading is a thorough examination of your essay. Just looking at the surface without going into detail will only marginally improve the quality of your essay. You should *want* to find problems with your essay – too often proofreading tends to ignore problems. To do this, you need to read your essay critically (see Step 8).

- ■ **When?**
  Most people, when they finish writing their essay, want to hand it in as soon as possible. Many students have no choice about this, as they only finish their essay a few minutes before the deadline. Whenever possible, however, you should wait *48 hours* after finishing your essay before proofreading it. It is important to get some distance from your essay so that you can gain some freshness and clarity. If you do not have 48 hours, even a short break will help. Although proofreading is a process which can be time-consuming and boring, it is necessary. Any time which is spent proofreading will be time well spent. It is much better to spend an hour on proofreading than an hour on additional research or writing.

> **Focusing your proofreading**
> By knowing your own strengths and weaknesses, you can focus your proofreading more effectively. Analyze those specific areas where you know you have problems.

D Activation

In one paragraph, summarize the importance of proofreading.

_____

_____

_____

_____

_____

_____

_____

_____

_____

_____

_____

 # E Personalization

- **Identify a friend with whom you can proofread. Ideally, the friend will either be a native English speaker, or else will have a different mother tongue from you.**
  - Give your friend a piece of your writing and ask him or her to identify any problems.
- **Think about (a) your own problems with English and (b) problems which are linked with your mother tongue.**
  - Write a list of these issues so that you can focus on them in future proofreading.
- **Identify a paragraph from a previous piece of writing which contains a number of mistakes.**
  - Rewrite it – you will see how much it can improve, highlighting the value of proofreading.

F Extension

- Step 12 helps develop your **time-management skills**, thus ensuring that you have time to include proofreading in your planning.
- Step 47 focuses on the '**how**' of **proofreading** – looking at different strategies which you can use.
- Step 48 highlights some of the **common errors** which students make, which you should look out for.
- Step 50 looks at **final checks** which you need to make before your final submission.

What proofreading strategies can improve my final draft?

'I believe more in the scissors than I do the pencil.'

Truman Capote

A Reflection

The following are all important cross-cutting themes in your essay, which should be considered when proofreading.

- *How could you check whether these themes have been used effectively in your essay?*

Argument _____

Structure _____

Layout _____

Relevance _____

Grammar _____

Clarity _____

Language _____

B Contextualization

This is the conclusion to a student-written essay entitled 'Why is proofreading important, and what are the major problems students face in doing it successfully?'

- *Thinking at a more general/macro-level, what problems can you identify?*

> This essay has identified four key reasons why essays should be proofread, all of which show how important this skill is. It seems like a very important area to focus on. One key reason is that students run out of time in writing their essays and so consequently have no time left for proofreading. The overwhelming majority face this problem, so it is an important one to examine.

c Analysis

What section-by-section strategies can I use?

As noted in the previous step, it is important to be active in your proofreading. It can therefore be highly productive to think of a specific set of questions to ask yourself about each of the different sections of the essay. If the answer to any of the questions is 'no' (or you are not sure), you need to consider rewriting parts of that section. Questions that you might consider include:

- **Does your introduction:**
  - provide an overview of the whole essay?
  - indicate the direction in which the essay will be going?
  - engage the reader's interest?
- **Do your body paragraphs:**
  - focus on the main points of the essay?
  - present a consistent argument throughout?
  - give the quantity and quality of detail necessary to support your ideas?
- **Does your conclusion:**
  - highlight the main ideas of the essay?
  - leave the reader with a positive impression of your work?
  - answer the question?

Top ten general tips for proofreading

1. Print the essay out. It is very difficult to proofread properly on your computer screen.
2. Look for mistakes in groups. Mistakes will often come together, so if you find one, there may be others nearby.
3. Use different-coloured pens to indicate different types of mistakes (e.g., blue for grammar, red for language, etc.).
4. If you are having problems with particular sections of the text, read them aloud. It is often easier to hear mistakes than to read them.
5. Get others involved in proofreading. Work with a colleague or friend to increase the effectiveness (and interest) of the task.
6. Leave time between finishing writing and proofreading – 48 hours is ideal.
7. Proofread more than once – you will not find all your mistakes the first time.
8. Search actively for your mistakes.
9. Note the comments from the marker of your previous essays. You may have repeated previous mistakes.
10. Include proofreading in your planning. Do not see it as an 'extra' but as a fundamental aspect of your work.

Using these questions, we can say that the conclusion outlined in part B is problematic for the following reasons:

- It did not answer the second part of the question.
- It did not highlight the main points of the essay (e.g., it stated that there were four key reasons why essays should be proofread but only focused on one point, in too much detail).
- It is poorly written, leaving a bad impression (e.g., vague language such as It seems like a very important area to focus on).

What general proofreading strategies can I use?

As well as a section-by-section review, it is important to consider a number of cross-cutting themes that run throughout the essay. To ensure that the essay's argument and ideas are solid, and that an appropriate academic style has been used, you need a detailed analysis of these themes. The table identifies some themes and strategies you can use to analyze them.

Theme	Questions to ask	Strategy and rationale	Support
Argument	Do you justify all your points? Do you use appropriate evidence?	**Criticize your own essay.** Play devil's advocate: read your essay with the *deliberate* intention of finding as many problems as possible.	Steps 6, 7, 25, 28
Structure	Is there a clear path through the essay? Does it have a good backbone?	**Read the topic sentences.** Read the first sentence of every paragraph. From this, can you understand the main direction of the essay?	Steps 18–20
Layout	Have you laid out the essay correctly? What about **bold**, *italics* and underline? Is the essay spaced correctly?	**Visually check the essay.** Look at the essay as a painting. Ignore the actual words and content and decide whether it *looks* like an essay. Is there enough white space? Are there any paragraphs which are too long or too short? Is the correct font used?	Check your departmental handbook.
Relevance	Is everything you write necessary and important, or could some parts be deleted?	**Write the essay title on a piece of paper and reread your essay.** An essay must answer the question. Be constantly reminded of the title. Delete or rewrite any sections as needed.	Step 13
Grammar	Are all the tenses you have used appropriate? What about articles? Is there any MOTHER-TONGUE INFLUENCE?	**Read the text backwards, sentence by sentence.** This strategy will force you to only look at the words and to focus on the SYNTAX rather than the *meaning*. Reading the text aloud can be particularly effective.	Steps 41–45
Clarity	Can the reader understand your essay, or is it very difficult to understand the core meaning?	**Write a 100-word summary of your own essay.** Write this based only on what is in your essay (i.e., on what you have *written* rather than what you *know*). If you find this difficult, it may be that the essay lacks clarity. You could ask a friend to do this, and in return summarize their essay.	Step 29, Step 37
Language	Are there words or phrases which you use too frequently? Is the language the right level of formality?	**Search your essay.** Use your computer to search for terms which you know you tend to overuse (e.g., in Word, use *Ctrl-F*). This will show you all the places where these words appear, and you can make appropriate changes.	Step 36

Step 47

D **Activation**

Below is a body paragraph from the same essay as in part B.

- *Using some of the strategies outlined in part C, proofread and rewrite this passage.*

> Another important consideration is the benefit of using other people to proofread your writing. A lot of data suggests that proofreading is more successful when colleagues are also involved. Colleagues will be a useful resource because they could act as a 'critical friend', meaning that they can give you useful, knowledgeable advice in a way which is constructive. The colleague you chose can be someone you sit next to in class, or who you attend lectures with, or even someone you only occasionally see in the library.

_____

_____

_____

_____

_____

_____

_____

E **Personalization**

- Proofread a recent essay that you wrote – ideally, one which received a low mark – and ask the section-by-section questions listed in part C.
- Experiment with all the strategies listed on the previous page and decide which ones work for you. You may find some useful and others not.
- Compile a list of all the comments made by your essay markers. Consider this feedback when proofreading.
- Consider which of the cross-cutting themes identified in part C are the biggest problems for you and try to implement some of the strategies outlined.

F **Extension**

- A list of specific steps which can help with proofreading are presented in part C.
- Steps 46 and 48 also focus on the issue of **proofreading**.

What language/grammar mistakes are particularly common?

> *'The man who makes no mistakes does not usually make anything.'*
>
> **Edward Phelps**

Reflection

From what you have read so far, what are the major problems in using appropriate language and grammar in academic English?

- *Review the appropriate steps as necessary.*

Major problems in grammar	Major problems in language
Choosing the right voice (active or passive)	*Using the right level of formality*

B Contextualization

PROOFREADING SYMBOLS can be used to identify specific problems in a text. Here is an example. Based on the way these symbols are used, guess their meaning.

Proofreading symbols may be used by some of your teachers in order to identify some of your language and grammar mistakes. Understanding what these symbols represent, and the areas which you need to improve, can help minimize your mistakes in future essays. As Grobbelaar (1986) argues, Following feedback from your tutors is an important effective way of improving your essay quality.

Symbol	Meaning	Explanation / rationale
	Delete space, close up	There should not be a space here – *language* is one word.

C Analysis

What different types of mistakes are there?

Whereas the previous step focused on macro-level mistakes (either in different sections of the essay, or cross-cutting issues throughout the essay), the focus of this step is micro-level mistakes, particularly those related to grammar and language. These problems can be divided into three main types: slips, mistakes and errors. Understanding each of these issues can be important in terms of knowing the best strategy for solving the problem.

Slips

- *Overview*: A slip occurs when you can immediately recognize the problem and correct it easily. As such, slips are not the result of a lack of knowledge, but a lack of attention. Common examples would include subject–verb agreement, misspellings and word confusion (see box).

- *Problem*: While in isolation slips may not be a major problem, if they are frequently repeated they may suggest to the marker that you are careless. This may create a negative impression.

- *Solution*: Better, more focused and more active proofreading is needed. It does not necessarily matter if these slips occur in your *first* draft, but they should be corrected by your final draft.

Mistakes

- *Overview*: A mistake occurs when you can identify the problem and, with careful analysis, correct it.

- *Problem*: It may be that you have not thought about the particular topic in enough detail when writing.

- *Solution*: Active proofreading, specifically by use of the 'question-and-answer' methodology presented in the following section.

Errors

- *Overview:* An error represents a more fundamental problem. Generally speaking, you are not able to recognize your own errors because either you think what you have written is correct, or you lack the English-language knowledge to correct the problem.

- *Problem*: Errors are serious and may prevent the reader from understanding your text. Some errors may have become FOSSILIZED; that is, they have been problems for such a long time that they are now virtually impossible to correct.

- *Solution*: You need to study these particular areas, and perhaps 'unlearn' some of your English.

Commonly confused words

Such words can be divided into two main lists: homophones (words which sound the same but have different spellings) and words which have similar meanings/spellings.

Homophones

there/their	*to/too/two*
where/wear	*by/bye*

Words with similar meanings/spellings

less/fewer	*affect/effect*
as/like/such as	*than/then*
comprise/compose	*accept/except*
passed/past	*advice/advise*
practice/practise	*of/off*

How can I identify slips, mistakes and errors?

As noted before, being active in your proofreading is critical. One effective strategy for becoming more active is to ask yourself a series of questions as you proofread. Consider the following questions, which focus on use of language and grammar, as you read through your essay.

Language

- Have you used any informal language? (Step 1)
- Have you used collocations properly? (Step 38)
- Are you sure the phrase you have used exists? (Steps 37, 40)
- Are you sure there is no mother-tongue influence? (Step 11)
- Have you made any silly spelling mistakes?
- Have you repeated any language unnecessarily? (Step 37)

Grammar/structure

Word/phrase level

- Are the verbs in the right tense? (Step 41)
- Have you used the right voice? (Step 41)
- Do the subject and verb agree?
- If necessary, are nouns preceded by an article? (Step 44)
- Have adjectives/adverbs been placed in the appropriate position? (Step 45)
- Do the adjectives/adverbs genuinely add value, or are they unnecessary? (Step 45)

Sentences

- Is the word order correct? (Step 17)
- Do all your sentences have a verb in them?
- Is the punctuation correct? (Step 43)

Paragraph level

- Are all the paragraphs of roughly equal length? (Step 18)
- Does each paragraph have a good topic sentence? (Step 18)
- Is there a good balance of different types of sentence within the paragraph? (Step 26)

Using Microsoft Word

The overwhelming majority of academic essays are written in Microsoft Word. As such, it is important to know how this program works, and where it can be useful (or unhelpful) in identifying language/grammar problems in your writing.

✓ Identifies common grammatical and punctuation problems such as fragment sentences, lack of subject–verb agreement and misplaced commas.

✓ Detects words which have been misspelt.

✓ Can automatically correct certain idiosyncrasies which you might have.

✗ Provides advice based on standard rather than academic writing. As such, some of the conventions/requirements are different (e.g., increased use of the passive voice).

✗ May automatically 'correct' a misspelling to something which is actually incorrect.

✗ May switch between languages, or different varieties of English.

What symbols can be used to indicate problems?

When you receive feedback on your essays, your tutor may use a system of symbols to indicate particular problems, as indicated in the table below. Knowledge of these will help you identify and learn from your problems. It may be useful to learn these symbols and use them yourself. This can improve the efficiency and effectiveness of your proofreading. You may find it useful to develop your own system, or other symbols, in order to identify personal problems.

Symbol	Meaning	Symbol	Meaning	Symbol	Meaning
℈	Delete something	∽	Swap around	⑦	Missing/confusing info
∧	Insert something	☰	Capitalize	⊙	Insert a full stop
# or ⅄	Add space	/	Make lower-case	⋏	Insert a comma
◠ or ⌒	Delete space, close up	⌐ or ¶	New paragraph	⅋⅋	Insert quotation marks

D | Activation

Read the following sentences, each of which contains mistakes.

• *Identify the problems, note them in the lists below and rewrite the sentences accordingly.*

1. Proofreading are considered generally a really good academic skill.

_____

2. Commas, are the important piece of punctuation, which are often misused.

_____

3. Verbs will be areas where mistakes often find. Teh maximum reason for these verb problems is lack of knowledge of verbs.

_____

4. Disreal language, which is invention of non-native speakers, makes texts difficult to follow.

_____

Problem (grammar)	Mistake (sentence)	Problem (language)	Mistake (sentence)
Article	the important (2)	Incorrect form	invention (4)
Word order		Silly mistake/typo	
Subject–verb agreement		Collocation	
Tense		Invented language	
Voice		Repeated language	
Misplaced comma		Informal language	

E | Personalization

⬜ **Read through your academic writing and identify any problems.**

   • Divide these problems into slips, mistakes and errors.
   • Develop strategies, following the guidance in part C, to deal with them.

⬜ **Mark the questions in part C which you need to focus on specifically.**

F | Extension

⬜ Unit H provides you with strategies for improving your **academic language**.

⬜ Unit I develops your understanding of different aspects of **academic grammar** (including punctuation).

⬜ Steps 46 and 47 discuss more general aspects of **proofreading**.

⬜ Appendix 3, Step 48 lists words which are commonly misspelt in English.

How do I write a good abstract?

'To make abstract that which is concrete.'

Siegfried Sassoon

A Reflection

Answer the following questions about abstracts:

- When doing research for essays, why do you read abstracts?
- How long should an abstract be?
- What is the difference between an abstract and an introduction?
- At which stage of the writing process should you write your abstract?

B Contextualization

Read the following abstract, written for an essay entitled 'What are the characteristics of good abstracts?'

- *Identify the purpose of each section.*

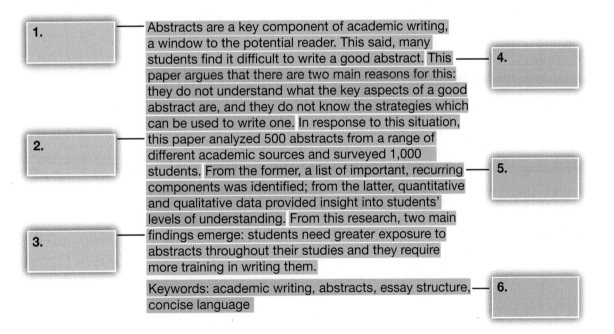

1.

2.

3.

4.

5.

6.

Abstracts are a key component of academic writing, a window to the potential reader. This said, many students find it difficult to write a good abstract. This paper argues that there are two main reasons for this: they do not understand what the key aspects of a good abstract are, and they do not know the strategies which can be used to write one. In response to this situation, this paper analyzed 500 abstracts from a range of different academic sources and surveyed 1,000 students. From the former, a list of important, recurring components was identified; from the latter, quantitative and qualitative data provided insight into students' levels of understanding. From this research, two main findings emerge: students need greater exposure to abstracts throughout their studies and they require more training in writing them.

Keywords: academic writing, abstracts, essay structure, concise language

Analysis

What is an abstract?

In simple terms, an abstract is a short passage which appears at the beginning of your essay, usually just after the title. The primary function of an abstract is to be a 'shop-window' – to provide the reader (or the potential reader) with an overview of the piece of writing which follows, and to indicate its key characteristics.

At the student level, abstracts are generally associated with longer pieces of writing, namely dissertations and theses. Additionally, professionally written academic articles will always have an abstract, which you can use to decide whether or not the article is relevant for your own writing (see Step 9).

There is no specific length for an abstract. Very often, they will be 100–150 words long. However, a PhD abstract can be in excess of 300 words, and an abstract for a paper given at a conference may only be 50–80 words.

Three top tips for writing abstracts:

- Does it 'sell' your essay? If you read the abstract, would you want to read the essay?
- Write the abstract at the very end, when you know the exact scope of your essay.
- Be patient – the abstract is not easy to write. It has many different functions and has to be extremely well-written. It will take time to do this.

What are the key 'structural' aspects of an abstract?

The following numbers refer to the order of the abstract sections presented on the previous page.

1. **Establish the context of the research**
   Abstracts are a key component of academic writing, a window to the potential reader. This said, many students find it difficult to write a good abstract.

2. **Establish the topic of the research/research problem**
   This paper argues that there are two main reasons for this: they do not understand what the key aspects of a good abstract are, and they do not know the strategies which can be used to write one.

3. **Indicate the methodology**
   In response to this situation, this paper analyzed 500 abstracts from a range of different academic sources and surveyed 1,000 students.

4. **Present the main findings**
   From the former, a list of important, recurring components was identified; from the latter, quantitative and qualitative data provided insight into students' levels of understanding.

5. **Indicate the main conclusion**
   From this research, two main findings emerge: students need greater exposure to abstracts throughout their studies and they require more training in writing them.

6. **Keywords**
   Academic writing, abstracts, essay structure, concise language

If your essay can be searched by means of an online database, you will be required to put in keywords, which will help potential readers narrow the search. You must therefore choose those words which most accurately and powerfully encapsulate your essay.

What are the key language/grammar aspects of an abstract?

Language

As the abstract needs to give a lot of information in few words (more so even than the introduction), the language used must be clear, concise and direct. To ensure this, it is important to use powerful CONTENT WORDS as far as possible.

- Abstracts are a key component of academic writing ...

Grammar

Use the present simple to introduce the topic and describe results and conclusions.

- From this research, two main findings emerge ...

Use the past simple (often in the PASSIVE VOICE) to describe research methodology and results.

- ... this paper analyzed 500 abstracts from a range of different academic sources ...

Style

An abstract should follow the same principles as any piece of academic writing. Short, powerful but grammatically correct sentences tend to be more common. Good cohesion and linking between sentences is critical. References may be included, if relevant.

Audience

A good abstract should be accessible and interesting to both experts and general readers. You want to encourage people to read your essay, but also to sound professional. You must, therefore, judge both the content and the language you use accordingly.

Format

Usually, abstracts are written as one paragraph and appear in a slightly smaller font than the rest of the essay.

Common problems associated with abstracts

The following list represents some of the main problems faced by students when writing abstracts. Explanations of these problems, and possible solutions, are outlined below.

Problem 1: The abstract is too long/overly detailed. It should just be a snapshot of your essay. They will often be fewer than 150 words.
Solution: Focus on key points; write in a more concise way; delete unnecessary information.

Problem 2: The abstract is poorly written/not well edited. Often, poor time management is the reason for this – students leave the writing of the abstract to the very last minute and do not have time to edit it. Its importance, however, demands that you spend more time on it.
Solution: Better time-management skills; include writing the abstract in your overall planning.

Problem 3: The abstract sounds like the introduction. Although they are related, the abstract and introduction have different purposes.
Solution: Be clear about the specific purpose/function of each (see Step 19).

Problem 4: The abstract misjudges its audience. It may be too complicated – or too simple.
Solution: Write in a style appropriate for the average or 'median' reader.

D Activation

Below are two 'first drafts' for the abstract which appears in part B. In each case, identify five problems.

Abstract 1	Abstract 2
An abstract is a short piece of writing which goes at the beginning of an academic essay in order to give an overview of the main points. Two main findings emerge from this study: students need greater exposure to abstracts throughout their studies and they require more training in writing them. This essay analyzed lots of abstracts from many different sources. It discovers that students have problems in understanding the key components of an abstract, and that they require skills development.	'Abstracts are easily accessible online and are useful as miniaturized texts, providing a rich source of characteristic patterns of text organization and language.' Abstracts are a really important bit of academic writing which appear at the beginning of a piece of academic writing and which, in this essay, are analyzed from 500 different sources and from the responses of 1,000 students.

Problems with abstract 1	Problems with abstract 2
1.	1.
2.	2.
3.	3.
4.	4.
5.	5.

E Personalization

- Look at abstracts in your subject area. Examine them in relation to the information presented in part C.
- Write an abstract for the last essay which you wrote, following the procedure outlined previously.

F Extension

- Steps 28 and 29 analyze ways to improve the **cohesion** and **coherence** of your academic writing, both of which help to make your abstract as clear as possible.
- Step 30 focuses on **linking words**, which are commonly used in abstracts.
- Step 37 develops your ability to use **concise and specific language**, an extremely important feature of an abstract.
- Appendix 3, Step 49 provides examples of abstracts from a range of subject areas.

What final checks do I need to make?

*'I have made this letter longer only because
I have not had time to make it shorter.'*

Blaise Pascal

A Reflection

Having finished *50 steps to improving your academic writing*, what are the five main things you have learnt about academic writing?

1. _____

2. _____

3. _____

4. _____

5. _____

B Contextualization

The following terms represent important final checks or useful strategies which can be used before submitting your essay.

- *In each case, write a question that could help you check if you are ready to submit.*

Abbreviations *If you have included any abbreviations, have you explained what they refer to?*	Number of copies	
Bibliography and citations	Official information	
Deadline	Page numbers	
Extension	Question	
Font	Reliability	
Gauging your audience	Sources	
Hook	Type of English	
Idiosyncrasies	Unnecessary slips	
Jargon	Vague language	
Keeping the reader interested	Word count *Have you written the appropriate number of words?*	
Labelling	X-rated language	
Mother-tongue interference	Your voice	

c Analysis

What final checks do you need to make before submission?

The following list represents an A–Z guide to some of the major areas which you need to consider in your final analysis. In each case, it may be useful to identify those areas which you personally need to address. Ask yourself which areas you need to think about before you submit your essay or, if possible, have a friend or colleague use the list when he or she checks your essay.

Abbreviations ☐ I need to think about this

If you have included any abbreviations, have you explained what they refer to?

Bibliography and Citations ☐ I need to think about this

Can all the texts you mention in your references be found in the essay as citations? Likewise, can all the work you quote in-text be found in your references?

Deadline ☐ I need to think about this

Are you sure when the deadline for the essay is? It is important to double-check, as the penalties can be very severe. You may be penalized a percentage of your mark (typically 5–10% per day you are late) or your essay may not be marked at all.

Extension ☐ I need to think about this

Do you need to request an extension for any reason? Depending on the circumstances (e.g., illness, personal reasons), you may be able to get an extension to your deadline. If you do need one, it is *always* better to ask earlier rather than later.

Font ☐ I need to think about this

Have you used the correct font for your essay? Sometimes, departments have strict requirements about this, so you should check your departmental handbook.

Gauging your audience ☐ I need to think about this

Have you judged your audience correctly?

Hook ☐ I need to think about this

Does your essay engage the reader from the beginning? Is there a 'hook' in the introduction? *Topic sentences are also a good place to include hooks.*

Idiosyncrasies ☐ I need to think about this

Have you checked the essay for your 'personal' mistakes? Double-check the feedback from previous essays to ensure that you have not repeated any mistakes.

Jargon ☐ I need to think about this

Have you used any unnecessary jargon? If so, replace it with simpler language.

Keeping the reader interested ☐ I need to think about this

Is there any part of the essay where the reader might become less interested? Essays sometimes have a middle part which is less interesting and less coherent than the rest of the essay.

Labelling ☐ I need to think about this

Are all your graphs, charts and tables labelled appropriately and clearly?

Mother-tongue interference ☐ I need to think about this

Have you identified and corrected all those issues which are the result of mother-tongue interference? Getting a native speaker (or someone with a different mother tongue) to check your essay can be helpful.

Number of copies ☐ I need to think about this

How many copies of your essay do you need to submit? Do you need to submit it in print/electronically/both?

Official information ☐ I need to think about this

Have you included all the relevant details – e.g., course name/module – which are officially required?

Page numbers ☐ I need to think about this

Have you included these? Even if they are not a requirement, they can be extremely helpful to the person marking the essay.

Question ☐ I need to think about this

Have you answered it properly? The most important thing you have to do in any essay is answer the question.

Reliability ☐ I need to think about this

Have you used reliable and authoritative sources? If not, delete those which weaken your essay and find alternative sources of evidence.

Sources ☐ I need to think about this

Have you sourced all the information which you need to? Are you sure you have not committed plagiarism, even 'accidentally'?

Type of English ☐ I need to think about this

Have you been consistent in your use throughout? You can use either British English or American English. The most important thing is not to mix the two forms.

Unnecessary slips ☐ I need to think about this

Have you checked your writing several times to ensure that you haven't made any unnecessary mistakes?

Vague language ☐ I need to think about this

Is there any unnecessarily vague language used?

Word count ☐ I need to think about this

Have you written the appropriate number of words? The majority of universities have very strict penalties if you are over or under the stated word count.

X-rated language ☐ I need to think about this

Have you used any language which is more commonly used, for example, in e-mails or text messages?

Your voice ☐ I need to think about this

Is your 'voice' clear in the essay? While it is important that you use relevant academic sources and evidence, it is important that your own view/opinion is clear as well.

Zzzzzzz ☐ I need to think about this

Now you have planned, written, rewritten, finished and submitted your essay … go and have a good rest! You deserve it!

Activation

The following table presents examples of some of the problems listed in part C.

- *Identify each problem and correct the sentence.*

Sentence	Problem area	Correction
'The United Nations (UN) is composed of 192 countries. The United Nations was created in 1945.'	Abbreviation	'The United Nations (UN) is composed of 192 countries. The UN was created in 1945.'
'This essay is going to look at the interesting issue of neuroscience, and relevant issues which are being discussed at the moment.'		
'When the gas turns to vapor, the colour changes to green.'		
'Teh practise has been observed four many years.'		
'Religion is often thought to be an important issue for some people while others do not seem to really see the point of it.'		

E Personalization

- Ensure that you have been through the A–Z list and ticked the boxes which apply to you.
- As noted elsewhere, it can be useful to get a friend/colleague to check through your work, using the list. Often, he or she will be able to identify mistakes which you cannot.
- What do you still need to work on in terms of your academic development?
  - How are you going to improve your existing weak areas?

F Extension

- Steps 1–50! Go back through the book. Hopefully, you have developed your writing skills and feel more confident writing in English. Writing an academic essay in any language is a difficult task; doing so in a second language is an even bigger challenge. Therefore, focus on those areas which are still weak and learn from the feedback which you get from your essays. Appendices 1–4 provide additional information and support which may help to develop further your skills and knowledge.

ANSWERS

Step 1, part D

1. Aspects which need changing:

- Repetition (really really)
- Speech-specific words (um)
- Informal and vague language (how they're done)

Original	'Written' version
'Speaking and writing are really really different skills … um … there are three ways this is true – how they're learnt, what they contain, and how they're done.'	Speaking and writing can be seen as very different skills in three main areas: their development, content and presentation.

2. Aspects which need changing:

- Contraction (it's)
- Checking understanding (isn't it)
- Standardization of written form (yer, gotta)
- Non-specific language (better)

Original	'Written' version
'It's clear, isn't it, that yer grammar has gotta be better in writing.'	It is clear that your grammar has to be more formal in writing.

3. Aspects which need changing:

- Speech-specific devices (*intonation rises*)
- Informal grammar (no question word)

Original	'Written' version
'The main differences in speaking and writing *[intonation rises]*. Difficult question.'	What are the main differences between speaking and writing? That is a difficult question.

4. Aspects which need changing:

- Informal linking word (but)
- Vague language (things, loads)

Original	'Written' version
'Things don't really change in writing, wherever you are, but in speaking they can change loads.'	There are a number of differences which exist in speaking which do not exist in writing.

Step 2, part D

1b. is more objective. We do not tend to use *I* in academic English.

2b. employs appropriate academic convention, referencing the source of information.

3b. uses hedging language (more likely to be), thus making the statement less direct and more balanced.

4a. has a higher lexical density and more specific, richer language.

Step 3, part D

1. Plagiarism **is** considered to be a serious offence by universities.

All universities have plagiarism committees where they consider cases of plagiarism. Punishment can range from deduction of marks to expulsion.

2. If found guilty of plagiarism, you **can** be expelled from the university.

Although it is not common, every year there are a number of students who are expelled from British universities for plagiarism.

3. I **am not** allowed to copy and paste material directly from electronic sources into my essay.

While you can, of course, use electronic resources in your essays, copying and pasting (without proper referencing) is plagiarism.

4. I **am** allowed to discuss my essay with a friend.

You may discuss the essay with a friend, but ensure that whatever you submit for assessment is all your own work. If you incorporate any of your friend's original ideas, you must acknowledge this.

5. Universities **do** have a range of electronic software to detect plagiarism.

Programmes such as Turnitin are used in almost every university and place of higher education.

6. I **do not have to** reference every single fact in my essay.

Knowledge which is considered 'common' does not need to be referenced.

7. If I pay someone to proofread my essay, they **cannot** change the content and ideas as well.

Proofreaders should really only focus on issues such as language and grammar. If they change the content/structure/ideas, this is plagiarism.

8. I **cannot** resubmit a piece of my work for assessment.

You are only allowed to submit a piece of work once for assessment. Resubmitting an essay is an example of self-plagiarism.

9. I **should** use other people's ideas in my essays.

You absolutely should use other people's ideas in your essays, but make sure you correctly and appropriately reference them.

Step 4, part D

Original	Paraphrase
1. 'Such investigations are likely to play a crucial role in our larger efforts to help university students become confident and successful academic writers.'	In all probability, this research will be an integral part of our endeavours to support university students in becoming skilled writers (Keck, 2006).
2. 'The study aimed to establish a reliable, replicable method.'	The aim of this research was the establishment of a method which you could rely on and replicate (Keck, 2006).
3. 'Many believe that the teaching of paraphrasing can help students to move beyond copying as a textual borrowing strategy.'	There is a consensus that understanding paraphrasing can assist students in developing strategies which replace copying as a means of 'textual borrowing' (Keck, 2006: 278).
4. 'Judgments of paraphrase acceptability depend upon a number of factors, including, but not limited to, the length of the borrowed phrase, word frequency, and the grammatical structure of the paraphrase.'	Judging whether a paraphrase is acceptable is dependent upon several factors, such as how long the phrase is, how often it is used, and the design of its grammatical structure (Keck, 2006).

Step 5, part D

According to (Gibaldi and the Modern Language Association of America 2003)[1], good referencing is important because it enables you to become part of the academic community. This view is supported by Tara[2] (2010) who argues that the success or failure of a PhD can rest on good references. Oshima and Hogue (1991)[3,4], meanwhile, emphasize the importance of referencing in avoiding plagiarism when stating 'if you neglect to mention whose ideas you are using, you are guilty of … plagiarism'.

References

Brabazon, T. (2010). How not to write a PhD thesis. *Times Higher Education Supplement*, 28 January. www.timeshighereducation.co.uk/story.asp?sectioncode=26&storycode=410208. [5]

Gibaldi, Joseph, and Modern Language Association of America (2003). *MLA Handbook for Writers of Research Papers*. 6th ed. New York: Modern Language Association of America, 2003[6].

1. When the name of the author is introduced in 'open text', the brackets should only go around the year, i.e., … Gibaldi and the Modern Language Association of America (2003). Another alternative way of writing this sentence would be: Good referencing is important because it enables you to become part of the academic community (Gibaldi and the Modern Language Association of America, 2003).

2. The student has used the author's first name in their in-text referencing. You should always use his or her surname (family name). This may be a problem for countries (e.g., China) where names are presented surname–first name, rather than in the West, where it is first name–surname.

3. Although this is a direct quotation, no page reference is given. It should read Oshima and Hogue (1991: 140).

4. The in-text citation does not appear in the list of references. We should find: Oshima, A. and Hogue, A. (1991). *Writing Academic English*. New York: Addison-Wesley.

5. All sources taken from the Internet should indicate the date when they were accessed. This is in case the details change, i.e., www. … Retrieved 28/03/10.

6. This reference does not follow the author–date system, but rather the MLA system. It is important to be consistent in the system of references which you use. In the author–date system, it should appear as: Gibaldi, J. and the Modern Language Association of America (2003). *MLA Handbook for Writers of Research Papers*, 6th edn. New York: Modern Language Association of America.

The corrected version should look as follows:

According to Gibaldi and the Modern Language Association of America (2003), good referencing is important because it enables you to become part of the academic community. This view is supported by Brabazon (2010), who argues that the success or failure of a PhD can rest on good references. Oshima and Hogue (1991: 140), meanwhile, emphasize the importance of referencing in avoiding plagiarism when stating 'if you neglect to mention whose ideas you are using, you are guilty of … plagiarism'.

References
Brabazon, T. (2010). 'How not to write a PhD thesis. www.timeshighereducation.co.uk/story.asp?sectioncode=26&storycode=410208. Retrieved 28/03/10.

Gibaldi, J. and the Modern Language Association of America (2003). *MLA Handbook for Writers of Research Papers*, 6th edn. New York: Modern Language Association of America.

Oshima, A. and Hogue, A. (1991). *Writing Academic English*. New York: Addison-Wesley.

Step 6, part D

1. General books and Wikipedia® can both be useful starting points to help you get going with your research.

2. Google Scholar and your reading list are both almost certain to contain only academic information.

3. Academic books and academic journals.

4. Online lectures and podcasts provide a 'listening' alternative which may stimulate your research.

Step 7, part D

1. A useful online source of journals.

2. May be useful research material, but be careful about plagiarism – and quality.

3. A good source (though note that this is a good magazine, not a specifically academic source). It also has a right-wing bias, which may not be immediately obvious.

4. Recognized as impartial, but as the information is not academic (as the results suggest), it may not be appropriate to include in your essay.

5. Although some of the information may be useful, there is no external or authoritative checking of the information contained here.

Step 8, part D

Students from countries which can broadly be said to have a 'Confucian system' (particularly China, Japan and South Korea) have difficulty with critical thinking because of the academic cultures found in these countries[1]. I have taught many people from this part of the world, and they always seem to have difficulties[2]. Clearly, therefore, your mother tongue is also an important factor[3]. In my opinion, French and German speakers also have significant problems in this respect[4]. Recent research (e.g., Smith, 2001; Barton, 2004) indicates that it is not only overseas students who have problems with critical thinking, but British students as well[5]. This research is supported by www.criticalthinkingcourses.com[6].

1. This is fine. However, although an explanation is offered, you are of course able to challenge the premise if you wish.

2. The evidence provided is weak and is based on personal experience. You cannot draw such strong conclusions from unscientific sources.

3. There is no justification for this assertion. Specific language is being used to try to convince you of the strength of the argument – *clearly* (i.e., you are stupid if you cannot see this) and *therefore* (i.e., there is a cause and effect link), but no reasoning is provided.

4. This statement is not based on reason, but on personal experience. This is not appropriate in academic writing.

5. Makes reference to recent research. Also, it uses some hedging devices and does not try to claim too much. This assertion is appropriate.

6. The Internet suffix indicates that this site belongs to a company, and the website name suggests that the company has a vested interest in students who may have weak critical thinking skills (i.e., the company can sell such students its products).

Step 9, part D

1. [Increased flexibility] [comes from] [not slavishly following] [the linear order] [of the text], [but] [by adapting] [your reading strategies] [accordingly] [(e.g.,] [reading the conclusion] [first]).

   The benefit of dividing up the text in this way can be seen more clearly if it is presented in a single column:
   Increased flexibility
   comes from
   not slavishly following
   the linear order
   of the text, ·
   but
   by adapting
   your reading strategies
   accordingly
   (e.g.,
   reading the conclusion
   first).

2. Increased flexibility comes from not slavishly following the linear order of the text, but by adapting your reading strategies accordingly (e.g., reading the conclusion first).

   Note: Some words (e.g., adverbs) may be considered 'content' depending on the context – e.g., *slavishly/accordingly*.

3. *Slavishly* – can be guessed by knowledge of the word *slave*. The ~*ly* ending indicates an adverb.

   Linear – can be guessed by knowledge of the word *line* and its contextualization with the word *order*.

   Accordingly – can be guessed by knowledge of *according to*.

4. *E.g.,* – indicates an example; brackets – indicate less important information; parallel structure of adverb + ~*ing* form (*slavishly following … adapting accordingly*).

Step 10, part D

Topic: Listening skills	Authors: Alexander, O., et al. (2008)
Relevance: I want specific strategies to help me follow my lectures, as I have been finding it difficult.	**Publication year:** 6 January 2011
Summary	**Main notes**
	Ss – shd take notes
How can lecturers help?	Ls – can help with:
	Visuals
	Handouts
	Intonation
	Textual signalling e.g., macro/micro-markers
Possible danger	But: Ss with poor L skills
	hard 2 diff. signals & content
	Listening + reading + NT = difficult
	Also NB: 'fact' vs 'opinion'

Step 11, part D

Verbs: has been developed (present perfect) should be was developed (past simple)

Articles: an *influence of your mother tongue*. This is a specific idea, and therefore needs the definite article – i.e., the *influence of your mother tongue*.

Word order: *order* specific (noun–adjective) should be specific *order*.

Vocabulary: vivid *understanding* should be clear *understanding* or good *understanding*.

Spelling: *populer* should be *popular*.

Collocations: *high relationship* should be strong *relationship*.

Step 12, part D

The relevant quotation from the text (which contains the answer) is given.

1. 'If you only plan your workload over the short term, you will forget your deadlines.'

2. 'You must prioritize your workload – focus on the tasks which are (i) most important and (ii) have the closest deadline.'

3. 'When a task starts to make you feel tired, you should do something different. For example, writing an essay when you have no motivation will result in bad writing and you will just have to rewrite it.'

4. 'The brain needs to be refreshed. Being a good student is about quality, not quantity.'

5. '"Spending time in the library' does not always equate to 'reading for your essay'. Progress should be measured by outcomes rather than activities."

6. 'Creating artificial deadlines (e.g., showing a draft to a friend) can help you focus on important tasks.'

7. 'Task management is important: you need to plan out an individual task, developing a series of mini-deadlines.'

8. 'Many people find electronic calendars a useful tool for managing schedules.'

Step 13, part D

Please note that these are 'model' rather than 'final' answers. Many other examples exist.

1. Account for the dominance of the English language in the 21st century.

2. How did English come to be the dominant world language?

3. Evaluate the advantages and disadvantages of a world language?

4. The dominance of the English language: a force for good or the continuation of empire?

5. Assess the impact of the English language on communication technology in the modern world.

6. 'The English language no longer belongs to the English.' Do you agree with George Lamming's assertion?

Step 14, part D

Basic outline	Expanded outline
1. Introduction	*Topic sentence:* Writing an essay without a plan is like going for a walk without a map: you may get to your destination, but it will take much longer and be much more difficult.
2. Makes writing more efficient	*Topic sentence:* Contrary to what many students believe, brainstorming and outlining your essay can actually save you time.
3. Makes writing higher quality	*Notes:* Coherence – logic – cohesion
4. Makes writing more enjoyable	*Topic sentence:* The writing process has to be enjoyable.
5. Conclusion	*Notes:* Recap three main points.

Step 15, part D

Remember: these are only model answers. There are many other acceptable thesis statements.

1. This essay will strongly argue that the scientific evidence for global warming is overwhelming, and that if multilateral action is not taken, a crisis will occur.

2. I will challenge Fitzpatrick's assertion, and argue that while higher education should, in certain circumstances, be free, it is impossible to make it free for all.

3. Overseas students, it is argued, have a predominantly positive impact on the British universities, although there are a number of areas where negative impacts can be seen.

4. This paper strongly advocates democracy as the most effective political system, and maintains that all countries should adopt it.

Step 16, part D

1. **Descriptive**: Outline the main types of academic writing in common use in British universities.

2. **Evaluative**: Assess the essay-based system of assessment which is common in most British universities.

3. **Argumentative**: Justify the importance of the essay as a means of assessment.

4. **Critique**: A critique of *50 steps to improving your academic writing* by Chris Sowton.

Step 17, part D

Student's own answers.

Step 18, part D

1. Sentence is written in too much detail. A good topic sentence should just give an overview of what is to follow rather than go into specifics.

2. Sentence is the best topic sentence as it is short, concisely written and provides a good overview of the paragraph.

3. Sentence is too general. Although it focuses on the main theme, it does not give any real indication of the specific direction in which the paragraph is going.

Sample paragraph

When creating topic sentences, there are two particularly important aspects to consider: content and language. The content should be a preview of the rest of the paragraph, highlighting certain key features. As with all good academic writing, the language should be concise and focused. In the topic sentence this is especially important, because if the language is unclear or confusing, the reader will soon lose interest. In fact, these two areas are not exclusive of each other, but should be considered together, for if either one is missing then the paragraph is significantly weakened. Needless to say, it does not matter how good your topic sentence is if the supporting statement does not develop the main theme of the paragraph.

Step 19, part D

1. **Interesting opening statement**
   (b) is better because it is an interesting idea which, presumably, the writer is going to develop as the paragraph continues. Most importantly, it is a *hook* which gets the reader interested. (a), meanwhile, merely states the obvious, telling the reader nothing new.

2. **Attention-grabbing data**
   (a) is irrelevant and uninteresting. It is certainly not a statistic which will make the reader more engaged in the essay. (b), however, immediately demonstrates to the reader why this essay is important.

3. **Relevant and interesting quotation**
   (a) is written in a good, compact academic style (using *parallelism*, for example) and is a well-chosen quotation as it is full of content (rather than structure) language. Conversely, (b) uses vague and redundant language, and is overly long.

4. Outline of sections

(a) feels like it has been written by a robot – as if the writer is just trying to tell the reader the information without any variation in style. (b) has a preferable style and also gives an indication of the kind of information to expect in these sections. It also uses the present simple tense, which is most common when outlining sections.

Step 20, part D

Since the essay is 1,500 words long, the length of the conclusion should be c. 75–150 words. It should relate directly back to the thesis statement, and provide a summary of some of the key points (which will often be outlined in the topic sentences).

To conclude, this essay has shown that even if it was desirable to standardize English, it would be impossible to develop a system. The majority of the world has some competence in English, with the language being commonly used in both work and personal life. To say that it still somehow 'belongs' to the English is absurd. Lamming's conclusion, therefore, seems inescapable. However, the slightly negative implication of his assertion (i.e., that this phenomenon is a bad thing) could be challenged because the process of internationalization can bring many benefits. English truly is a world language and, as the electronic revolution continues, it will probably only become more dominant. If managed carefully, this is to be welcomed.

Step 21, part D

You[1] might think that the sort of[2] words[3] you use in academic writing is not important[4]. But[5] nowadays[6], it's[7] becoming really[8] important for you[9] to choose your language and grammar carefully[10]. The fact of the matter[11] is that many students are influenced by the writing style of mags and papers[12]![13] They just do the same[14].

[1]Second-person pronoun
[2]Unspecific language
[3]Unspecific language – a broader generalization needed
[4]Informal negative expression
[5]Sentences should not start with *but*
[6]Informal language
[7]Contraction
[8]Informal language
[9]Second-person pronoun
[10]Adverbial position – placing the adverb at the end of the sentence is associated with a more informal writing style
[11]Cliché
[12]Slang
[13]Punctuation
[14]*Do* + word

Corrected passage:

The kind of language used in academic writing may be considered unimportant. Currently, however, it is becoming extremely important for students carefully to choose their language and grammatical structures. Many students are influenced by the writing style of magazines and newspapers. They simply copy what they find.

Step 22, part D

Please note that these are only model answers. Other alternatives are possible.

1. **This paper** discusses the advantages and disadvantages of depersonalization in academic writing.

2. From this, more about the nature of academic writing **can be understood**.

3. **It** has been clearly argued that academic writing uses *I* at certain times.

4. **This author** has previously referred to this issue.

5. Following analysis of the data, **one** can clearly identify the main theme.

6. **The data** clearly demonstrate that academic writing is considered challenging.

Step 23, part D

1. The Earth's diameter ~~might be~~ **is** 12,756 kilometres.
   Overhedging: this is an unambiguous fact, so using a form of to be *(is, here) is acceptable.*

2. The opinion polls ~~prove~~ **suggest/indicate** that the Liberal Party will win the election.
   Underhedging: this sentence can only be a prediction – therefore the verb prove *is too strong.*

3. One of the main functions of the pancreas is to produce hormones.
   This is a fact – therefore there is no need for hedging language.

4. There is ~~always~~ a tendency for the graph to rise sharply.
   Unbalanced hedging: always *is an extremely strong word, whereas* tendency *is weak.*

5. The data seem to suggest that Sowton's argument is correct.
   Appropriate hedging.

6. ~~It is assumed that~~ civil law and criminal law are different.
   Overhedging: they are clearly different.

7. The USA's lies created disorder.
   Underhedging: this is too direct – and a controversial statement. Perhaps add the word alleged *before* lies.

8. Undoubtedly, these problems may have begun last year.
   Unbalanced hedging: undoubtedly *is an extremely strong word, whereas* may have *suggests doubt.*

Step 24, part D

Sample paragraph:

Complex language, which is a challenge for many students, is often a normal expectation at British universities. Importantly, many universities have responded to this problem through the provision of in-sessional writing courses. Predictably, while many students only attend one or two classes and then leave, others attend the whole course.

Step 25, part D

1. Arguments based on personal experience are not considered 'academic'. They should be based on appropriate evidence.

2. Simply because a lot of information is presented does not mean the argument is right. It is quality, not quantity, that is important.

3. You cannot assume that the book is right just because your tutor wrote it. The quality of the *argument* has to be considered.

4. This is an assertion, as indicated by the phrase *In my opinion*.

5. The conclusion is extremely strong (*it should <u>definitely</u> ...*) based on the evidence (i.e., what about the 48% of people who disagreed?).

Step 26, part D

There are four types of sentences in English[1]. The most basic type, which is known as a 'simple sentence', consists only of an independent clause[2]. Compound sentences have two independent clauses, which are joined by a coordinating conjunction[3]. Complex sentences, however, contain both an independent and subordinate clause, and are particularly useful for comparing and contrasting ideas[4]. This is an important skill in academic writing[5]. The last type of sentence is a mixture of these last two forms and can be quite challenging to write[6]. These sentences, which form an important part of academic discourse, contain at least two independent clauses and one dependent clause and are known as 'complex-compound sentences'[7].

Sentences 1 and 5 are simple.

Sentences 2 and 3 are complex.

Sentences 4 and 6 are compound.

Sentence 7 is complex-compound.

Step 27, part D

1. The purpose of this essay is to interpret the data clearly, concisely and specifically.

2. English is the lingua franca of India.

3. Above all, globalization is largely understood as the rapid shift of power from the state to the market.

4. Money was the motivation.

Step 28, part D

Major problems	Rewritten paragraph
1. Poor topic sentence – too detailed and specific. **2.** The term *argument* is analyzed/ discussed before it is defined. **3.** Overcomplicated grammar which is used incorrectly.	Coherence is an important, but often ignored, academic skill. The logical progression of your argument, meaning the position you take with regard to the essay title, should occur on a step-by-step basis. Concerning arguments, you need to ensure that you have been particularly careful and that your position is consistent throughout.

Step 29, part D

This is a model answer only. The table that follows examines the aspects of cohesion that this paragraph demonstrates.

It can be said that English is an important world language for three key reasons, which are outlined below. To begin with, it is the international language of business: this can lead to significant economic development. Furthermore, as a world language which people from all countries can use, English has a role in developing relationships and increasing diplomacy (among other things, it is also one of the official languages of the United Nations). Lastly, English has an importance in developing cultural relations between countries.

Aspect of cohesion	Examples
Enumerators	**Three** key reasons … to **begin** with … **furthermore** … **lastly** …
Personal pronouns	**it** is the international language of business
Demonstrative pronouns	**this** can lead to significant economic development
Words referring backwards/forwards	which **are outlined below**
Word family	**important** … **importance** …
Academic punctuation	… it is the international language of business**:** this can lead to significant economic development.

Step 30, part D

Teacher feedback
1. These two sentences could be more cohesive if a contrastive linking device such as *while* or *whereas* was used.
2. It is not common academic practice to start a sentence with *because*. *Since* would be more appropriate.
3. The linking device (*but*) is informal and the sentence is poorly written. An improvement would be: *Although students could benefit significantly by learning 15 to 20 key linking devices, they do not want to take the time to learn them.*
4. Since this linking device is linking a sentence to a previous sentence, a comma is required.
5. Repetition of the same idea – a tautology.

Step 31, part D

1. *Argues* introduces a new idea that requires a balanced/neutral verb. Additionally, *illustrate* is not followed by a *that*-clause, and *conjecture* is too weak.

2. *Analysis* and *examination* are both acceptable.

3. The conjunction *however* suggests an opposing point of view. Therefore, **challenged** is correct.

4. *Affirms* indicates that Matthewman (2011) is following Otaqui (2011).

5. Using **reveals** would unbalance the sentence (with the subsequent hedging). Therefore, **notes** and **suggests** are appropriate.

Step 32, part D

Sample paragraph:

If you use cause and effect language in your essays, your ideas are developed in a more logical way. The result of this is that your arguments are more coherent which, in turn, leads to an improvement in the overall quality of your essay. Finally, as a result of all this, your essay will achieve a higher mark.

Step 33, part D

1. Economics is a field which focuses on the financial relations of different factors.

2. Malaria is a terrible disease which is carried by mosquitoes and kills around two million people per year.

3. Cirrhosis is a liver disease which is characterized by serious damage to liver tissue.

4. In simple terms, photosynthesis is a process which converts carbon dioxide into an organic compound using the energy from sunlight.

5. For the purposes of this essay, modern history is defined as the period from the end of the First World War to the present day.

6. In legal terms, 'duty of care' is a legal obligation which represents the first action which must be proved before an action in negligence.

Step 34, part D

Student's own answers.

Step 35, part D

Note: these are five example sentences; there are many other possibilities.

1. Between 2004 and 2009, the number of students from EU countries increased significantly.

2. The number of non-EU students rose sharply between 2006 and 2007.

3. Compared with the previous year, the number of students from non-EU countries rose slightly in the period 2005 to 2006.

4. The number of British undergraduates peaked between 2006 and 2007.

5. Since 2004, there has been an upward trend in the number of undergraduate students at British universities.

Step 36, part D

Reusing identical language in academic writing is considered bad style by most academics. Repeating the same words gives the impression that your knowledge of the subject is also poor, whereas you might actually have a good understanding. A range of vocabulary will make your texts sound more professional and interesting.

Step 37, part D

Following the completion of their first draft, overseas students ~~from abroad~~[1] often choose not to recognize ~~the fact~~[2] that their essay ~~is in possession of~~ contains[3] ~~an excessive number of~~ too many[4] words. For many, their ~~usual~~[5] habit is to avoid ~~carrying out an evaluation of~~ evaluating[6] their work. The ~~honest~~[7] truth of the matter is that ~~the majority of~~ most[8] students do not proofread properly. Proofreading, ~~on most occasions~~ usually[9], is too brief ~~in duration~~[10]. Students do not want to edit their work in case they need to ~~make their essay longer in length~~ lengthen their essay[11].

A key to the changes made above appears below, referring to the three-problem system outlined in Step 37, namely:

Problem 1. Too many words are used, making the phrase difficult to understand.

Problem 2. An unnecessarily complicated phrase is used, where a simpler version is available.

Problem 3. Language is used which only repeats the information already there.

1. Problem 3 – *overseas* means *from abroad*.

2. Problem 1 – *the fact*, while not being *wrong*, adds nothing to the meaning.

3. Problem 2 – *contains* is a much more precise phrase (one instead of four words).

4. Problem 2 – as above, two instead of four words.

5. Problem 3 – if something is a *habit*, it is, by definition, *usual.*

6. Problem 1 – *evaluating* is a much neater, easier way of saying the same thing.

7. Problem 3 – *truth* is, by definition, *honest.*

8. Problem 2 – *most* conveys the same idea in a third of the words.

9. Problem 2 – *usually* is only one word instead of *on most occasions*, which is three.

10. Problem 3 – if something is described as *brief*, it implicitly contains the idea of *in duration.*

11. Problem 1 – an example of a complicated *make* + noun phrase structure (i.e., *make … longer in length*). A one-word verb is much more powerful (i.e., *lengthen*).

Step 38, part D

Word	Collocates
development (noun)	economic D; early D; rapid D; industrial D; child D; language D; research and D; D grant; facilitate D
significant (adjective)	very S; S number; S changes; S differences; S contribution; S role; statistically S
completely (adverb)	C different; C free; C wrong; C new; C gone; C satisfied
confidence (noun)	total C; increased C; lack of C; crisis of C; rebuild C; vote of no C
indicate (verb)	reports I; studies I; I whether; may I; figures I; clearly I; seem to I

Step 39, part D

1. Ranke came to his conclusion **on the basis of** earlier research.

2. It thereby recognizes **the role of** psychology in determining the origins of social behaviour.

3. This could also be linked **to the fact that** many have a lack of language skills and familiarity with British institutions.

4. The gradual increase before the peak is **as a result of** the general effect of increasing temperature.

5. **One of the most important** books of the Enlightenment era was undoubtedly Adam Smith's *The Wealth of Nations*.

6. *Theory of International Politics* was written by Waltz **in the context of** the pluralist challenge to classical realism.

Step 40, part D

1. The appendices should **be referred to** as necessary.
2. These proposals **are based on** research undertaken by Dyer (2007).
3. The delegates **vote for** the candidate they wish to take control.
4. Many scholars **are convinced of** the need for further research.
5. It is hoped that this paper **will result in** practical implementation in the appropriate sectors.
6. This setback should not **subtract from** the excellent achievements of the project.
7. Both engines **were equipped with** a particular type of flywheel.
8. Despite overwhelming support, the government **decided against** supporting the project.
9. This feedback **will be incorporated into** the overall report.
10. She **is regarded as** one of the finest scholars of her generation.

Step 41, part D

1. It was therefore precisely in those areas where it **had developed** a unique function ... that the structure of the court **made** it chronically inefficient.
2. The World Health Organization **predicts** that by 2020, depression **will be** the second leading contributor to the global burden of disease.
3. Historically, thrombelastography **was first used** clinically for haemostatic monitoring during liver transplantation.
4. The potential in developing countries also correlates with the high population growth **currently being experienced.**
5. The Third Legion **had been stationed** in Syria before **being transferred** to Moesia.

Step 42, part D

Note: These modal verbs are simply suggestions – there are others that are also correct.

Students **should** use modal verbs to make the meaning of their texts more specific. It is common to find whole essays where modal verbs are not used, even though they **would** be better if modal verbs were used on a relatively frequent basis. As a result of mother-tongue influence, it **can** be argued that a lack of confidence in how they are used is the main reason for this. If students take the time to learn the specific functions of modal verbs, their essay **will** improve. It **must** be concluded, therefore, that modal verbs are an important aspect of academic writing.

Step 43, part D

1. It is important to be able to distinguish important from less important information **(**particularly in academic writing**),** otherwise sentences look extremely long and are difficult to follow.
2. According to Otaqui (2000), **'P**unctuation is **...** a critical factor in high-quality academic writing.'
3. Comma splicing is a serious problem in academic writing**;** proofreading is a good strategy for eliminating this problem. *[Note: a full stop could also be used here.]*
4. **C**apital letters should be used for proper names, the first word of a sentence and, as **S**toddart (2001: 208) argues in his book *Guide to Punctuation*, 'At the beginning of direct quotations'.
5. In addition to their use in references, there are three main areas where colons can be used**:** series, examples and explanations.

Step 44, part D

Articles[1] are **a very important part**[2] of **the English language**[3]. This is demonstrated most clearly by the fact that *the* is **the most frequently used word**[4] in English. *A* and *an* are also in very common use, as can be demonstrated by listening to **any conversation**[5] in **Britain**[6].

1. No article needed as a general idea is being referenced.

2. *A* is needed here because this refers to one of many important parts of the English language.

3. The English language is a unique, specific idea, and therefore *the* is needed.

4. A superlative form.

5. Already has a determiner (*any*) so no article is needed.

6. Country name but no countable noun. Note the difference with *the United Kingdom*.

Step 45, part D

Sentences from a range of subject areas (as well as generic academic sentences) are presented below.

1. In the UK, law cases are **seldom** decided in the House of Lords.

2. In most cases, the plays of Shakespeare are no longer performed in traditional costume.

3. In fact, heart disease is one of the biggest health problems in the United Kingdom.

4. Unfortunately, reliable data on this mountain range does not exist.

5. Additionally, a further reason for this could be a lack of sufficient analysis.

6. The research paper was finally completed **last week**.

7. This archaeological discovery may **even** be more important than was originally thought.

Step 46, part D

Student's own answer.

Step 47, part D

Argument:

This statement is extremely vague and needs more support/detail.

Language:

The word 'colleague' is used three times throughout the paragraph. The use of synonyms would be appropriate.

Another important consideration is the benefit of using other people to proofread your writing. A lot of data suggest that proofreading is more successful when colleagues are also involved. Colleagues will be a useful resource because they could act as a 'critical friend', meaning that they can give you useful, knowledgeable advice in a way which is constructive. The colleague you choose can be someone you sit next to in class, or who you attend lectures with, or even someone you only occasionally see in the library.

Relevance:

This is irrelevant detail and does not push the argument forward at all.

Grammar:

Inconsistent use of tenses.

Corrected paragraph:

Another important consideration is the benefit of using other people to proofread your writing. Many writers, such as Smith (2001) and Jones (2005), have argued that proofreading is more successful when colleagues are also involved. Classmates are a useful resource because they can act as a 'critical friend', meaning that they can give you useful, knowledgeable advice in a way which is constructive.

Step 48, part D

1. Proofreading is generally considered a very important academic skill.

2. Commas are pieces of punctuation which are often misused.

3. Verbs are areas where mistakes are often found. The main reason for this is lack of knowledge.

4. Unreal language, which is invented by non-native speakers, makes texts difficult to follow.

Problem (grammar)	Mistake (sentence)	Problem (language)	Mistake (sentence)
Article	*the important* (2)	Incorrect form	*invention* (4)
Word order	*considered generally* (1)	Silly mistake/typo	*the* (3)
Subject–verb agreement	*proofreading are* (1)	Collocation	*maximum reason* (3)
Tense	*will be areas* (3)	Invented language	*disreal* (4)
Voice	*often find* (3)	Repeated language	*verbs ... verb ... verbs* (3)
Misplaced comma	*commas* (2)	Informal language	*really good* (1)

Step 49, part D

Problems with abstract 1:

1. Audience/style – not the place for a definition; inappropriate for audience – it is likely they will know what an abstract is.

2. Chronology – does not follow the prescribed order that information should follow.

3. Tense – present simple used to describe results.

4. Methodology – too vague/unspecific.

5. Language – some informalities, e.g., *lots of.*

Problems with abstract 2:

1. Style – quotations are not generally found in abstracts.

2. Style – very long sentence at the beginning of the second paragraph – abstracts should be more direct.

3. Format – unusual to find an abstract divided into two paragraphs, unless it is extremely long and they are needed for clarity.

4. Language – some informalities, e.g., *really, bit.*

5. Content – no context, findings or conclusion.

Step 50, part D

Sentence	Problem area	Correction
'The United Nations (UN) is composed of 192 countries. The United Nations was created in 1945.'	Abbreviation	'The United Nations (UN) is composed of 192 countries. The UN was created in 1945.'
'This essay is going to look at the interesting issue of neuroscience, and relevant issues which are being discussed at the moment.'	Hook	'This essay focuses on neuroscience, a field which has experienced radical developments in recent times.'
'When the gas turns to vapor, the colour changes to green.'	Mixed types of English (AmE/BrE)	'When the gas turns to **vapor**, the **color** changes to green.' 'When the gas turns to **vapour**, the **colour** changes to green.'
'Teh practise has been observed four many years.'	Unnecessary slips	'**The practice** has been observed **for** many years.'
'Religion is often thought to be an important issue for some people while others do not seem to really see the point of it.'	Vague language	'Religion is considered important by many, while others have no need for it.'

Glossary

ABSTRACT
A short text which provides an overview of a piece of writing. The term may also refer to a short description of the main themes of a conference paper.

Related steps: 6, 9, 49

ABSTRACT NOUN
A noun that refers to an idea or a general quality, not to a physical object, e.g., *love*, *art*, *beauty*, *democracy*.

Related steps: 33, 44

ACADEMIC COMMUNITY
The group of people – real or imagined, known or unknown – for whom you are writing. When writing, your aim is to sound as if you belong to your chosen academic community.

Related entry: audience

Related step: 39

ACCIDENTAL PLAGIARISM
Where you use, but do not acknowledge, somebody else's ideas *by accident* – for example, through poor note-taking. Accidental plagiarism is treated just as seriously as deliberate plagiarism.

Related entry: plagiarism

Related steps: 3, 4

ACTIVE VOICE
See **VOICE**.

ACTIVE READER
When reading, it is extremely important that you know *why* you are reading a particular text, and that you engage directly with it. This process is known as active reading.

Related step: 9

ACTIVE VOCABULARY
The set of words which you are immediately able to use in speaking or writing.

Related entry: passive vocabulary

Related step: 30

ADVERB/ADVERBIAL PHRASE
A word class whose function is usually to modify a verb, but sometimes an adjective or another adverb. Adverbs in English can be divided into different types (e.g., function, manner) and often end with ~ly (e.g., *quickly*, *slowly*).

An adverbial phrase is a two-, three- or four-word term which has an adverb as its main focus.

Related entry: stance adverbial

Related steps: 24, 34, 45

AMBIGUITY
Where a piece of text can have more than one meaning. Academic writing should **not** be ambiguous – it should be clear exactly what is meant.

Related entry: vagueness

Related steps: 1, 21

AMERICAN ENGLISH (AmE)
The variety (dialect) of English spoken in the USA. In terms of writing, the differences between American and British English are relatively small, e.g., spelling (~or rather than ~our in words like AmE *favor*/BrE *favour*, ~er rather than ~re in words like AmE *center*/BrE *centre*).

Related entry: British English

Related step: 1

ANGLO-SAXON
Also known as 'Old English'. The form of the English language spoken between about the 5th and 12th centuries. Much of the vocabulary of modern English comes directly from Old English.

Related entries: French, Latin

Related step: 1

APPOSITION
Where two noun phrases are placed next to each other and one noun phrase modifies the other.

Related entry: noun phrase

Related step: 43

ARGUMENT
In academic writing, a reason, or reasons, someone uses to show that something is true or correct.

Related entry: logical fallacy

ARTICLE
a/an and *the*, words which come before a noun phrase and show whether the noun phrase is indefinite or definite.

Related entries: determiner, demonstrative pronoun, quantity word

Related steps: 11, 44

AUDIENCE
The people (or person) who will read your essay. It is important to consider your audience when you write, in terms of language used, level of detail, etc.

Related entry: academic community

Related steps: 1, 28

AUTHOR–DATE SYSTEM
See **HARVARD SYSTEM**.

AUTHORIAL COMMENT
The way in which an author indicates his or her position or attitude in a text.

Related entry: stance

Related step: 31

AUXILIARY VERB
Provides additional information (related to voice and tense) about the main verb which follows. In addition to *modal verbs* the main auxiliary verbs in English are *be*, *have* and *do*. For example, *I am going* or *I have gone*.

Related entries: main verb, modal verb, voice

Related steps: 11, 41, 42, 45

AVOIDANCE
The act of deliberately not using certain language because you are not confident about using it correctly.

Related entries: fossilization, mother-tongue influence, transfer

Related step: 11

AXES
The horizontal and vertical lines on a graph.

Related entry: legend

Related step: 35

BIAS
Prejudice towards a particular point of view. Academic writing should be free of bias, as it should be as objective as possible.

Related entries: objectivity, vested interest

Related steps: 7, 8

BODY LANGUAGE
Non-verbal communication (e.g., gestures) which engages an audience and may reveal something about the speaker's position.

Related entries: eye contact, hand movement

Related step: 1

BRITISH ENGLISH (BRE)
The variety (dialect) of English used in the United Kingdom. If you are at university in the UK, you will be expected to use British English. If you use Microsoft Word, ensure that the appropriate language setting is selected.

Related entry: American English

Related step: 1

CAUTIOUS LANGUAGE
See **HEDGING LANGUAGE**.

CHRONOLOGICAL ORDER
When information is presented in time order (i.e., earliest to latest).

Related step: 9

CLAUSE
A group of words composed of a subject and a verb.

Related entries: independent clause, phrase, subordinate clause

Related step: 16

CLUSTER DIAGRAM
See **MIND MAP**.

COHERENCE
The logical organization of a piece of writing.

Related entries: cohesion, subject–verb–object, weighting, word order

Related steps: 2, 18, 28, 29

COHESION
The relationship between parts of a sentence which helps give it meaning. Cohesion may be either grammatical (e.g., parallel structures) or lexical (e.g., linking devices).

Related entries: coherence, linking devices

Related steps: 9, 17, 28, 29, 40, 43, 44, 46

COLLOCATION
Where two or more words frequently appear together. For example, in English, if someone smokes a lot they are a *heavy smoker* (rather than a *large smoker*). Collocations are an effective way of sounding more natural.

Related steps: 11, 29, 34, 35, 38

COMPARATIVE
The form of an adjective (or adverb) which indicates a contrast with another person or object.

Related entry: superlative

Related step: 35

COMPOUND ADJECTIVE
See **COMPOUND WORD**.

COMPOUND WORD
A combination of two or more words which form a single word or phrase (e.g., *bus stop*). Sometimes, in writing, such words may be linked by a hyphen (e.g., *first-class*).

Related step: 43

CONCLUSION
The last paragraph(s) of a piece of academic writing. A conclusion tends to follow a number of conventions, including providing a summary of the essay and linking back to the thesis statement.

Related entries: introduction, main body, thesis statement

Related steps: 2, 19, 20

CONJUNCTION
A class of words which link words, phrases or clauses together.

Related entries: linking device, word class

Related steps: 28, 30, 34

CONNOTATION
The secondary, suggested or implied meaning of a word in addition to its core meaning.

Related entry: denotation

Related steps: 24, 31, 32, 35, 36

CONTENT WORD
A content word carries meaning, specifically nouns and verbs. The use of these words should be maximized in academic writing.

Related entries: noun phrase, structure word, verb phrase, word class

Related steps: 2, 9, 13, 24, 36, 37, 38

COORDINATING CONJUNCTION
A type of conjunction which links two independent clauses together. Common examples include *and*, *but*, *for* and *or*.

Related entries: conjunction, independent clause, subordinating conjunction

Related steps: 26, 43

COUNTER-EVIDENCE
Evidence which is presented to challenge or disprove an argument.

Related step: 8

DEMONSTRATIVE PRONOUN
A pronoun is used to identify the person or thing that is being referred to. The main demonstrative pronouns are *this*, *that*, *these* and *those*.

Related entries: cohesion, determiner

Related steps: 44

DENOTATION
The core, central meaning of a word.

Related entry: connotation

Related steps: 24, 31, 32, 36

DETERMINER

A word used before a noun phrase to indicate something specific about it. Determiners include articles (*a*, *an*, *the*), demonstrative pronouns (*that*, *those*) and quantity words (*enough*, *either*).

Related entries: article, demonstrative pronoun, quantity word

Related step: 44

DISCUSSION SECTION

The part of a piece of writing (often scientific writing) which discusses the implications of any results.

Related step: 20

EMPHASIS

The process of highlighting information which is of particular importance.

Related steps: 1, 27

EMPIRICAL RESEARCH

Research based on gathering information through a variety of mechanisms, such as experiments and interviews.

Related step: 35

END-WEIGHTED

See WEIGHTING.

EYE CONTACT

The extent to which you look directly at your audience when delivering a presentation.

Related entries: body language, hand movement

Related step: 1

FIGURATIVE LANGUAGE

Language which may have a non-literal meaning, e.g., idioms.

Related entry: idiom

Related step: 21

FILLER

A word which you use in conversation to indicate to the speaker that you are listening, e.g., *ah* and *mmm*.

Related step: 1

FIXED PHRASE/EXPRESSION

A phrase whose parts cannot be changed.

Related entries: figurative language, idiom, lexical bundle

Related step: 44

FORMALITY

The type of language which is used in academic writing should be formal and appropriate – for example, no slang words. Formal language will often come from Latin.

Related entries: Anglo-Saxon, Latin, slang

Related step: 21

FOSSILIZATION

The process by which a language mistake becomes 'normalized', and consequently very difficult to remove from your own language.

Related entries: avoidance, mother-tongue influence, transfer

Related steps: 11, 48

FRENCH

A language which, like Latin, has had an important influence on the vocabulary of English (especially from the 11th century onwards). Many French-derived terms are considered formal.

Related entries: Anglo-Saxon, Latin

FRONT-WEIGHTED

See WEIGHTING.

GERUND

The usage of a verb as a noun (in its ~*ing* form). For example, 'I enjoy *writing*'.

Related entry: infinitive

Related step: 27

HAND MOVEMENT

The use of your hands to help convey meaning when speaking.

Related entries: body language, eye contact

Related step: 1

HARVARD SYSTEM

A type of referencing system, also known as the Author–Date system.

Related entry: referencing

Related step: 5

HEDGING LANGUAGE
Language which reduces the strength and directness of a particular claim, such as modal adverbs (e.g., *probably*) and particular verbs (e.g., *seem*). Hedging language is a particularly common aspect of academic writing.

Related entries: adverb, modal verb

Related steps: 23, 32

IDIOM
A phrase or clause whose meaning is not literal. For example, *to throw in the towel*, taken from boxing, means 'to quit'. Idioms should not generally be used in academic writing.

Related entry: figurative language

Related steps: 21, 39

INDEPENDENT CLAUSE
A clause which can exist by itself and requires no other information to support it (contrasting with a subordinate clause).

Related entries: clause, subordinate clause

Related steps: 26, 30, 43

INDEX
The section at the end of a book which details its main themes. An index can help you pinpoint the pages of a book which you want to read. Indexes are usually alphabetical, so that you can find the term as easily as possible.

Related entry: table of contents

Related step: 6

INFINITIVE
The basic form of the verb, usually preceeded by *to* (e.g., *to run*). There are four types of infinitive in English: the perfect (*to have* + past participle), the continuous (*to be* + present participle), the perfect continuous (*to have been* + present participle) and the passive (*to be* + past participle). Sometimes an infinitive is 'bare', i.e., it is not preceded by *to* (e.g., *she can run*).

Related entry: gerund

Related steps: 27, 42

INFLECTION
A change in the form of a word, especially the endings, according to its grammatical function in the sentence.

Related steps: 11, 40

INFORMATION-MANAGEMENT SYSTEMS
Ways in which you can organize your time more efficiently, e.g., using lists, Gantt charts, electronic calendars.

Related step: 12

INTONATION
The rise and fall of the voice in speaking so as to affect meaning.

Related entries: pitch, tempo, tone

Related step: 1

INTRANSITIVE VERB
See **TRANSITIVE VERB**.

INTRODUCTION
The opening section of your essay. In shorter essays, the introduction will only be one paragraph; in longer essays, it may be more.

Related entries: conclusion, main body, thesis statement

Related steps: 2, 19

IRREGULAR VERB
See **REGULAR VERB**.

JARGON
Language or terminology which is used by a particular group. Jargon can show that you 'belong' to a specific academic community; however, overuse of jargon is considered poor academic style.

Related entries: academic community, audience

Related step: 36

KEYWORDS
Those words in a text which are frequently repeated and which are vital to know if you want to understand the text.

Related steps: 6, 9, 33

LANGUAGE FRAME

A fixed set of structure words which can be used in a number of different situations (e.g., *according to X*).

Related entry: fixed phrase/expression

Related step: 33

LATIN

The language originally spoken by the Romans, which had considerable influence on English, particularly on its vocabulary. Words which come from Latin are often considered to be formal.

Related entries: Anglo-Saxon, formality, French

Related step: 1

LEGEND

Information which explains the various components of a graph.

Related entry: axes

Related step: 35

LEXICAL BUNDLE

A type of fixed phrase.

Related entry: fixed phrase/expression

Related steps: 38, 39

LINKING DEVICE/WORD

A linking device joins text together, thereby improving both the cohesion and coherence of writing. These are usually adverbs or conjunctions. Linking devices may join either clauses or sentences.

Related entries: adverb, clause, coherence, cohesion, conjunction

Related steps: 1, 30, 34

LOGICAL FALLACY

A mistake which arises from poor reasoning and argumentation, which may lead to an incorrect conclusion.

Related entry: argument

Related step: 25

MAIN BODY

The middle part of an essay, which is neither the introduction nor the conclusion.

Related entries: conclusion, introduction

Related steps: 2, 13

MAIN VERB

The verb in a sentence which carries the main meaning.

Related entries: auxiliary verb, modal verb

Related step: 11

MID-POSITION

One of the positions in which an adverb can come in a sentence – either between the subject and the verb, or immediately after *be* when used as a main verb.

Related entry: adverb

Related step: 17

MIND MAP

A diagram which represents ideas linked to a central concept. Mind maps are useful techniques for generating ideas when planning an essay.

Related step: 14

MODAL VERB

A type of auxiliary verb which indicates something about a speaker's opinion or attitude towards a main verb (e.g., *might*, *could*, *must*).

Related entry: auxiliary verb

Related steps: 23, 42

MOTHER-TONGUE INFLUENCE

The extent to which your mother tongue (your first language) can influence the way you learn English. Often this influence is negative, though it can also be positive.

Related entry: transfer

Related steps: 11, 39, 40, 47

NECESSARY AND SUFFICIENT CONDITIONS

Term used in critical thinking. A *necessary* condition is one without which something could not happen (e.g., being female is necessary for giving birth). A *sufficient* condition is one where, if a particular situation is achieved, a particular outcome will follow (e.g., a lack of water is sufficient for a plant to die).

Related step: 8

NEGATIVE TRANSFER

See TRANSFER.

NICHE
The specific area of research on which you are focusing.

Related step: 22

NOMINALIZATION
The process of forming a noun from a verb or adjective.

Related entries: content word, noun phrase, word class

Related step: 24

NOUN PHRASE
A phrase in which the main word is a noun. Information may be added before a noun phrase (e.g., an adjective) or afterwards (e.g., a relative clause).

Related entries: phrase, postmodification, prepositional phrase, relative clause, verb phrase

Related steps: 2, 9, 40

OBJECTIVITY
An impartial, unbiased attitude which is based on evidence and analysis. Subjectivity, by contrast, indicates an attitude which comes only from an individual's thoughts and feelings.

Related entries: bias, vested interest

Related step: 22

ONLINE CORPUS
A collection of academic essays which can be searched electronically. Searching an online corpus can be useful to see if a particular word or phrase is commonly used in academic writing.

Related steps: 23, 32, 35, 36, 37, 40

PARAPHRASING
Rewriting text from another piece of writing, using your own words.

Related entries: quotation, referencing, summarizing

Related step: 4

PASSIVE VOICE
See VOICE.

PASSIVE VOCABULARY
The group of words which you are able to *understand* (either in listening or reading) but not use when speaking or writing.

Related entry: active vocabulary

Related steps: 30, 35

PEER-REVIEWED ARTICLE
An article which has been evaluated and checked by experts in the relevant field.

Related step: 7

PERSONAL LEARNING STYLE
The different ways in which people learn languages, e.g., some people are 'visual' learners (i.e., they learn best when presented with images), while others are 'auditory' learners (i.e., they learn more through listening).

Related step: 36

PHRASAL VERB
A type of verb composed of a main verb and one or more preposition (e.g., *look for/look into*). Academic writing tends to prefer one-word verbs (e.g., *search/investigate*).

Related entries: formality, preposition

Related steps: 21, 38

PHRASE
A group of words that forms a component of a sentence.

Related entries: noun phrase, prepositional phrase, verb phrase

Related steps: 1, 9, 21, 33, 37, 39

PITCH
The way in which a particular syllable or word is given prominence or emphasis in a sentence.

Related entries: tempo, tone

Related steps: 1, 43

PLAGIARISM
Academic theft: the act of stealing another person's idea and pretending that it is your own. There are very strict penalties for plagiarism in British universities.

Related entries: accidental plagiarism, paraphrasing, referencing, summarizing

Related steps: 3, 4

POSITION
The writer's attitude towards the subject matter.

Related step: 8

POSITIVE TRANSFER
See **TRANSFER**.

POSTMODIFICATION
Where a phrase (often in the form of a relative clause) follows a noun, providing more specific information about the noun.

Related entries: phrase, relative clause

Related step: 44

PREMISE
A statement on which an argument is based, and which may lead to a conclusion.

Related entries: argument, logical fallacy, necessary and sufficient condition

Related steps: 8, 25

PREPOSITION
A word or group of words used before a noun/pronoun to show place, position, time or method (e.g., *at, on, in*).

Related entries: phrasal verb, prepositional phrase, structure words

Related steps: 11, 28, 39, 40

PREPOSITIONAL PHRASE
A phrase which has a preposition (or prepositions) as its main component.

Related entries: noun phrase, preposition, verb phrase

Related step: 40

PROOFREADING SYMBOLS
A specific set of symbols used by proofreaders which indicate problems in the text in areas such as layout, punctuation and grammar.

Related step: 48

QUANTITY WORD
A kind of determiner which precedes a noun, and says something about its quantity (e.g., *any, some*).

Related entry: determiner

Related step: 44

QUOTING
Using the exact words from somebody else's writing in your own essay.

Related entries: paraphrasing, plagiarism, referencing, summarizing

Related step: 4

READING LIST
The set of books which your university recommends that you read for a particular module/course.

Related step: 6

REFERENCING
The mechanism by which you show the source of your quotations, paraphrases and summaries. Referencing is an important tool for reducing the possibility of plagiarism. There are several different referencing systems.

Related entries: Harvard system, paraphrasing, plagiarism, quotation, summarizing

Related steps: 2, 5

REFLECTIVE WRITING
The kind of writing which you do only for yourself, whereby you think about what you have learnt in order to improve in the future. This may often be in note or diary form.

Related step: 16

REGISTER
The level and style of a piece of writing (or speech) appropriate to the situation in which it is used.

Related step: 21

REGULAR VERB
A type of verb which follows the *~ed* pattern when forming past forms (e.g., *look ~ looked*). Irregular verbs have various past forms (e.g., *go ~ went*).

Related entry: main verb

Related step: 41

Relative clause

A type of subordinate clause, often starting with *which*, *that* or *who*, which provides additional information about a noun phrase.

Related entries: noun phrase, relative pronoun, subordinate clause

Related steps: 2, 33, 44

Relative pronoun

A word which introduces a relative clause. The relative pronouns used in English are *who*, *whom*, *which*, *whose* and *that*.

Related entry: relative clause

Related steps: 26, 28

Rhetorical question

A question for which no answer is expected. Its main function is to highlight or emphasize a particular point (e.g., *So what is the reason for this?*). Note that question marks are still needed for rhetorical questions. Rhetorical questions are more common in spoken English.

Related step: 21

Root

The root is the base form of a word. Words with the same base form are in the same word family, e.g., noun *sign*; verb *signify*; adjective *significant*; adverb *significantly*).

Related entry: word class

Related steps: 9, 29, 36

Scan-reading

The act of quickly reading a text looking for specific information (e.g., a particular name or data).

Related entries: active reading, skim-reading

Related step: 9

Scepticism

To adopt a questioning attitude towards information. The British university system has this concept at its centre.

Related step: 8

Shorthand

An abbreviated form of writing which can be particularly useful for taking notes quickly.

Related step: 10

Signposting language

Words which indicate to the reader the direction in which a text is going and can help guide him/her through (e.g., *as mentioned above*, *this said*).

Related entries: authorial comment, linking device

Related steps: 9, 30

Skim-reading

The act of reading through a piece of writing quickly in order to understand the main point.

Related entries: active reading, scan-reading

Related step: 9

Slang

Very informal words and expressions which should be avoided in academic writing.

Related entry: formality

Related step: 21

Stance

An author's position on or attitude towards an idea.

Related entries: audience, authorial comment, stance adverbial

Related step: 24

Stance adverbial

An adverb used as the first word of a sentence which provides a general comment on the whole sentence. For example, *Clearly*, *it can be seen that …*

Related entry: adverb, stance

Related step: 45

Stream of consciousness

A style of writing which is unedited – as if the ideas have come directly from your brain without any changes.

Related step: 14

Stress

To pronounce a word or part of a word (syllable) with greater force than other words or syllables.

Related entry: emphasis

Related step: 1

STRUCTURE WORD

A class of words, such as prepositions and conjunctions, which have no meaning by themselves. They only have a meaning when combined with a content word. Structure words help glue language together.

Related entries: content word, preposition, syntax

Related steps: 2, 9, 37, 38, 39

SUBHEADINGS

Mini-titles which may appear in a text, to provide an ongoing summary of the contents.

Related entry: title

Related step: 9

SUBJECT–VERB–OBJECT

The basic order of words in English, as well as many other languages (e.g., Chinese, Russian, Thai). Some languages have a different basic word order.

Related entries: voice, word order

Related steps: 11, 17, 22, 26, 41

SUBJECTIVITY

See **OBJECTIVITY**.

SUBORDINATE CLAUSE

A clause which is not a complete sentence. A subordinate clause must be linked to an independent clause to have meaning.

Related entries: clause, independent clause, subordinating conjunction

Related steps: 26, 30

SUBORDINATING CONJUNCTION

A conjunction which links a subordinate clause to an independent clause. Common examples include *although*, *because*, *until* and *while*.

Related entries: conjunction, coordinating conjunction, independent clause, subordinate clause

Related step: 26

SUMMARIZING

Condensing whole paragraphs, pages, articles or even books to provide a short account of the most important facts or features.

Related entries: paraphrasing, quotation, referencing

Related step: 4

SUPERLATIVE

The form of an adjective (or adverb) that expresses the highest degree of something (e.g., *the biggest/longest/most interesting*).

Related entry: comparative

Related step: 35

SYNONYMS

Words which have a similar but not identical meaning.

Related entry: paraphrasing

Related step: 4

SYNTAX

The rules which govern the way words and phrases are put together to form sentences, including aspects such as grammar and word order.

Related entry: word order

Related steps: 26, 47

TABLE OF CONTENTS

The part of a book which provides an overview of what it contains.

Related entry: index

Related step: 6

TARGET LANGUAGE

The foreign language, or parts of it, which you are in the process of learning.

Related step: 36

TASK MANAGEMENT

The way in which you can organize your time according to a particular task, i.e., thinking and planning all the specific stages which are required.

Related step: 12

TAUTOLOGY
Repetition of words or phrases with essentially the same meaning consecutively, e.g., *final result*, *absolute beginning*.

Related steps: 30, 35, 37

TEMPO
The speed at which somebody speaks.

Related entries: intonation, pitch

Related steps: 1, 43

TEXT ENGLISH
The abbreviated, restricted type of written English which is commonly used on mobile phones. This is not acceptable in academic English.

Related entries: formality, slang

Related steps: 1, 21

THESIS STATEMENT
The sentence in your introduction which states your overall position.

Related entries: introduction, position

Related steps: 15, 19, 20

TITLE
Heading which provides an overview of an essay or other piece of writing.

Related entry: subheadings

Related steps: 9, 13

TONE
The way in which something is said. Tone may indicate the stance of the writer or speaker.

Related entries: pitch, position, stance

Related steps: 1, 43

TOPIC SENTENCE
The sentence which provides an overview of the whole paragraph. The topic sentence is usually the first sentence in a paragraph.

Related steps: 13, 15, 20

TRANSFER
Where speakers apply rules from their mother tongue to the new language which they are learning. Transfer may be positive (i.e., may help understanding) or, more often, negative.

Related entries: avoidance, fossilization, mother-tongue influence

Related step: 11

TRANSITIVE VERB
A type of verb which requires a direct object (e.g., *give*, *eat*, *see*). Intransitive verbs, however, require no object (e.g., *sleep*, *arrive*, *sit*).

Related step: 41

UMBRELLA TERM
A broad, wide-ranging term which categorizes ideas. For example, economics, philosophy, law, etc., could be grouped under the umbrella term *field* or *subject*.

Related steps: 29, 33

UNCOUNTABLE NOUN
A noun which cannot be preceded by a number (i.e., it cannot be counted). Examples include *air*, *water*, *flour*.

Related step: 44

UNIVERSITY PRESS
The publishing division of a university which often produces high-quality, well-researched academic books. Two particularly well-known university presses are Cambridge University Press (CUP) and Oxford University Press (OUP).

Related entry: vanity publishing

Related step: 6

VAGUENESS
Language which is not used in a precise or specific way. Words such as *things* and *stuff* which are common in spoken language have no place in academic writing.

Related entry: ambiguity

Related steps: 1, 21, 37

VANITY PUBLISHING

A kind of publishing where people pay their own money for their books to be published. The academic quality of such books should be questioned.

Related entries: university press

Related step: 6

VERB PHRASE

A phrase whose main component is a verb. A common type of verb phrase in academic writing is verb + adverb (e.g., *go quickly*).

Related entries: noun phrase, prepositional phrase

Related steps: 9, 11, 33, 34, 40

VESTED INTEREST

Where somebody has a particular personal interest in an issue which might influence their judgement.

Related entry: bias

Related step: 8

VOICE

The form of a verb which shows whether the subject of a sentence performs the action (active voice) or is affected by it (passive voice). The active is the more common, but in academic English the passive is used frequently as well. Verbs which are in the active voice follow the subject–verb–object word order. The passive, however, follows an object–verb–subject order.

Related entry: subject–verb–object

Related steps: 2, 4, 23, 41

WEIGHTING

English tends to be an end-weighted language, meaning that new/detailed information comes at the end of the sentence. Occasionally, front-weighting may also be used for emphasis or variety.

Related step: 17

WORD CLASS

A group of words which have the same grammatical properties. The major word classes in English are nouns, verbs, adjectives, adverbs, prepositions, conjunctions and pronouns.

Related entries: adverb, conjunction, preposition

Related step: 4

WORD ORDER

The order in which words appear in a sentence. For example, in English, prepositions precede nouns, and auxiliary verbs come before main verbs.

Related entries: auxiliary verb, preposition, subject–verb–object

Related steps: 11, 26

APPENDIX 1: DOCUMENT LIST

Step 6

Document 1: Source analysis

Source	Relevant?	Authoritative?	Recent?	Reliable?	Comments	Read?

APPENDIX 1: DOCUMENT LIST

Step 9
Document 2: Pre-reading checklist

1. *Read the title* and predict what the text will focus on.	
2. *Write down two to three bullet points* about what you want to learn from this text.	<ul><li></li><li></li><li></li></ul>
3. *Read the topic sentence* (the first sentence of the paragraph). What is the focus going to be?	

APPENDIX 1: DOCUMENT LIST

Step 10

Document 3: Blank note-taking form

Topic		Author(s)	
Relevance		Publication year	

Summary	Main notes

APPENDIX 1: DOCUMENT LIST

Step 11

Document 4: Analysis of the influence of your mother tongue on learning English

Area	Academic English	My language	Positive/negative transfer?
Verbs	12 x verb forms (3 x tenses, 4 x aspects); active/passive voice		
Articles	Frequent (c. 10% of words used); definite and indefinite		
Word order	Subject–Verb–Object the norm		
Choice of vocabulary	Words from different sources, especially native Anglo-Saxon; French; Latin		
Spelling	Spelling and sound do not necessarily match		
Sentence length	Shorter, more concise sentences generally preferred		

APPENDIX 1: DOCUMENT LIST

Step 18

Document 5: Paragraph self-evaluation

Factor	Guideline target	Self-feedback
Length	c. 100–150 words	
Unity	One central idea	
Transition	Is it linked to the previous/next paragraph?	
Topic sentence	Is it clear and well-written?	
Supporting sentences	Do they develop the topic sentence sufficiently?	
Summary sentence	Does it reflect the main theme?	

APPENDIX 1: DOCUMENT LIST

Step 18
Document 6: Paragraph step-by-step guide

Sentence type	Your sentence
Transition sentence	•
Topic sentence	•
Supporting sentences (c. 3–5)	•
Summary sentence	•
Transition sentence	•

APPENDIX 1: DOCUMENT LIST

Step 19

Document 7: Planning your introduction

Interesting opening statement	
Definition of terms	
Quotation	
Thesis statement	
Outline of sections	

APPENDIX 2: EXTENSION ACTIVITIES

Step 7

Activity 1: Using the Internet for research

Complete the following sentences in your own words.

1. Wikipedia is ...., but ....

   ....

2. Anyone can set up an Internet site. Therefore, ...

   ....

3. Although it is generally easier to search for information online, you must ....

   ....

4. It is difficult to identify whether information on the Internet is academic or not because

   ....

Model answers on page 246.

Step 8

Activity 2: Challenging the specialists

Just because a specialist in a subject says something, this does not mean you cannot challenge what has been said. Consider the following claims and criticize them accordingly:

- 'Democracy passes into despotism.' (Plato)

- 'Women have no sense of justice.' (Arthur Schopenhauer)

- 'If there were no God, it would have been necessary to invent him.' (Voltaire)

- 'All socialism involves slavery.' (Herbert Spencer)

- 'Businessmen are the one group that distinguishes capitalism and the American way of life from the totalitarian statism that is swallowing the rest of the world.' (Ayn Rand)

APPENDIX 2: EXTENSION ACTIVITIES

Step 33

Activity 3: Defining words

Define the following words. Your language should be as specific and precise as possible.

The words come from a range of academic disciplines.
1. oceanography
2. jurisprudence
3. history
4. virus
5. dialect

Sample definitions are provided on page 246.

Step 42

Activity 4: Modal verbs in context

Fill each gap below with an appropriate modal verb.

1. If this occurs, it _____ lead to many further problems.

2. It _____ be argued that Stone (2004) follows the same line.

3. The machine _____ be connected as stipulated, otherwise it will not function properly.

4. This research is extremely important and _____ lead to many new applications.

5. The results _____ have been more revealing, but the data were imperfect.

6. If the data had been more carefully analyzed, Smith (2002) _____ not have misinterpreted the main argument.

Answers on page 246.

APPENDIX 2: EXTENSION ACTIVITIES

Answers and sample definitions

Activity 1: Using the Internet for research (model answers)

1. Wikipedia is *a good place to start your research,* but *you should not rely on it completely.*
2. Anyone can set up an Internet site. Therefore, *it is unlikely to have been peer-reviewed and so the content may be inaccurate.*
   Anyone can set up an Internet site. Therefore, *the chances of the source being biased are increased.*
3. Although it is generally easier to search for information online, you must *employ good note-taking skills to ensure you do not accidentally plagiarize information.*
4. It is difficult to identify whether information on the Internet is academic or not because *anyone can set up an Internet site and post material.*

Activity 3: Defining words

Oceanography
- 'The scientific study of phenomena found in the world's oceans.' (www.babylon.com/define/48/Geography-Dictionary.html)
- 'The branch of science dealing with physical and biological aspects of the oceans.' (Word net 2.0)

Jurisprudence
- 'The philosophy or science of law.' (www.thefreedictionary.com)
- 'The branch of philosophy concerned with the law and the principles that lead courts to make the decisions they do.' (www.wordnetweb.princeton.edu/perl/webwn)
- 'Jurisprudence is about the nature of law and justice. It embraces studies and theories from a range of disciplines such as history, sociology, political science, philosophy, psychology and even economics.' (Ratnapala, 2006: iii)

History
- '"History" in academic study is either the study of the past or the product of our attempts to understand the past, rather than the past itself.' (http://europeanhistory.about.com)
- 'A chronological record of significant events (as affecting a nation or institution) often including an explanation of their causes.' (http://www.merriam-webster.com/)
- 'History is a confused heap of facts.' (Lord Chesterfield)

Virus
- 'Any of a large group of submicroscopic infective agents that are regarded either as extremely simple microorganisms or as extremely complex molecules, that typically contain a protein coat surrounding an RNA or DNA core of genetic material but no semipermeable membrane, that are capable of growth and multiplication only in living cells, and that cause various important diseases in humans, animals, or plants.' (www.merriam-webster.com)
- 'A virus is a small infectious agent that can replicate only inside the living cells of organisms.' (http://en.wikipedia.org)
- 'Viruses are ubiquitous companions of cellular life forms: it appears that every cellular organism studied has its own viruses or, at least, virus-like selfish genetic elements.' (Koonin et al., 2006)

Dialect
- 'One of the subordinate forms or varieties of a language arising from local peculiarities of vocabulary, pronunciation, and idiom. (In relation to modern languages usually *spec.* A variety of speech differing from the standard or literary "language"; a provincial method of speech, as in "speakers of dialect".) Also in a wider sense applied to a particular language in its relation to the family of languages to which it belongs.' (www.oed.com)
- 'A dialect is distinguished by its vocabulary, grammar, and pronunciation (phonology, including prosody). Where a distinction can be made only in terms of pronunciation, the term *accent* is appropriate, not *dialect*.' (http://en.wikipedia.org)
- 'A language is a dialect with an army and navy.' (Max Weinreich)

Activity 4: Modal verbs in context

1. If this occurs, it may lead to many further problems.
2. It can be argued that Stone (2004) follows the same line.
3. The machine must be connected as stipulated, otherwise it will not function properly.
4. This research is extremely important and will lead to many new applications.
5. The results could have been more revealing, but the data were imperfect.
6. If the data had been more carefully analyzed, Smith (2002) would not have misinterpreted the main argument.

APPENDIX 3: ADDITIONAL INFORMATION

Step 4

Common academic words with the same root form

Here are 20 sets of words used in academic English that have a common root. Related noun, verb, adjective and adverb forms are shown. Note: (a) where a particular form does not exist or is rarely used, the box has been left blank; (b) in some cases, more than one option may be possible.

Noun	Verb	Adjective	Adverb
analysis	analyze	analytical	analytically
association	associate	associated	–
consideration	consider	considerate	considerately
context	contextualize	contextual	contextually
creation	create	creative	creatively
development	develop	developmental	developmentally
emphasis	emphasize	emphatic	emphatically
exclusion	exclude	exclusive	exclusively
evidence	evidence	evident	evidently
influence	influence	influential	influentially
method	–	methodological	methodologically
prime	prime	primary	primarily
procedure	proceed	procedural	procedurally
selection	select	selective	selectively
significance	signify	significant	significantly
strategy	strategize	strategic	strategically
sufficiency	suffice	sufficient	sufficiently
symbol	symbolize	symbolic	symbolically
theory	theorise	theoretical	theoretically
transformation	transform	transformative/ transformational	–

Step 4

Passive voice

The table below lists passive forms of the verb that are common in academic English (note that the perfect continuous has not been included since it is extremely rare).

Sentences in the passive voice are made up of an appropriate auxiliary construction with *be* followed by the past participle of the main verb. Note that in the table, the subject of each sentence is in brackets – in passive sentences the subject is not essential but may be used to clarify meaning.

Verb form	Object	Auxiliary construction (with *be*)	Main verb (past participle)	Subject
Present simple	The data	are	understood	(by everyone)
Past simple	The idea	was	challenged	(by specialists)
Future simple	The paper	will be	disseminated	(by the journal)
Present continuous	The matter	is being	researched	(by scientists)
Past continuous	The specimen	was being	dissected	(by postgraduates)
Future continuous	The essay	will be being	written	(by the student)
Present perfect	A system	has been	developed	(by the company)
Past perfect	The position	had been	accepted	(by the director)
Future perfect	A plan	will have been	created	(by the organizers)

APPENDIX 3: ADDITIONAL INFORMATION

Step 9

High-frequency prefixes in academic English

Prefix	Meaning	Examples
a~, an~	not, without, lacking in	anarchy 'without order' anonymous 'with a name that is not known'
ab~	away	absent 'not present' abduction 'taking somebody away illegally'
acro~	high	acrobat 'entertainer who balances on high ropes' acropolis 'castle on a hill in an ancient Greek city'
aero~	air	aeroplane 'a flying vehicle with wings' aeronautics 'the science of building and flying aircraft'
alter~	another	alternative 'another option' alter ego 'another personality'
alti~	high	altitude 'height above sea level' altimeter 'instrument for showing height above sea level'
anglo-	English	anglocentric 'focused on England' anglophone 'a person who speaks English'
ante-	before	a.m. (*ante meridian*) 'before 12 o'clock midday' antenatal 'during pregnancy (i.e., before birth)'
anti~	against	antisocial 'harmful or annoying to other people' anticlockwise 'opposite of clockwise'
auto~	self	autobiography 'biography written by oneself' automobile 'vehicle that moves under its own power – a car'
bi~	two	bicycle 'two-wheeled road vehicle that you ride using pedals' biped 'animal with two feet'
bio~	life	biology 'the study of living things' biography 'the story of a person's life'
cent~	hundred	centimetre 'one-hundredth of a metre' century 'one hundred years'
co~	together	cooperation 'working together' coordinate (v) 'enable people to work together'
con~	with, together	congregation 'group of people gathered together in church to worship God' congress 'large meeting of representatives of different groups'
contr~	against, opposite	contradict 'say that something someone said is wrong, and the opposite is true' controversy 'public argument over something people widely disagree about'
crypto~	secret, hidden	cryptography 'the art of writing or solving codes' cryptogram 'secret message'
culp~	guilty, at fault	culprit 'someone who has done something wrong or illegal' culpable 'blameworthy'
de~	opposite of, removing something	decelerate 'reduce speed, get slower' decentralization 'to move organizational power away from the centre'
dec~	ten	December 'tenth month of the year (in old calendar)' decimal 'counted in units of ten'

Step 9

Prefix	Meaning	Examples
demo~	people	democracy 'government of the people' demographics 'data relating to the population'
dis~	not, the opposite of	disinformation 'false information that is given deliberately' disprove 'show that something is wrong or false'
dynam~	movement, power	dynamics 'science of the forces involved in movement' dynamite 'a type of explosive'
eco~	home	economy 'domestic finance' ecosystem 'creatures living in a particular area considered in relation to their physical environment'
ethno~	nation, race, people	ethnic 'connected with or belonging to a nation, race or people' ethnology 'the scientific study of human races'
eu~	good	eulogy 'speech or piece of writing praising someone' euphemism 'an indirect expression referring to something unpleasant, sometimes to make it seem more acceptable'
ex~	former, previous	ex-wife 'former wife' ex-president 'former president'
extra~	outside, more than usual	extra time 'time at the end of a sports match' extraterrestrial 'connected with life outside planet Earth'
hydro~	water	hydrogen 'gas combined with oxygen to form water' hydroelectric 'using water power to obtain electricity'
hyper~	more than normal	hyperactive 'too active' hypersensitive 'too sensitive'
hypo~	below, under	hypodermic syringe 'a syringe that injects under the skin' hypocrite 'someone who pretends to have moral standards that they do not actually have'
in~	not	inability 'the fact of not being able to do something' inaudible 'not able to be heard'
inter~	between	intervention 'to become involved in a situation in order to improve it' interlocutor 'a person taking part in a conversation'
intra~	within	intravenous 'into a vein' intranet 'computer network within an organization'
kilo~	thousand	kilogram 'one thousand grams' kilometre 'one thousand metres'
mal~	bad	malnutrition 'poor condition of health due to lack of (good) food' malice 'feeling of hatred for someone that causes a desire to harm them'
maxi~	most	maximum 'greatest amount, size, speed, etc., that is possible, recorded or allowed' maximal 'as great or large as possible'
mega~	million (lit) large (colloq)	megawatt 'a million watts' megalith 'very large stone'
micro~	small (colloq)	microgram 'a millionth of a gram' microchip 'a very small piece of a material that is a semiconductor'
milli~	thousandth	millimetre 'a thousandth of a metre' millilitre 'a thousandth of a litre'

Step 9

High-frequency prefixes in academic English – *continued*

Prefix	Meaning	Examples
mini~	small/tiny	miniskirt 'very short skirt' minimum 'smallest that is possible or allowed'
mis~	dislikes, bad, wrong	misanthrope 'person who hates and avoids other people' misbehaviour 'bad behaviour'
mono~	one, single	monorail 'railway system in which trains travel along a single-rail track' monotony 'boring lack of variety'
multi~	many	multiple 'involving many different people or things' multilingual 'speaking many languages'
non~	not	nondescript 'having no interesting or unusual features' nonsense 'ideas, statements or beliefs you think are ridiculous or untrue'
omni~	all	omnipotent 'all-powerful' omnivore 'animal or person that eats all types of food'
out~	greater, better, further	outrun 'run faster or further than someone' outperform 'perform better than someone'
post~	after, following	postnatal 'after giving birth' post-op 'after a surgical operation'
pre~	before	prediction 'a statement of what you think will happen' preview 'to see a film or show before it is shown to the general public'
pro~	in favour of, supporting	promote 'to help something happen or develop' propose 'to put forward a plan'
re~	again	redo 'do something again' review 'carefully look at something again'
retro~	backwards	retrospective 'thinking about something that happened in the past' retrograde 'returning to how something was in the past'
semi~	half	semi-detached 'house joined to one other house by a shared wall' semicolon 'half a colon'
sub~	below, under, less than	substandard 'not as good as normal' subway 'path underneath a road' (BrE); 'underground train' (AmE)
super~	above, over	superhuman 'having greater power or knowledge than is normal' supersonic 'faster than the speed of sound'
tele~	far, distant	television 'device for watching pictures from far away' telephone 'device for speaking to somebody far away'
trans~	across	transfer 'move from one place to another' transatlantic 'crossing the Atlantic Ocean'
tri~	three	triangle 'flat shape with three straight sides and three angles' triptych 'picture in three panels'
ultra~	extremely	ultraviolet light 'very high-frequency light' ultrasonic 'higher-pitched than humans can hear'
un~	not, the opposite of	unattractive 'not attractive' undeniable 'cannot be denied'
uni~	one, single	unicycle 'cycle with one wheel' uniform 'special set of clothes worn by all members of an organization'

APPENDIX 3: ADDITIONAL INFORMATION

Step 9

High-frequency suffixes in academic English

Suffix	Meaning	Examples
~able	can be, has the quality of	This piece of equipment is still *usable*. I am being very *reasonable* about this.
~arch(y)	rule, leadership	Queen Elizabeth II is Britain's current *monarch*. *Anarchy* is a situation in a country, organization, etc. where nobody is in charge.
~athlon	athletic event	She's competing in the Olympic *heptathlon*. The *decathlon* is made up of ten events.
~cide	killing	They think it was *suicide* – that he killed himself. He works in the police *homicide* department.
~cracy	government, rule	In a *democracy* people can vote how they like. An *aristocracy* is the rule of many by a few.
~dom	condition or state of	I value my *freedom* above anything else. I get bored easily – my *boredom* threshold is very low.
~duce	bring, lead	I'd like to *introduce* you to my friend. I'm trying to *reduce* the amount I smoke.
~ess	female	Can you ask the *waitress* for our bill? The air *stewardess* will show you to your seat.
~ful	full of	Are you *hopeful* about your interview? I am rather *fearful* about this new job.
~fusion	mixing together	All these ideas have created a lot of *confusion*. When you have a blood *transfusion*, you receive somebody else's blood.
~gress	go, walk	To *regress* means 'to go backwards'. People came to the *congress* from all over the world.
~holic	someone who is addicted to something	I used to be an *alcoholic*, but I don't drink any more. I'm such a *chocoholic* – which is why I'm so fat.
~hood	state or quality of	They were a *brotherhood*, helping each other all the time. *Parenthood* is difficult to begin with, but you get better at looking after your children.
~ics	scientific study of something	*Physics* was his favourite subject at school. *Ballistics* is the study of missiles.
~(i)fy	to make or become	Can you please *clarify* your name and address? The seawall needed to be *fortified* against higher tides.
~illion	large number	If you are a good businessman, you might earn a *million* dollars. If you are a really good businessman, you might earn a *billion* dollars.
~ism	state or quality of, teachings of	*Alcoholism* is an increasingly serious problem. *Hinduism* is the predominant religion in India.
~ist	member of a profession or business activity	The *receptionist* will be able to help you. You should go to the *chemist* and get something to help your headache.
~ity	quality or state of	Thank God *normality* has returned to the streets. It would be a *calamity* if we were late.

Step 9

High-frequency suffixes in academic English – *continued*

Prefix	Meaning	Examples
~*ium*	metallic element	*Magnesium* and *calcium* are well-known metals.
~*ize* (also ~*ise*)	become, make	It *materialized* from nowhere! Have you *organized* your wedding yet?
~*ject*	throw	Why were you *ejected* from the meeting? The proposal was *rejected*.
~*less*	without	My husband is *useless* at buying presents. Why does he look so sad? He is so *joyless*.
~*let*	small, not very important	There's a tiny *droplet* of water on the window. A *hamlet* is a very small village.
~*ly*	in the way mentioned	He ran home very *quickly*. She was *terribly* fat.
~*man*	person	When I grow up I want to be a *policeman*. A *cameraman* filmed the entire wedding.
~*mania*	uncontrollable belief, desire	A *kleptomaniac* can't help stealing things. The dictator was a *megalomaniac* – he loved power.
~*meter* ~*metre* ~*metry*	measurement	A *thermometer* tells us how hot or cold it is. *Geometry* is about the measurement of angles.
~*mit*	send	Marconi successfully *transmitted* a radio message across the Atlantic. How much light do these lamps *emit*?
~*ography* ~*ograph*	writing, study	*Geography* is the study of the Earth. A *tachograph* measures a vehicle's travels.
~*ology* ~*ologist*	concerning study, science of … someone who studies a particular subject	*Theology* is the study of religion. His father was an *archaeologist* who specialized in ancient Egypt.
~*onym*	word, name	'Happy' is a *synonym* of 'cheerful'. 'Happy' is an *antonym* of 'sad'.
~*phile*	a person who likes a particular thing	An *Anglophile* loves all things English. A *Francophile* loves all things French.
~*phobia*	fear	I am *claustrophobic* – I hate being in small spaces. *Agoraphobia* is the fear of open spaces.
~*phone*	to do with sound	Can I use your *telephone* to call a taxi? I would like to live in an *Anglophone* country,
~*plete*	to fill	Have you *completed* that form yet? I am quite *replete*, thank you – I couldn't eat any more.
~*polis*	referring to city or urban area	Tokyo is the largest *metropolis* I have been to. Greek cities were often built around a fortified *acropolis*.
~*port*	to carry people or goods	I like *airports* – they bring people from all over the world. My company *exports* to over 50 countries worldwide.

Step 9

Prefix	Meaning	Examples
~pose	to put	Have you submitted your *proposal* yet? These laws have been *imposed* on us unfairly.
~potent ~potence	having power power	The President can do nothing about the situation – he is *impotent*. Many believe in the *omnipotence* of a mighty God.
~science ~scient	what is in the mind knowing	My *conscience* is clear – I have nothing to be ashamed of. How does the boss know everything that is going on? Is he *omniscient*?
~script	something written	This 2,000-year-old *manuscript* was written with a reed pen. I've written a *transcript* of our meeting with the boss.
~semble	to be like or with other people	Your daughter really *resembles* you. As evening came the crowd started to *assemble*.
~sert	to join	*Insert* the needle into your arm and press the plunger. Why did you *desert* me when I needed you most?
~ship	state or quality of	*Friendship* is so important in this life. The *authorship* of this book is unknown.
~stan	country, land	*Afghanistan* and *Pakistan* are both countries in Asia.
~ster	person of a particular type	A *youngster* is a person less than 18 years old. A *fraudster* is somebody who commits fraud.
~struct	to place, be placed	How was the building *constructed* so fast? It seems it was put up overnight! A fallen tree was *obstructing* the road.
~tain	to hold, keep	I won't *detain* you any longer. I've *obtained* the documents you require.
~th	ordinal number	This is the *fourth* time I have been to Paris. For the *millionth* time, stop exaggerating.
~voke	to call	I *revoke* my promise to you. He hit you because you *provoked* him.
~vore ~vorous	an animal that eats a particular kind of food eating a particular kind of food	*Carnivores* only eat meat. Chimpanzees, like humans, are *omnivorous* – they eat a range of foods.
~ward(s)	in the direction of	I wish I was *homeward* bound. During the 17th century, English settlers headed *westwards*.
~where	location, place	I don't know *anywhere* like this! The key must be *somewhere* – just look for it.
~y	full of, having the quality of	It's a lovely *sunny* day today. He's an extremely *funny* person who makes me laugh all the time.

APPENDIX 3: ADDITIONAL INFORMATION

Step 10

Useful symbols and abbreviations for note-taking

The following symbols and abbreviations are commonly used in written English. You may wish to use them when taking notes yourself.

Symbols

Prefix	Meaning
→	lead(s) to, cause(s)
←	come(s) from, is/are the result of
↑	increase(s), rise(s)
↓	decrease(s), decline(s)
&	and
@	at
/	per
+	in addition, and
−	minus
=	is/are equal to; is/are
≠	is/are not equal to; is/are not
~ or ±	about, approximately
×	times, multiplied by
>	greater than
<	less than
£, $	money; cost, price
∴	therefore
#	number

Abbreviations

Abbreviations	Meaning
w/	with
w/o	without
i.e.	that is
e.g.	for example
etc.	et cetera, and so forth
b/c	because
b/4	before
re:	regarding, about
esp.	especially
min.	minimum
max.	maximum
no.	number
ASAP	as soon as possible
yr	year
c.	circa, about (with dates)
vs	versus, against
Q, A	question, answer
ref.	reference
diff.	difference

APPENDIX 3: ADDITIONAL INFORMATION

Step 13
Sample essay titles

Examples of essay titles from four academic fields are presented below.

Law

1. 'The decision in *R.* (Jackson and others) vs. Attorney-General (2005) can be used to support both the orthodox and the alternative (or new) view of parliamentary sovereignty.' Discuss.
2. Outline the main remedies provided by the Human Rights Act 1998.
3. 'The Human Rights Act 1998 continues to provide a justiciable declaration of rights which gives citizens effective safeguards against the misuse of public power.' Discuss

Health sciences

1. Discuss the process of type 1 hypersensitivity, explaining how it arises, how it is mediated, and the range of pathological symptoms it produces.
2. Explain how certain HLA antigens can predispose the possessor to develop particular diseases. Show, with examples, how this predisposition is detected and quantified and discuss why it might occur.
3. Describe how *Agrobacterium tumefaciens* may be used to engineer commercially useful traits into crop plants.
4. Discuss the mechanisms whereby the integrity of the female reproductive system can be altered by exposure to xenobiotics.
5. Describe how tissues are prepared for light microscopy and discuss process by which dyes bind to the tissues and how this is exploited in clinical histopathology.
6. Discuss the mechanisms of action and problems of drugs used in anaerobic therapy.

Social sciences

1. 'The Cold War was inevitable'. Discuss with reference to competing explanations of the origins of the Cold War.
2. 'The UN Security Council is a relic of the immediate aftermath of the Second World War and as such is ill-suited to the management of security in today's world.' Discuss.
3. Is armed intervention by the international community the best way to deal with large-scale human-rights abuses within states?
4. Outline what you understand by the term 'globalization' and assess its key implications for international politics.
5. Show how competition between land uses in tropical moist forests can result in deforestation.
6. In what ways are virtual communities different from place-based communities?

Humanities

1. 'China in 1600 is the most sophisticated realm on earth'. (Jonathan Spence). Discuss.
2. To what extent can *Yojimbo* (1961) be considered a 'typical' Kurosawa film?
3. In what ways and to what extent does 'refugee studies' differ from 'refugee history'?

APPENDIX 3: ADDITIONAL INFORMATION

Step 14
Brainstorming ideas

Here is additional information about techniques and mechanisms you can use for brainstorming. There are three main categories of brainstorming techniques – those which generate ideas, those which evaluate ideas and those which aggregate ideas.

1. GENERATING IDEAS
To begin with, you want to write all your ideas down as a list so that you can see the scope of your essay. There are two main ways in which you can do this.

A. Creating a list
What is good academic writing?
Structure v. important
Coherence – needs to be logical
Suitable layout
Simple–to–complex style
Linking words (conjunctions) important
Bad things include: v. long sentences, bad punctuation, jargon
Transitional devices

The most basic method for most brainstorming is simply to list ideas that you think will be relevant to your essay. You can do this electronically, although some people find it easier and more effective to write it by hand.

B. Using a cluster diagram
This allows you to develop ideas in a linear fashion (i.e., *x* leads to *y*, which in turn leads to *z*). Drawing a cluster diagram (Figure 1) is useful in that it can allow you can see the flow of ideas. The size and range of your cluster diagram is entirely up to you, depending on how many ideas you have about a particular subject.

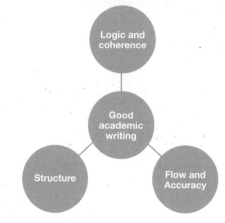

Figure 1: Cluster diagram

2. EVALUATING IDEAS
Having listed your ideas, you want to put them into some kind of order. Here are two ways you can do this.

A. Creating a hierarchy of ideas
In trying to build your argument, it is crucial to know how different ideas relate to each other and what the relationship is between these different ideas. The distinction is not always clear, but to help you identify the hierarchy of ideas you can place them in the following diagram (Figure 2) according to whether they are at the macro-level (general), meso-level (middle) or micro-level (specific). Take the following example looking at logic and coherence (Step 28).

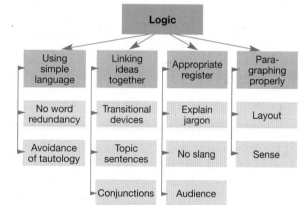

Figure 2: Hierarchy of ideas diagram

B. Assessing the importance of your ideas
One of hardest things to do when confronted with a long list of ideas is to decide which are the most important. Normally, you want to start each section with your strongest or most general idea, and then to work down to less important or more specific levels.

A 'cross diagram', as outlined in Figure 3 on page 258, can help you place each idea at an appropriate point. Note: you can change the label on the *x* and *y* axis accordingly, depending on what type of essay you are writing and the essay's content.

Step 14

Brainstorming ideas – *continued*

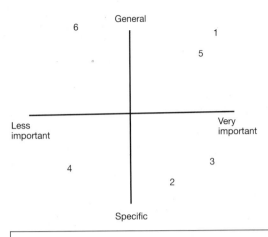

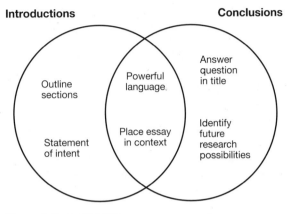

Figure 4: Venn diagram

Selected ideas (adjusted from 'Creating a list', p. 257)
1. Structure
2. Transitional devices
3. Using conjunctions
4. Explaining jargon
5. Logic and coherence
6. Layout

Figure 3: Cross diagram

3. AGGREGATING IDEAS

Once you have a list of *all* your ideas, it becomes easier to see the patterns, themes and links between them. The following two types of diagram help you to categorize and aggregate your ideas.

A. Venn diagram

The Venn diagram is more normally associated with mathematics, but it also provides a useful way to identify the connections between two or more ideas. For example, the diagram in Figure 4 considers introductions and conclusions. If desired, a further circle (e.g., 'body of the essay') could be included, and so on.

This Venn diagram indicates that both introductions and conclusions should include 'powerful language' and should 'place the essay in context', since these items occur in the subset (the overlap between the circles).

B. Logframe

A logframe (Table 1) is a more advanced analytical tool, requiring more thought and consideration than some of the other brainstorming techniques. However, creating a logframe will give you a very good overview of how your essay might develop. A logframe is essentially a table with different categories for the columns and rows. In a logframe you can analyze information both horizontally and vertically; this lets you identify crosscutting themes in your essay. You can use as many rows and columns as you feel appropriate. The headings used in this logframe (which focuses on the essay as a whole) can be used generally. 'Outputs' (what you are aiming to do), 'rationale' (why this is important) and 'areas to cover' (specific items that you will be examining) are all useful analytical functions.

Table 1: Logframe

Cross-cutting themes		Outputs	Rationale	Areas to cover
Sections of the essay	**Structure**	To identify the core components of a well-structured essay.	Without a good structure, essays (however good the content) can be poor.	Mindmaps, logframes, cluster diagrams, Venn diagrams.
	Logic and coherence	To identify how to build your argument.	Convincing arguments must be logical, clear and concise.	Topic sentences, transitional devices, proper paragraphing, simple–to–complex style.
	Flow and accuracy	To keep the essay moving forward, to be readable and to ensure quality.	A good essay is not just about the content, but also the way in which it is presented.	Sentence variation, tautology, circumlocution, punctuation.

APPENDIX 3: ADDITIONAL INFORMATION

Step 15

Sample thesis statements

Here are thesis statements from four academic articles from a range of disciplines.

Law

'For the good of others: censorship and the third-person effect'

This study argues that the existence of a 'third-person effect' in communication is an important factor contributing to pro-censorship attitudes towards media.

Health sciences

'Factors associated with self-care activities among adults in the United Kingdom: a systematic review'

Our aim was to generate hypotheses about who uses self-tests by reviewing evidence for factors that are associated with self-testing and, because of a lack of evidence about self-tests, similar activities.

Social sciences

'The ecological footprint as a key indicator of sustainable tourism'

Despite the undoubted demand for appropriate indicators of ST, these authors argue (p. 365) that research in this area is 'still in its incipient stages', a view echoed by others (e.g., Li, 2004; Miller, 2001; Rebollo and Baidal, 2003).

Humanities

'Change and development in a pluralistic world: the view from the classics'

Building on this insight, we summarize three reasons for the relevance of classic work to the understanding of change, development, and pluralism.

APPENDIX 3: ADDITIONAL INFORMATION

Step 18
Examples of good paragraphs

The following body paragraphs come from academic articles in a range of disciplines.

Law
'For the good of others: censorship and the third-person effect'

The first regression was run with the overall censorship scale as the dependent variable and the corresponding effects gap as the final independent variable (see Table 4). This analysis demonstrated that the media effects gap was significantly related to the willingness to censor even after accounting for the influence of demographic, media use, and attitudinal variables. The conventional variables did account for a considerable amount of variance in the censorship scale: variables included in the first three blocks explained a combined 23 percent of variance in the measure. In total, the four blocks accounted for 26 percent of variance in the measure. All significant relationships were in the expected direction: women were more willing to censor than men, while age, religiosity and conservatism were positively associated with censorship. Consistent with the perspective offered by many researchers, a particularly important, and statistically significant, variable block was individual attitudes.

Health sciences
'Factors associated with self-care activities among adults in the United Kingdom: a systematic review'

A link with poor health was supported by several studies. Using adjusted analyses, the high quality population-based survey found that people with a long-standing illness or who saw their GP more often were more likely to have seen a CAM practitioner recently than other people [11, 12], and a medium quality study found that CAM patients were more likely than GP patients to have psychiatric morbidity [29]. Using unadjusted analyses, a low quality population-based survey found that CAM users had higher GP attendance rates and were more likely to have severe or chronic conditions than non-users [18], and two medium quality studies found that CAM patients were more likely than GP patients to have had a serious illness [30], chronic illness [30] and longer illness [30, 32]. Two medium quality studies also looked at symptom length: one described most Chinese medicine patients as having symptoms for over a year [20], and the other described new CAM patients as having longer symptoms than GP patients, although CAM patients also had lower pain scores [31].

Social sciences
'The ecological footprint as a key indicator of sustainable tourism'

Gössling et al. (2002) provide a component-based framework for the calculation of a leisure tourism EF for the Seychelles, using secondary data sources. These authors found that the per tourist EF to be some 1.9 gha/year (similar to the fair earthshare value of some 2 gha/capita/ year), with an average holiday in the Seychelles equivalent to 17–37% of the annual EF of a citizen of an industrialised country. Well over 90% of the total leisure tourism footprint was found to be due to air travel to and from the destination. Critically, the authors conclude that, in part, the Seychelles maintains a high quality local environment for tourists at the expense of a much larger hinterland, and that traditional approaches used to assess sustainability, such as limits of acceptable change or environmental impact assessment, would fail to provide the required global perspective on the sustainability of tourism activity in the Seychelles. Indeed, focusing on the air travel component, the authors argue (p. 210) that '[t]aking these results seriously, air travel should, from an ecological perspective, be actively discouraged'. The key point here, echoing that made by Gössling et al. (2002), is that locally derived and based indicators of ST are not, by their very nature, capable of providing a global perspective on tourism's resource demands and impacts.

Humanities
'Change and development in a pluralistic world: the view from the classics'

Crozier (1964) carefully analyzed the tendency for bureaucratic organizations to resist change and maintain inertia in a French setting. In a startling anticipation of the punctuated equilibrium model, Crozier described how the rhythm of bureaucratic organization consisted of long periods of reliance on a protective system of rules and regulations punctuated by 'very short periods of crisis and change' (1964: 196). The rules and regulations were maintained with such consistency because they guaranteed a degree of independence from arbitrary authority. To focus only on this apparent stability, however, was to omit a 'distinctive and necessary element of the bureaucratic system' (Crozier, 1964: 196).

APPENDIX 3: ADDITIONAL INFORMATION

Step 19

Examples of good introductions

The introductions below come from four academic articles, representing a range of disciplines. **Note:** These introductions have been taken from journals, and may be longer and include more paragraphs than you would be expected to write in your essays.

Law
'For the good of others: censorship and the third-person effect'

The first amendment to the U.S. Constitution states that Congress shall make no law abridging the freedom of speech. Yet, despite this amendment, there appears to be a growing trend towards the support of censorship for several types of communication. These areas include: pornography (Ritts and Engbretson, 1991, Cowan, 1992), books (Wellborn, 1982, Yudof, 1983), the press (Schwartz, 1977, Picard, 1982), television violence (Rowland, 1983) and neo-fascism (Hentoff, 1989, Brown, 1990).

Expectations about the potentially 'dangerous' effects of communication messages seem to lie at the heart of the censorship phenomenon. One area of research that may shed some light on pro-censorship attitudes is the third-person effect (Davison, 1983). According to the third-person effect hypothesis, individuals exposed to a mass media message will expect the communication to have a greater effect on others than on themselves. Individuals assume that the effects of communication 'will not be on "me" or "you", but on "them" – the third-persons' (Davison, 1983: 3). Furthermore, it has been suggested that the observer's expectation of the communication's impact may lead that individual to take some action. The third-person effect may lead to greater support for media censorship because of exaggerated expectations about media effects on others.

Advocates for censorship seem particularly likely to be overestimating the effects of media on others – the 'gullible' public. This study argues that the existence of a third-person effect in communication is an important factor contributing to pro-censorship attitudes towards media. The discrepancy between perceived media effects on others and self is expected to contribute to explaining variance in censorship attitudes. This will be examined regarding the media in general, as well as two important areas of media content: violence on television and pornography.

Health sciences
'Factors associated with self-care activities among adults in the United Kingdom: a systematic review'

Self-care is 'the care taken by individuals towards their own health and well being' [1]. The Government has promoted self-care on the basis that the public favour more control over their health [1] and self-care improves health outcomes and appropriate use of health and social care services [2].

Diagnostic self-tests for over 20 conditions can be bought in pharmacies or over the internet [3]. Some provide results at home or a sample is sent to a laboratory and results are returned by post or email. Either way, people who self-test do not need to discuss why they decided to have the test or the results with a clinician. Members of the public may consider that using self-tests is self-care and, therefore, desirable, but direct access to self-tests has the potential to reduce or reinforce inequity. People who can afford a test may simply wish to check on their health, for example with a home cholesterol test, and this could free up conventional services for other people. Alternatively, people who are unable to communicate their needs to a health professional could buy expensive and perhaps undesirable tests for home use. It is, therefore, important to understand who uses self-tests so that targeted education about appropriate testing can be provided and equitable access to corresponding conventional services can be assured. Our aim was to generate hypotheses about who uses self-tests by reviewing evidence for factors that are associated with self-testing and, because of a lack of evidence about self-tests, similar activities.

Social sciences
'The ecological footprint as a key indicator of sustainable tourism'

The importance of learning from related fields and disciplines is increasingly being recognised in the sustainable tourism (ST) literature, both as a means of advancing knowledge and understanding of ST, and as a means of avoiding 're-inventing the wheel' in ST practice (e.g., Farrell and Twining-Ward, 2003; Hunter, 2002a; Ko, 2001). Potentially, one area where a great deal may be learned from the broader sustainable development (SD) and environmental management literature is in the development and use of suitable indicators of ST. This is explicitly recognised by Twining-Ward and Butler (2002), in one of the very few works to date specifically designed to formulate indicators of ST. Despite the undoubted demand for appropriate indicators of ST, these authors argue (p. 365) that research in this area is 'still in its incipient stages', a view echoed by others (e.g. Li, 2004; Miller, 2001; Rebollo and Baidal, 2003).

Humanities

'Change and development in a pluralistic world: the view from the classics'

Change, development, pluralism: these seemingly innocuous words have an edgy, contemporary ring to them. They suggest the threat of competition and conflict, as well as the promise of new opportunities and the discovery of diversity. These three words summarize preoccupations at the end of a thousand years that has transformed the earth and its people. Among the changes most relevant to our field have been the growing dominance of formal organizations and the emergence of professional managers. In order to understand these developments and their implications, we often turn to a body of work referred to as the 'classics'.

What do we mean when we refer to works of scholarship as classics? One plausible answer is that by classics we mean 'earlier works of human exploration which are given a privileged status vis-a-vis contemporary explorations in the same field' (Alexander, 1989: 9). Within the field of management and organizations, various lists of classics have been presented over the years (e.g., Merrill, 1960; Shafritz and Ott, 1987). In our brief essay we offer not a systematic sampling but a personal selection of classic work that seems relevant to the themes of this special issue.

First, we must justify the attention devoted to the privileged works of the past. Everyone impatient with historical scholarship likes to quote Whitehead's dictum that 'a science which hesitates to forget its founders is lost' (1974: 115). A deliberate neglect of outmoded work is excusable for researchers in fields such as physics and chemistry, for whom new and better theory eclipses old in a predictable process of amelioration. Those who champion the importance of the classics in the social sciences (e.g., Alexander, 1989) have argued that these sciences resemble the humanities more than they do physics and chemistry in their reliance on potentially contested interpretations of evidence and theory. Building on this insight, we summarize three reasons for the relevance of classic work to the understanding of change, development, and pluralism.

APPENDIX 3: ADDITIONAL INFORMATION

Step 20
Examples of good conclusions

The conclusions below come from four academic articles, representing a range of disciplines. **Note:** These conclusions have been taken from journals, and may be longer and include more paragraphs than you would be expected to write in your essays.

Law
'For the good of others: censorship and the third-person effect'

The results of this study support the third-person effect hypothesis and offer evidence of its relationship with the censorship phenomenon. A significant part of the apprehension caused by media effects results from the overestimation of its effects on others. This knowledge has direct implications for public policy concerning speech and its limitations. If part of the public drive to curtail certain types of messages results from the third-person effect, policy debates have to recognize this and concentrate on measuring actual media effects and not perceived media effects.

The theoretical relationship discovered between the third-person effect gaps and pro-censorship attitudes deserves further exploration. Beyond testing this question using more generalizable samples, researchers may wish to explore whether the third-person effect gap is related to other censurable topics, such as school books, and hate speech. This may also be particularly applicable to a number of advertising issues including the use of advertising for potentially 'harmful' products such as cigarettes and alcohol, and the use of specific techniques such as negative political ads or host selling. Additionally, the third-person effect gap may help to explain the outcry against some targeting efforts in advertising aimed at minority groups.

Finally, researchers interested in the third-person effect phenomenon should explore the behavioral component with greater scrutiny. This study examined reported behavior for a hypothetical situation. Additional research should examine actual behavior in both naturally occurring and experimentally controlled situations. In general, future research examining the third-person effect would appear to have great promise in explaining both ethical attitudes regarding media practices and individual and even regulatory actions to limit them.

Health sciences
'Factors associated with self-care activities among adults in the United Kingdom: a systematic review'

This review suggests that people who engaged in self-care activities were likely to be affluent and/or educated. Self-care is, therefore, likely to require targeted promotion to ensure that use is equitable. People who have used some self-care activities may also have poorer health than non-users or people attending conventional services. It seems reasonable that people would use self-care activities when they feel unwell, but it is important to ensure that self-care is not a second choice for people who have been dissatisfied with, or not had their needs met by conventional services. There is weak evidence that dissatisfaction with orthodox medicine was a factor in some people's decision to use CAM and that some people used OTC medicine because their doctor was unable to help them. This requires further investigation as part of the evaluation of the promotion of self-care.

Social sciences
'The ecological footprint as a key indicator of sustainable tourism'

It is likely that the use of ST indicators that are wholly derived from a local perspective and through local processes of participation will underplay the recognition of tourism activity as a user of natural resources at the global scale. Furthermore, different sets of locally derived and contextualised indicators make it less easy to compare different areas or products in terms of environmental impact and sustainability. At the very least, therefore, it would appear appropriate to recognise the potential benefits of the widespread adoption of a unique indicator capable of providing a global perspective on tourism's environmental impact. The use of EF analysis as an indicator of environmental sustainability allows quantitative comparison between different impact components (e.g., the transit zone and destination area footprints), and can provide an indication of the overall ecological impact of tourism products on global biological resources. The simple methodology outlined in this paper could

Step 20

be widely adopted for the environmental appraisal of international tourism products and destination areas. It should be stressed again, however, that the methodology is as yet rather crude, providing indicative estimates of the likely minimum potential tourism EF.

This said, it would appear critical in any tourism EF analysis to determine the net tourism EF; i.e. to account for the EF that a tourist would normally produce at home while s/he is abroad. Otherwise, the additional burden on the planet's resources created by the tourist trip/product may be greatly over-estimated, in contravention of the tradition in EF analysis work. Furthermore, as we sought to demonstrate above, it may be that some tourism products could actually alleviate the consumption of the world's biological resources. The potential for this rather surprising outcome is greatest for some products to low EF countries, but involving tourists from high EF (generally developed) countries, and where short to medium haul flights are involved if the length of stay is of sufficient duration. By way of defining one avenue for future research, some types of 'hard' (Page and Dowling, 2002) eco-tourism product, at least on the face of it, exhibit the necessary characteristics for a 'zero' or 'negative net EF' outcome. However indicative it may be at this stage, EF analysis offers the prospect of more 'rounded' evaluations of eco-tourism (and other tourism) products, and suggests that any automatic dismissal of eco-tourism on environmental grounds – certainly if short to medium haul flights are involved – may be rather premature. Furthermore, it is by no means clear that even eco-tourism products involving long haul flights will, in net EF terms, tend to be more environmentally demanding than many mass tourism products. What is clear, however, is the danger of assessing the sustainability of tourism products without considering the transit zone.

Avenues for further research in the application of EF analysis to tourism are many and varied. Many more simple estimates of the EF of different tourism products could be made using, for example, the methodology outlined in this paper. These might also attempt to incorporate different modes of transport to the destination. Ways of estimating the EF of domestic tourism activities could also be explored. Perhaps the greatest need, however, is to collect 'real world' primary data for the resources consumed during the life-cycle of a range of different tourism products, including low-impact, 'genuine' ecotourism holidays of various kinds, and very up-market, luxury hotel-type holiday resorts.

Humanities
'Change and development in a pluralistic world: the view from the classics'

Rather than reach back into medieval times for the future of our discipline (an idea advanced by Burrell, 1996: 657), we suggest a re-evaluation of the classic readings in our field and in related fields for critical insights, diversity of views, and taken-for-granted assumptions. The more our research and teaching concern change, development, and pluralism, the more we need to guard against a premature abandonment of the rich variety of our existing writing. Rather than conceptualizing our developmental journey as a linear process, we may be better served by visualizing ourselves as a constantly enlarging circle of inquirers. The circle metaphor allows us to incorporate existing writings with new writings in a hermeneutic process of scholarship. Classic writings, from the circle perspective, provide a common ground of concepts, theories, and ideas about which competing schools can agree or disagree. This common ground is a prerequisite for the disciplined reflexivity that Weick (1999) sees as intrinsic to theory development. The one sure way to avoid the slavish repetition of ideas and theories already well established is through a sophisticated acquaintance with classic work. Change and pluralism in our research and theory are best served by development journeys that revisit and critique the best work of the past and the present.

APPENDIX 3: ADDITIONAL INFORMATION

Step 21

Phrasal (multi-part) verbs and their one-word verb equivalents

Here are 20 frequently used phrasal verbs with one-word verb equivalents that are more appropriate in academic writing.

Phrasal verb	One-word verb
call off	cancel
find out	discover
get away	leave; escape
get in	arrive; enter
give up	quit
hand in	submit
help with	aid, assist; support
hold up	delay
leave out	omit
look for	seek
look into	investigate
look over	examine
put off	postpone
put out	extinguish
put up with	tolerate
read through	peruse
step up	increase
talk over	discuss
try out	test
use up	exhaust

Step 25
Examples of logical fallacies

Here are examples of different types of logical fallacy that you may encounter in your academic reading – or commit yourself in your academic writing.

Fallacies of relevance: there is no relationship between the premise and conclusion of an argument

'Only a traitor would agree with what you've just said.' – *Appeal to emotion:* reason is replaced by an emotional reaction.

'If you vote for them then you'd better start praying.' – *Appeal to force:* reason is replaced by military, political, legal or other power.

'If he agrees, the idea must be ridiculous.' – *Argument against the person:* the validity of an argument is questioned because of the individual personality of its proponent.

'Everyone else agrees with me, so you must be wrong.' – *Irrelevant conclusion* ('red herring'): the central point of an argument is replaced by irrelevant detail – for example, majority opinion.

Fallacies of defective induction: the premise is irrelevant to the conclusion

'You may disagree with me, but Aristotle says very much the same thing.' – *Argument from authority:* the 'who' of an argument is considered more important than the 'what'.

'If my teacher teaches well, she is happy. Since she is happy now, she must have taught well.' – *Affirming the consequent:* a conclusion is drawn from an irrelevant premise, i.e., assuming that Q implies P because P implies Q. In the example, the teacher's happiness could easily be due to something other than how well she has taught.

'If I do lots of background reading, I write a good essay. I didn't do lots of background reading; therefore I wrote a bad essay.' – *Denying the antecedent:* the opposite of affirming the consequent (above), i.e., assuming that Q does not imply P because P does not imply Q. In the example, the high quality of the essay could easily be due to other factors, not just the amount of background reading – e.g., good time management, quality of writing.

'I spent lots of time on my essay and so it will get a high mark.' – *Non sequitur* (Latin: 'it does not follow'): there is confusion between cause and effect, i.e., just because Q happened, this does not necessarily mean P was the result. More specifically, the example is a case of *post hoc ergo propter hoc* (Latin: 'after this, therefore because of this'): temporal succession (things happening one after the other) is mistaken for causal relation (one thing that

happens necessarily being caused by something else that happened earlier).

'Every teacher I have met has been nice, so all teachers must be nice.' – *Reverse accident:* arguing that a general case can be made on the basis of a specific fact or rule.

Fallacies of presumption: the conclusion of an argument is based on a false premise

'Killing people is a crime. Soldiers kill people. Therefore, soldiers are criminals.' – *Fallacy of accident:* a generalization is made which disregards any exception.

'Have you been cheating in your exams again?' – *Many questions:* a single question is asked; however, in reality it is made up of several different questions that require different answers. In the example, even if the person responding answers 'no' he or she is still having to admit to cheating.

'My professor is always right, so he must be right about this too.' – *Assuming the answer:* circular reasoning is used – i.e., the conclusion is demonstrated by a premise which intrinsically assumes the conclusion.

Fallacies of ambiguity: the precise meaning of the language or grammar used in the argument is unclear

'Neo-conservatives believe in a liberal economic theory. Neo-conservatives dislike liberals. Therefore, neo-conservatives dislike themselves.' – *Equivocation:* in setting out the argument a word is used in two different senses; this leads to a faulty conclusion.

'She only likes chocolate.' – *Amphiboly:* there is grammatical ambiguity. In the example, the adverb only can modify any of the other words so the sentence could mean several different things. In spoken English this problem typically does not arise because the meaning is made clear by means of prosody (stress and/or intonation patterns).

'Every flower in my garden is beautiful, therefore my garden is beautiful.' – *Fallacy of composition:* the individual elements of a word or phrase do not necessarily lead to a correct conclusion for the sentence as a whole.

'I will prove my point by looking at all the data from 1648 to the present day …' – *Proof by verbosity:* facts are submerged beneath a mass of information and the reader or listener is asked to merely accept that they are true.

APPENDIX 3: ADDITIONAL INFORMATION

Step 27

Latin words and phrases in common use in academic English

a posteriori	derived by reasoning from observed facts
a priori	derived from a general law to a specific instance
ad absurdum	to the point of absurdity
ad hominem	appealing to feelings or emotions rather than logic
ad infinitum	without limit
addenda	things to be added
bona fide (adjective)	genuine, sincere
bona fides (noun)	honest intentions
circa (c.)	about (used with dates)
compos mentis	sane, of sound mind
confer (cf.)	compare with
curriculum vitae	a summary of a person's career and skills
de facto	in fact
de jure	by right
emeritus	(of a professor) retired after long, distinguished service and holding an honorary title
ergo	therefore
errata	a list of errors (in a book)
et alia	and other things
et alii (et al.)	and others (often used in referencing, to refer to further authors)
et cetera (etc.)	and so on
ibidem (ibid.)	in the same place (often used in referencing, to refer again to a source just mentioned)
idem	the same
ipso facto	by that very fact
mutatis mutandis	the necessary changes being made
non sequitur	it does not follow (an example of a logical fallacy)
nota bene (NB)	note well
passim	in various places (used for citing sources)
per annum	per year
per se	taken alone
prima facie	on a first view
sic	thus (used in quoted passages to indicate that an error or apparent error has been deliberately reproduced)
status quo	the existing condition

APPENDIX 3: ADDITIONAL INFORMATION

Step 37

Reducing overcomplexity and redundancy in academic writing

Here are examples of phrases which are commonly used but are overcomplex or overlong or use redundant language (tautology), and how they can be improved. The phrases are relatively common in general academic English.

Overcomplex or overlong phrases

In these phrases either of the following has occurred:

1. A complex phrase, is used when a much simpler version is possible.

2. Too many words are used, making the phrase difficult to understand.

In each case, the overcomplex, longer and/or tautologous phrase is given in plain text and the shorter, more dynamic equivalent in **bold**.

along the lines of – **similar to**
at all times – **always**
at the time that – **when**
by the name of – **named, called**
came to an agreement – **agreed**
carry out an evaluation of – **evaluate**
comply with – **follow**
conduct a review of – **review**
despite the fact that – **although**
due to the fact that – **because**
employment opportunities – **jobs**
excessive number of – **too many**
extend an invitation to – **invite**
give an indication of – **show**
give rise to – **cause, lead to**
give consideration to – **consider**
has the capability to – **can**
if that/this is not the case – **if not**
if that/this is the case – **if so**

in addition to – **besides**
in advance of – **ahead of, before, by**
in conjunction with – **along with or with**
in excess of – **more than**
in possession of – **has, have**
in proximity to – **close to, near**
in spite of the fact that – **although**
in the absence of – **without**
in the course of – **during**
in the event that – **if**
in view of the fact – **because**
is able to – **can**
it would appear that – **apparently, it seems (that)**
make a statement – **say**
make an application – **apply**
make an examination of – **examine**
make reference to – **refer to**

is/are not in a position to – **will not be able to**
not many – **few**
not old enough – **too young**
not possible – **impossible**
not the same – **different**
on most occasions – **usually**
perform an assessment of – **assess**
refer to as – **call**
some of the – **some**
a sufficient number of – **enough**
take action – **act**
until such a point in time as – **until**
use up – **use**
with a view to – **to, for**
with regard to – **regarding**
with the exception of – **except**

Redundant language (tautology)

Here are examples of phrases where the language used just repeats information that is already there. In each case, the phrase can be cut down to include just the language in **bold**.

a total of **28 weeks**
brief in duration
CD disk
close **proximity**
completely **destroyed**
completely **unanimous**
consensus of opinion
cooperate together
costs a total of
CPU unit
current **status**
each and **every**
end **result**

exactly **equidistant**
exactly **the same**
few in number
filled to capacity
first **began**
foreign **imports**
free **gift**
future **plans**
group together
honest **truth**
HIV virus
join together
month of **January**

mutual **agreement**,
mutual **cooperation**
new **innovations**
period of **four days**
personally **responsible**
PIN number
postpone until later
potentially **dangerous**
potentially **hazardous**
present **incumbent**
red in colour
return again
safe **haven**

shorter in length
small in size
square in shape
still **remain**
sum **total**
summarize briefly
the reason is because
total **monopoly**
true **fact**
usual **custom**
usual **habit**
warn in advance
weather conditions

APPENDIX 3: ADDITIONAL INFORMATION

Step 44
Determiners: an overview

A. DEFINITION OF TERMS
Determiners are those little words that precede and modify nouns; they include articles, demonstratives and quantifiers. For example:
- Articles: *the teacher*, *a college*
- Demonstratives: *that person*, *those people*
- Quantifiers: *enough eggs*, *either way*

These words are usually short and may seem irrelevant – however, they actually tell us a lot about nouns. They tell us whether the speaker is talking about something in general or about a specific case, as well as about how much or how many of something the speaker is talking about.

The difficulty of understanding how determiners (and especially articles) are used in English will vary depending on what your mother tongue (L1) is like. For example, if your L1 has articles and uses them similarly to English, understanding the English system will be relatively easy; but if your L1 does not use articles at all, understanding the English system will be difficult.

B. ARTICLES
Articles are the most commonly used determiners in English. Indeed, the definite article *the* is the most commonly used word in English; the indefinite article *a(n)* takes fifth place. Therefore, a good understanding of how they are used is imperative.

The main uses of each type of article are set out below.

Definite article
In general, *the* is used when referring to things that the speaker/writer and listener/reader are assumed to know about already.
- **The** is used when we refer to something specific which has already been established or mentioned, e.g.:
  - *She told me a story the other day.* **The** *story was very funny.*
  - **The** *thing you just mentioned – could you repeat it?*
- **The** is used when we know which particular thing is meant, e.g.:
  - *I've just been to* **the** *zoo (i.e., it is obvious which zoo I am talking about) versus A zoo should look after its animals (i.e., any zoo, in general)*
  - *Have you fed* **the** *cats (i.e., the cats we own) versus Do you like cats? (i.e., cats in general)*
- **The** is used for unique objects – when there is only one thing that the speaker could be talking about, e.g.:
  - **The** *Moon rotates around* **the** *Earth.*
  - **The** *Japanese are a friendly people.*
- **The** is used with superlatives, e.g.:
  - *You're* **the** *best friend I've ever had.*
  - **The** *most annoying thing I ever heard was …*

Indefinite article
- **A(n)** is used when it is not known which one is meant (**the** is used subsequently), e.g.:
  - *I bought* **an** *apple on the way to work. The apple tastes lovely.*
  - **A** *thing of beauty is a joy forever.*
- **A(n)** is used when it does not matter which one is meant, e.g.:
  - *Could I borrow* **a** *pen, please?*
  - *I'd like* **an** *official to help me.*

No article
There are some instances where you might think an article was needed, but it is not.
- Use no article for things in general (when making a general, wide-ranging point about something), e.g.:
  - **Dogs** *are stupid.*
  - **Mobile phones** *are the curse of the modern world.*
- Use no article for the names of countries (except in the few cases which have a countable noun as part of the name), e.g.:
  - *I went travelling to France, Germany, Italy and* **the** *UK (because UK = United Kingdom).*
  - *I once went to America (versus I once went to* **the** *United States of America).*
- Uncountable nouns
  - *Water is wet (not* ~~*a water is wet*~~*).*
  - *Humans need air to breathe (not humans need* ~~*an air*~~ *to breathe).*

C. QUANTIFIERS
Quantifiers, like articles, precede and modify nouns. They tell us 'how many' or 'how much'. Selecting the correct quantifier depends on your understanding the distinction between countable and uncountable nouns.

The following quantifiers will work with countable nouns:
- **many** *trees*
- **a few** *trees*
- **few** *trees*
- **several** *trees*
- **a couple** *of trees*
- **none of the** *trees*

Step 44

Determiners: an overview – *continued*

The following quantifiers will work with uncountable nouns:

- *not much* water
- *a little* water
- *little* water
- *a bit of* water
- *a good deal of* water
- *a great deal of* water
- *no* water

The following quantifiers will work with both countable and uncountable nouns:

- *all of* the trees/water
- *some* trees/water
- *most of* the trees/water
- *enough* trees/water
- *a lot of* trees/water
- *lots of* trees/water
- *plenty of* trees/water
- *a lack of* trees/water

Notes

1. In formal academic writing, it is usually better to use *many* and *much* rather than phrases such as *a lot of*, *lots of* or *plenty of*.
2. There is an important difference between *a little* and *little* (used with uncountable nouns) and between *a few* and *few* (used with countable nouns). Look at the following sentences, for example:
   - *David has a **little** experience in teaching* (= David is no expert but has some experience, which may be sufficient).
   - *David has **little** experience in teaching* (= David doesn't have enough experience).
   - *Susan owns a **few** books about engineering* (= Susan owns enough for her needs).
   - *Susan owns **few** books about engineering* (= there are insufficient for her needs).
3. The quantifier *much* is reserved for questions and negative statements, unless it is combined with *of*. Compare:
   - ***Much of** the snow has already melted.*
   - *How **much** snow fell yesterday?*
   - *Not **much**.*
4. Note that the quantifier *most of the* must include the definite article *the* when it modifies a specific noun – whether the latter is countable or uncountable, e.g.:
   - ***Most of the** instructors at this college have a doctorate.*
   - ***Most of the** water has evaporated.*

However, with a general plural noun (when you are not referring to a specific entity), *of the* is dropped:
- ***Most** colleges have their own admissions policy.*
- ***Most** students apply to several colleges.*

D. Predeterminers

Predeterminers occur before other determiners (as you can guess from the name). This class of words includes:
- multipliers (e.g., *double, twice, four times, five times*)
- fractional expressions (e.g., *one-third, three-quarters*)
- the words *both, half* and *all*
- intensifiers (e.g., *quite, rather, such*)

APPENDIX 3: ADDITIONAL INFORMATION

Step 48

Words that are commonly misspelt

The following words, which are relatively common in academic English, are often misspelt.

accommodate, acknowledge, across, actually, analyze, appearance, appreciate, argument, beginning, belief, business, committee, criticism, definitely, dependent, difference, discipline, discussed, eighth, eliminate, environment, especially, exaggerate, excellent, experience, extremely, foreign, government, guarantee, height, immediately, independent, intelligence, interest, knowledge, laboratory, library, meant, neither, nuclear, occasionally, parallel, persuade, physically, possible, practical, privilege, probably, psychology, receipt, recommend, reference, repetition, rhythm, ridiculous, scene, schedule, separate, similar, sincerely, succeed, surprise, thoroughly, unusual, usually

APPENDIX 3: ADDITIONAL INFORMATION

Step 49
Sample abstracts

Adapted abstracts from four academic articles, representing a range of different disciplines.

Law

'For the good of others: censorship and the third-person effect'

The third person effect hypothesis, which states that individuals exposed to a mass media message will expect the communication to have a greater effect on others than on themselves, may help to explain the growing trend in support of media censorship. It is suggested here that overestimating the effect of media on others may play an important role in the forces underlying a willingness to restrict various types of communication. To examine this relationship, this study focused on the discrepancy between perceived media effects on others and self, and its relation to pro-censorship attitudes within three major topics: the media in general, violence on television, and pornography. The results of this study support the existence of the third-person effect in mass communication. The findings also indicate that as the gap between perceived firsthand third-person effects increases, individuals are more likely to manifest pro-censorship attitudes. This relationship remained for all three topics even when a variety of potentially confounding demographic, media use, and attitudinal variables were controlled. The data also suggest that for pornography the effects gap is related to a willingness to *act* in favor of censoring.

Health sciences

'Factors associated with self-care activities among adults in the United Kingdom: a systematic review'

Background: The Government has promoted self-care. Our aim was to review evidence about who uses self-tests and other self-care activities.

Methods: During April 2007, relevant bibliographic databases were searched, and potentially relevant studies were reviewed against eligibility criteria. Studies were included if they were published during the last 15 years and identified factors, reasons or characteristics associated with a relevant activity among UK adults. Two independent reviewers used proformas to assess the quality of eligible studies.

Results: 206 potentially relevant papers were identified, 157 were excluded, and 49 papers related to 46 studies were included. Available evidence suggests that users of complementary and alternative medicine (CAM) and over-the-counter medicine are female, middle-aged, affluent and/or educated with some measure of poor health, and that people who use the private sector are affluent and/or educated.

Conclusion: People who engage in these activities are likely to be affluent. Targeted promotion may, therefore, be needed to ensure that use is equitable. People who use some activities also appear to have poorer measures of health than non-users or people attending conventional services. It is, therefore, also important to ensure that self-care is not used as a second choice for people who have not had their needs met by conventional services.

Social sciences

'The ecological footprint as a key indicator of sustainable tourism'

This paper argues for ecological footprint (EF) analysis to become widely adopted as a key environmental indicator of sustainable tourism (ST). It is suggested that EF analysis provides a unique, global perspective on sustainability that is absent with the use of locally derived and contextualised ST indicators. A simple methodology to estimate indicative, minimum EF values for international tourism activities involving air travel is presented. Critically, the methodology accounts for the EF that would have been used by a tourist at home during the tourist trip, providing an estimate of the net, as well as the gross, tourism-related EF. Illustrations of the application of the methodology are provided, including the evaluation and comparison of specific tourism products. It is suggested that some (eco)tourism products may, potentially, make a positive contribution to resource conservation at the global scale. Areas for further research in applying EF analysis to tourism are outlined.

Keywords: Sustainable tourism; Indicator; Ecological footprint

Humanities

'Change and development in a pluralistic world: the view from the classics'

The study of the classics in our field is important to the themes of this special issue because (1) the classics have shaped the world we live in; (2) studying the classics enlarges our theoretical alternatives; and (3) the critique of taken-for-granted assumptions enshrined in the classics can spur change, development, and pluralism. We briefly review a selection of classic writings to illustrate how change and pluralism have been presented as threats, as opportunities for the management of innovation, and as intrinsic aspects of management.

APPENDIX 4: USEFUL HYPERLINKS

List of hyperlinks

Step 3: Plagiarism

- Full plagiarism statement (from King's College London): www.kcl.ac.uk/college/policyzone/assets/files/assessment/Plagiarism strategy for the web final.pdf
- Turnitin – the program used by many British universities to detect plagiarism and cheating: www.submit.ac.uk/static_jisc/ac_uk_index.html

Step 5: Referencing

General websites:
- Refworks: www.refworks.com
- Endnote: www.endnote.com
- Refman: www.refman.com
- Citeulike: www.citeulike.org

Specific referencing systems:
- American Psychological Association: www.apastyle.org
- Author–date (Harvard): http://libweb.anglia.ac.uk/referencing/harvard.htm
- Modern Languages Association: www.mla.org
- Modern Humanities Research Association: www.mhra.org.uk
- Chicago: www.chicagomanualofstyle.org
- Vancouver: www.nlm.nih.gov/citingmedicine
- Oscola: www.law.ox.ac.uk/publications/oscola.php

Step 5: Useful essay research websites

General:
- Google Scholar: scholar.google.co.uk
- Wikipedia: en.wikipedia.org

Academic journals/databases:
- Athens (gateway to academic journals): www.athens.ac.uk
- JSTOR (major source of academic content): www.jstor.org
- Cambridge University Press (more than 220 peer-reviewed journals): http://journals.cambridge.org/
- Archives Hub (enables searches across archives at nearly 200 UK institutions): www.archiveshub.ac.uk
- ScienceDirect (scientific database containing journal articles and book chapters): www.sciencedirect.com
- Open University (free learning units): www.openlearn.open.ac.uk
- Openculture (free educational and cultural media): www.openculture.com
- Glossary of the Humanities (explanations of words commonly used in humanities): http://web.mac.com/radney/humanities/glossary.htm

Online podcasts/lectures:
- Academic Earth (US-based site with lectures from a range of disciplines): http://academicearth.org
- University Channel (videos of academic lectures from all over the world): http://uc.princeton.edu/main/
- TED Talks (talks by 'remarkable people', free; often with PowerPoint presentations): www.tedtalks.com
- Massachusetts Institute of Technology (free videos, lecture notes and exams from MIT): www.ocw.mit.edu

Step 7: Using the Internet for research

A list of the sources referenced in the step.
- journals.cambridge.org
- www.guardian.co.uk
- www.richarddawkins.net
- metalib.kcl.ac.uk/V
- answers.yahoo.com
- www.archiveshub.ac.uk
- en.wikipedia.org
- www.sciencedirect.com
- www.jstor.com
- www.dailymail.co.uk

Step 9: Reading

- Readingsoft (reading speed and accuracy level): www.readingsoft.com

Step 12: Time-management resources

- Mindtools: www.mindtools.com/pages/main/newMN_HTE.htm
- Timemanagement: www.timemanagement.com

Step 14: Brainstorming and planning

- Mindmeister: www.mindmeister.com

Step 26: Online writing tools

- Online Utility (calculates the readability of text): www.online-utility.org/english/readability_test_and_improve.jsp

Step 31: Online corpora

- BAWE Corpus Search: http://ca.sketchengine.co.uk/open/corpus/bawe2/ske/first_form
- Corpus Concordance English (useful resource for spoken and written academic and general English): www.lextutor.ca/concordancers/concord_e.html
- Cobuild Concordance and Collocations Sampler: www.collins.co.uk/Corpus/CorpusSearch.aspx